CARP DIEM !

# Unintended Consequence

Transforming America
How and Why We Came to This Place

William L. Kane, Sr.

Copyright © 2020 William L. Kane, Sr.
All rights reserved
First Edition

PAGE PUBLISHING, INC.
Conneaut Lake, PA

First originally published by Page Publishing 2020

ISBN 978-1-64701-983-9 (pbk)
ISBN 978-1-64701-984-6 (digital)

Printed in the United States of America

*For Ryan and Lilly.
Carpe diem.*

# Contents

Acknowledgments .................................................................... 7
Prologue .................................................................................. 9
Chapter I: Athletics and Sports ............................................ 19
Chapter II: Economy ............................................................ 30
        American Currency, the Treasury,
           Banking, and the Federal Reserve ..................... 36
        Legislation that Shaped the Economy ................... 43
        Stock Market: Security and Exchange
           Commission ......................................................... 63
        The National Debt ................................................ 67
Chapter III: Education .......................................................... 71
Chapter IV: Environment ..................................................... 90
Chapter V: Health Care ...................................................... 102
Chapter VI: Immigration ..................................................... 116
Chapter VII: Media ............................................................. 134
Chapter VIII: National Moral Compass ............................. 151
        Abortion ............................................................. 157
        Aspiration versus Accomplishment ...................... 161
        Congressional Investigations ............................... 173
        Our Bible, Our Flag, and Our History ............... 192
        Slavery: America's "Original Sin" ........................ 204
        Supreme Court .................................................... 204
        Technology and Incivility .................................... 212
        The Sexual Revolution ....................................... 223
        Voting Rights ...................................................... 230
Chapter IX: Slavery, Racism, and Reparations ..................... 241
Chapter X: Wars and Conflicts ............................................ 264
Epilogue .............................................................................. 283

# Acknowledgments

With special thanks to Elizabeth Mallonee and Terence Foxe for being my more progressive foils.

With equal thanks to Leslie Ditta, Gina Long, and Bob Sheldon for their counsel on the "Education" chapter.

With appreciation to John Murray for ensuring that my work product was equal to the standards of our Jesuit training.

With gratefulness to Leigh MacKay for contributing his mastery of the English language in editing my drafts.

With admiration to Crystal Beetham for the cover art and, finally, to Pauline Levesque for guiding me through the myriad of technical hurdles of my computer.

# Prologue

*Carpe diem.*

If you plan to vote in 2020 and beyond, then you should read this book before you vote; if you do not intend to vote, then you should read this book to understand why you should vote.

> *Every government intervention creates unintended consequences, which lead to calls for further government intervention.*
> —Ludwig von Mises
> Austrian American Economist

"The road to hell is paved with good intentions" is an English proverb with an unclear origin sharing a universal truth: Attempts to improve the well-being or ethical behavior of segments of our population are often counterproductive. Efforts that benefit our population in its entirety are generally more successful.

> *Almost every time that any social group has attempted to build a Utopia—literally attempting to embody their good intentions in the creation of a perfect place—it has ended in tragedy, misery and the abandonment of their project.*
> —*Psychology Today*[1]

---

[1] *Psychology Today: The Road to Hell Is Paved with Good Intentions*—April 2019

This book is not intended to tell you *what to think*; instead, it is meant to *encourage you to think*, encourage you to question, challenge, validate, explore, and consider. It is intended to demonstrate how legislative policies have historically led to unintended consequences that then have required additional legislation to resolve the unforeseen outcome. Abraham Lincoln warned us almost two centuries ago, "To stand in silence when they should be protesting makes cowards of men."[2] Ronald Reagan cautioned that "we must act today in order to preserve tomorrow."[3]

I will attempt to speak out in hopes that the "silent majority" will understand, become vocal, and take a stand against the erosion of our democracy, economy, national security, and the basic moral fabric of our nation.

"Let us look at America, let us listen to America to find the answer.... As we look at America, we see cities enveloped in smoke and flame. We hear sirens in the night. We see Americans dying on distant battlefields abroad. We see Americans hating each other; fighting each other; killing each other at home. And as we see and hear these things, millions of Americans cry out in anguish."[4] Few will recognize this quote, for though it might describe our country today, these words were said by presidential candidate Richard Nixon in his nomination acceptance speech in August 1968, fifty years ago.

How can it be that after a half-century, we are still mired in the same social quagmire? What degree of success can we attribute to our legislative process? Politics have become so bizarre and chaotic. We seem to have entered a period of political paranoia, a period of ignorance and arrogance. Many democrats seem to believe that President Trump is the Antichrist. Trump may be loved or hated, but he cannot be ignored.

For the record, I am less pro-Trump and more pro-reality. It is not my purpose to defend Donald Trump—he can be crass, crude, and narcissistic. Admittedly, there is a bit of a narcissist in each of

---

[2] *The Collected Works of Abraham Lincoln—1953*
[3] President Reagans Inaugural Address—January 20, 1981
[4] Richard Nixon—Republican Nomination Acceptance Speech—August 1968

us; however, he has also been that rare politician that is committed to delivering on his campaign promises. I believe that any president should be judged upon his performance, his policies and their impact on our country, economy, and society, rather than some visceral bias.

Our history is riddled with enacted legislation that have led to unintended consequences. Our politics have become so party-polarized that moderation and compromise seem impossible. The most extreme factions of all three major parties, Democrat, Republican, and Libertarian, are insistent upon stretching the envelope to unreasonable extremes in pursuit of their own agendas. The nonparty-affiliated independents might appear most moderate.

Moderation and compromise are the proper pathways to governing our great nation. We must all share the same fundamental priority: nation over party. Many Americans might agree that it could be time for a new centrist force, a "third" party that could be more effective in dealing with our nation's problems. How far have we fallen?

In February 2019, the Senate failed to pass a bill that would *prohibit* aborting a child after its birth (infanticide). Forty-four Democrat senators voted against the bill. I find this to be profoundly disturbing.

While the "progressive agenda" did not begin with the Obama administration, it certainly was aggressively pursued by it. Candidate Barack Obama said, "We are five days away from fundamentally transforming the United States of America."[5] Michelle Obama told us, "We are going to have to change our conversation; we're going to have to change our traditions, our history; we're going to have to move into a different place as a nation."[6]

Surely, we might *influence* our future, but how can we reasonably expect to "change our history"? It is what it is.

Anti-Semitism is again becoming commonplace. In 2019, presidential candidate Senator Bernie Sanders (D-VT) declared Israel to

---

[5] Barack Obama Speech—October 30, 2008
[6] Michelle Obama,—May 14, 2008

be a "racist government run by a right-wing racist."[7] Congresswomen Ilhan Omar (D-MN) and Rashida Tlaib (D-MI) have made controversial remarks viewed by most as anti-Semitic. The goal of the BDS (Boycott, Divestment, and Sanctions) movement is to delegitimize and destroy Israel.

Some members of Congress insist on inflaming tensions with the goal of isolating and tearing down anybody who supports freedom, human rights, and stability in the Middle East. Liberals always seem to want to engage in a *national conversation* as opposed to *national action*, comfortable with identity politics and poisonous rhetoric. They don't oppose hatred; they appear to encourage it.

The Freedom Caucus, the uberconservative wing of the Republican Party, successfully blocked bills it didn't like with just three dozen members. In 2018, the incoming House Democratic majority had an expanded liberal faction that is already causing disruption. The uberliberal Progressive Caucus has grown to nearly one hundred members, giving it tremendous potential influence. This new breed of liberal is suggesting more radical policies. If they cannot win by the rules, they propose to change them.

*Restructure the Supreme Court.* This is nothing less than a blatant attempt to dilute the power of the recently appointed conservative Supreme Court justices, with the possibility of liberal Justice Ginsburg's seat looming.

While the Constitution is silent regarding the number of judges to be on the highest court of the nation, we have presided with nine justices since 1869. President Roosevelt attempted to flood the court but was unsuccessful. I can see no *judicial* advantage to increasing the number of justices, only *political*.

*Eliminate the Electoral College.* Representative Cohen (D-TN) introduced a bill to eliminate the Electoral College on the first night of the 116th Congress. Cohen is a vocal opponent of President Trump, and his action was purely political. Our founding fathers were prescient in the determination that the Electoral College system would

---

[7] Bernie Sanders Speech—American Jewish Committee Global Forum—Washington, DC—June 2019

provide the most unbiased method to elect a president, understanding that all states should participate in that process. In 2019, eight states—California, Texas, Florida, New York, Pennsylvania, Illinois, Ohio, and Georgia—accounted for 50 percent of the US population. If the Electoral College were eliminated, these eight states would determine the presidency of the United States, effectively disenfranchising the voters of the other forty-two states, or the remaining 50 percent of our population.

Democrats accuse Republicans and conservatives of voter suppression. They seem to encourage voter dilution. What could possibly suppress voters more than the elimination of the Electoral College?

*Reduce the voting age to sixteen.*

"If you are not a liberal when you are 30, you have no heart; if you are not a conservative when you are 40, you have no brain." This quote is often attributed to Winston Churchill, but its true origin is the subject of controversy. Most of academia attribute the expression to Lord Acton, a British politician and historian.

Should we really consider providing voting rights to adolescents that have been so poorly trained in basic civics and history? The voting franchise is too serious a responsibility to give to children. This is simply another ploy, a blatant attempt to increase Democrat voting power.

*Give incarcerated felons the right to vote.* Some states, Florida most recently, have passed laws allowing convicted felons of *nonviolent* crimes to regain their right to vote after having completed all the conditions set out at court sentencing. I suspect that this was intended to allow the rehabilitation of individuals convicted of minor drug charges who had unusually severe sentences applied to them. To take the next leap, enacting a federal law allowing the vote to be reinstated to convicted felons regardless of the crime committed while they remain incarcerated, seems to be on the lunatic fringe. This is another obvious ploy, an attempt to increase Democrat voting power.

However, all things may not be as they seem. When Florida passed the state law pertaining to convicts that had completed their sentences, Jared Kushner, senior adviser to President Donald Trump, in a Fox News interview, reported that the majority of those that registered to vote registered as Republicans. I have been unable to confirm, or refute, that statistic.

*Free college tuition.* This represents another liberal solution to a problem exacerbated by liberal policy.

In 2008, before the Obama administration passed a bill requiring that direct government lending replace the federally subsidized loans made by private banks, college tuition fees were much more affordable. When the federal government took over the student loan guaranty program, loan approval became almost automatic. With easy student loan approval, student application rates soared. Based upon the laws of supply and demand, college tuition rates increased faster than previously, close to doubling in a decade. An unintended consequence. In 2016, the average undergraduate was leaving school with $50,000 in debt, up from about $17,000 in 2008. Tuition debt now exceeds $1.6 trillion.[8]

To remedy this disaster and remove this legislative stain from our history, Democrat presidential hopefuls are promising free tuition. Presidential candidate Elizabeth Warren has proposed a plan to repay student loans by instituting a "wealth tax" on the superrich Americans.

Shouldn't we reward people for making the right choices, rather than compensate those that have made wrong choices? If America were to move to tuition-free college, where would the money come from? The simple answer is taxes; who gets taxed seems to vary based on who is being asked. I am certain that this promise would be a vote-getter for the sixteen-year-olds and their parents. Another example of shameless Democrat pandering.

*The Green New Deal.* While the program lacks specificity, there appear to be five goals that the resolution says should be accomplished in a ten-year mobilization effort: achieve net-zero greenhouse gas emissions; create millions of good, high-wage jobs; invest in the infrastructure and industry; and secure clean air and water. Climate and community resiliency, healthy food, access to nature, and a sustainable environment. Promote justice and equity by stop-

---

[8] *Forbs Magazine*—June 2018

ping current, preventing future, and repairing historic oppression of indigenous peoples, communities of color, migrant communities, deindustrialized communities, depopulated rural communities, the poor, low-income workers, women, the elderly, the unhoused, people with disabilities, and youth.[9]

Pollyanna. Clearly, this is more aspirational than practical.

How would this be funded? How could anyone realistically hope to achieve in 10 years what has not been achievable in 250? If you ask any thirty Democrat politicians what this plan means, I suspect that you would get as many explanations. This is not a serious proposal—it is fantasy.

*Medicare for all.* Intended to provide universal health care and eliminate the need for private health insurance. Advocates argue that this would provide coverage for those who are currently unable to afford health insurance.

Isn't this what the Affordable Care Act had promised to do? Critics suggest that the plan would be too costly.

Medicare accounted for 15 percent of all federal spending in 2017. Benefit payments were $709 billion, an increase of 65 percent over the last decade.[10] Almost 62 million Americans received Medicare benefits in 2017. Our total population is 326 million. By simple math, "Medicare for all" would cost $3.7 trillion each year. Medicare spending is projected to be 18 percent of all federal spending by 2028. The trust fund is expected to be depleted by 2026. Simple logic would dictate that expanding the Medicare population by a factor of 3 to 5 would accelerate the depletion of the fund. This plan would require enormous increases in individual taxes.

To see the future of government-run health care, one need only look as far as our Veteran's Hospital System, which has been a dismal failure by most accounts. It astounds me that our politicians are unable to see that the solution to resolving our medical expense crisis lies in the bending of the cost curve rather than promising unsustainable "free stuff."

---

[9] *New York Times: What is the New Green Deal*—February 2019
[10] US Department of Health and Human Services—*2017 Budget in Brief*

*Reparations for slavery.* The absurdity of this notion is farcical. What would reparations be but the extraction of money from people who never *owned* slaves, to give to people who never *were* slaves?

Socialism seems to be overtaking liberalism in the Democrat Party. The insanity of the "woke" folks will hopefully force a pushback at the ballot box from the more conventionally minded Americans. Socialism is not where most Americans are. Notwithstanding the naked political intentions of these proposals, new voices in Congress, like Ilhan Omar (D-MN), Rashida Tlaib (D-MI), and Alexandria Ocasio-Cortez (D-NY), should not be disregarded as "flakes." We would do so at our own peril. Alexandria Ocasio-Cortez has been mistakenly dismissed as a "pompous little twit."[11] The truth is that she is equally well-educated (Boston University) and uninformed. She is charming, charismatic, and has an unflinching belief in her socialistic views. I believe that AOC is representative of what our liberal colleges and universities have been graduating for the past decade.

Ocasio-Cortez, Tlaib, and Omar are illustrative of our millennial generation and our future political, business, and societal leaders. Underestimating their potential political influence would be foolhardy. This political discord, resurgence of racial strife, and Far Left-leaning policies are eroding the fabric of our society and nation.

Most government programs are based upon noble principles on their onset: to assist the economically disadvantaged, to provide a head start for those with inferior educational opportunity, or to provide a safety net for those who lack medical coverage. While some societal good and redressing of our national shortcomings have resulted from these efforts, the objectives of most remain unachieved. The cost has led to unsustainable national debt. Frequently, those programs are expanded beyond their original scope, for good or ill, and bastardized on the altar of political gain primarily to "buy" votes. It is truly a simple equation: free stuff equals votes equals political power. I do not believe that it is the purpose of government to pro-

---

[11] *The Western Journal: Greenpeace Co-Founder Slams Ocasio-Cortez over GND—March 2019*

vide free stuff; rather, it should provide a fair shot, a hand-up rather than a handout.

Oftentimes, they do not think of the longer-term implications and/or the unintended consequence of their legislative actions. A blatant example being Speaker Nancy Pelosi announcing, "You have to pass it to know what's in it," regarding the Affordable Care Act.[12]

Walter Lippmann, a prominent writer, journalist, and commentator in the 1960s, cautioned the American people to make personal sacrifices in order to overcome the nation's challenges. He admonished, "You took the good things for granted. Now you must earn them again, for every right that you cherish, you have a duty which you must fulfill. For every good which you wish to preserve, you will have to sacrifice your comfort and your ease. There is nothing for nothing any longer."[13]

It has been said that there is no such thing as a free lunch. All free stuff will eventually have to be paid for. Politicians have been mortgaging our future, and the future of our grandchildren, for five decades. What are we becoming? How did we get here? As a house is built brick by brick, it can also be dismantled brick by brick. Let's try to understand the "dismantling" of America, brick by brick.

My intent is to retrace our history, to understand how we came to this place. Where does government responsibility end and personal responsibility begin? Shouldn't Americans take personal liability for their own progress and advancement? Let us examine these progressive laws, assess their success, and consider their cost to the US taxpayer.

While I will attempt to be level-handed and unbiased in my research, to ignore the facts does not change the facts. As Senator Daniel Patrick Moynihan (D-NY) admonished, "You are entitled to your own opinion, but you are not entitled to your own facts."[14]

---

[12]  Speaker Nancy Pelosi—2010
[13]  *Respectfully Quoted: A Dictionary of Quotations. 1989.*
[14]  Daniel Patrick Moynihan: *A portrait of Letters of an American Visionary*

President Eisenhower once wrote that "the American mind, at best, is both Liberal and Conservative," suggesting that balance and civility are required in a democracy.

I will endeavor to cover the many facets of our country—economy, education, environment, immigration, health care, media, our national moral compass, slavery, racism and reparations, and wars and conflicts. I will attempt to weave an intellectual understanding of how and why we have come to this point, how, over two and a half centuries, we have been transforming America.

# Chapter I

# Athletics and Sports

One might question why I would begin this book with a chapter on athletics. The answer is simple: with my personal penchant for structure and order, I simply chose to organize the chapters alphabetically.

Once upon a time, a seemingly long, long time ago, in a world far, far away, young boys would settle disagreements on the sandlot ball field, or the playground, by wrestling one another to the ground, holding him in a headlock until he cried "Uncle!" After which, they would shake hands and resume playing. (I have no knowledge how young girls resolved disputes, if they even had disputes!) Today, those disputes are resolved through cyberbullying or, worse, physical violence.

In my youth, we played sports all year-round, spending countless hours playing sandlot games: football, baseball, basketball, etc. We also participated in organized leagues and school teams, but much of our time was spent playing games organized by ourselves. We found the playing venue, a street, empty lot, or schoolyard. We organized teams, set the rules, and figured out everything ourselves: equipment, preparing the field, and dealing with fights or injuries. There were no parents around. If you drive by any baseball field or basketball court today, it is unlikely to find kids just playing sports without parental control and oversight. The days of kids just going out and playing without formal organizations and leagues are quite rare. Almost everyone is now on a "travel team," is in special sports camp, or has a sports tutor. Today kids primarily participate in athletics organized and controlled by parents or schools, some starting as early as five years old.

On those playgrounds and ball fields we would stumble, suffer scrapes and bruises, and be told to "rub some dirt on it" or that "it won't kill you, it's a long way from your heart." It was in our nature to get up and resume play.

Today, scrapes and bruises are viewed as medical emergencies.

Sports play an important part in developing character, skill sets, and the notion of teamwork. Talent could be identified, recognized, and appreciated. Winning could be enjoyed and a sense of accomplishment felt and developed. Losing would be endured, lessons in coping with failure and disappointment learned, salved with the acquired "wait till next time" attitude always present.

Aren't these experiences, these opportunities to develop character lost in our age of participation trophies, bubble-wrapped children, and couch-borne smartphone game play?

Some children are gifted with athletic skills. We cannot all be stars in sports; others might be gifted with talent in math, art, writing composition, or science. Where are the participation trophies for those skill sets? *The New York Times* reported, "Trophies used to be awarded only to winners but are now little more than party favors: reminders of an experience, not tokens of true achievement. When awards are handed out like candy to every child who participates, they diminish in value. If every soccer player receives a trophy for merely showing up to practice and playing in games, the truly exceptional players are slighted. The same applies to teams. Regardless of individual effort or superior skills, all who participate receive equal acknowledgement. Trophies for all convey an inaccurate and potentially dangerous life message to children: We are all winners. This message is repeated at the end of each sports season, year after year, and is only reinforced by the collection of trophies that continues to pile up. We begin to expect awards and praise for just showing up—to class, practice, after-school jobs—leaving us woefully unprepared for reality. Outside the protected bubble of childhood, not everyone is a winner. Showing up to work, attending class, completing homework and trying my best at sports practice are expected of me, not worthy of an award. These are the foundations of a long path to potential success, a success that is not guaranteed no matter how much effort I put in."[15]

Competition is a part of life, even if it is not organized. There will be times in each person's life when something sought will be lost to someone else. Not allowing our youth to experience loss or failure during one's formative years is denying them the opportunity to develop the essential emotional skills of resilience and perseverance. This may very well have led us to today's surge in therapist appointments. Wouldn't our children be better developed physically and mentally if they just went outside and played in the sunshine, experienced firsthand success and failure, and had the opportunity to develop the ability to deal with success and failure gracefully and compassionately?

Ancient cultures, Greek and Roman, considered physical training as a philosophical ideal and an essential component to a complete education. Sports have become part of growing up with youth leagues, high schools, and colleges. Organized sports for youth are now an institution in America. Baseball, football, ice hockey, and soccer attract forty-four million youngsters, according to the National Council of Youth Sports.[16]

Regrettably, some parents have found a way to spoil the youthful sports experience, trying to coach from the sidelines and criticizing performance after the game. Many parents treat sports as an investment in a future scholarship and have diminished the value of "pickup" games and playground experience, in hopes of creating the next "phenom." As a result, some youngsters who are quite-good athletes get burned out and quit playing altogether by high school. Kids are leaving sports way too early. A survey conducted by the Aspen

---

[15] *The New York Times—Participation Trophies Send a Dangerous Message—* October 2016

[16] *Play and Playground Encyclopedia—National Council on Youth Sports*

Institute and the Utah State University found that kids, on average, quit playing sports by age eleven, the sixth grade.[17]

The Sports and Fitness Industry Association and the Aspen Institute published new data that shows athletic participation by children between six and twelve has dropped almost 8 percent in the last decade because of skyrocketing cost, sport specialization, and coaches needing training.[18]

Sadly, there was a recent news article in the sports pages of my hometown newspaper, *The Record*, lamenting the state of the sports program at my alma mater, Tenafly High School, in Tenafly, New Jersey: "One of the oldest programs in Bergen County is now dealing with low participation....It wasn't long ago that the Tigers were a playoff mainstay. This year will be the 70th anniversary of the first Thanksgiving Day game between Tenafly and Dumont. Once a fixture of North Jersey football…people who are 70 or 80 years old coming…" It follows that if student participation wanes, so will the ability to field a competitive team, then so will the student and adult audience.

The World Health Organization has advised that the United States has a physical inactivity epidemic that has been getting worse over the past three decades. Not getting enough physical activity can lead to overweight issues and obesity during childhood and into adulthood. These, in turn, can lead to a range of medical problems such as diabetes. Sports should be fun, but for many kids, sports just aren't fun anymore.[19]

Baseball is considered America's pastime; Sunday without the NFL would be unimaginable by many.

Athletes have always been role models for children. What young boy did not want a Mickey Mantle baseball card? Who didn't point to the fence like Babe Ruth when at bat? What young girl didn't idolize Mary Lou Retton, Olga Korbut, or Nadia Comaneci? What young baseball player didn't imitate Derek Jeter's "time, hand up"

---

[17] *Forbes: Age 11 Is When Kids Quit Sports*—August 2019
[18] *The Washington Post—Youth Sports Study: Declining Participation*—September 2017
[19] *Forbes: Age 11 Is When Kids Quit Sports*—August 2019

signal when at bat? What aspiring football player didn't emulate Joe Namath's white shoe style and flair? These were positive influences. Athletics have always been an important part of American culture. Professional sports—baseball, basketball, football, soccer, and hockey—have become huge industries.

In April 1967, sports became a political platform.

Though it was never intended to be a forum for expressing political philosophy, its nature was dramatically changed when Muhammad Ali refused to be inducted into the US Army. Ali cited religious reasons, saying, "I ain't got no quarrel with those Vietcong. Those Vietcong never called me nigger." He was immediately stripped off his heavyweight title. There was no disrespect for the flag or anthem. Ali made his *personal* choice and paid a *personal* price.

Ultimately, the Supreme Court ruled in favor of Ali, eight to zero, and his boxing license was reinstated.

This action was followed by a series of other athlete protests over the decades:

- During the 1968 Olympics in Mexico City, gold medal winner Tommie Smith and bronze medal winner John Carlos raised their black-gloved fists in a black-power salute during the playing of the US national anthem. This act of nonviolent civil disobedience was in protest of racial strife in the United States.
- In 1996, Chris Jackson, basketball player for the Denver Nuggets, refused to stand for the national anthem at the NBA games because he viewed the American flag as a symbol of oppression. He was suspended for one game.
- After the September 11, 2001, attack on the World Trade Center, Pat Tillman, NFL player for the Arizona Cardinals, turned down a $3.6-million-dollar contract offer and enlisted in the US Army Rangers. He was killed in Afghanistan. The ultimate act of patriotism, serving what he saw as a higher calling, a greater good.
- In 2010, after Arizona passed a law that allowed police to demand to see documentation regarding legal status, the

Phoenix Suns wore "Los Suns" jerseys on Cinco De Mayo to express solidarity with the Latino community. There was no act of disrespect of the flag or anthem.
- In 2012, LeBron James and the rest of the Miami Heat basketball team posed for a photo donned with hoods and lowered heads, to express solidarity with the Florida community torn apart by the Trayvon Martin killing. There was no disrespect of the flag or anthem.
- In 2014, several of the St. Louis Rams players walked out of the tunnel during pregame introductions with their hands up in the air, depicting the "hands up, don't shoot" gesture, to protest the shooting of Michael Brown in Ferguson, Missouri. There was no disrespect of the flag or anthem. In each of these instances, the price for the athlete's action was borne by the athlete.
- In 2016, Colin Kaepernick, quarterback for the San Francisco 49ers, refused to stand and instead took a knee during the playing of the national anthem. He later stated, referring to the series of black men that had been shot and killed by police, "I am not going to stand up to show pride in a flag for a country that oppresses black people and people of color.... There are bodies in the street and people getting paid leave and getting away with murder."

Kaepernick eventually paid the price for his action—his career ended. Some will speculate that he was blacklisted; others might conclude that team owners did not want his distraction in the clubhouse.

Several other NFL players would copy this action in the months ahead. In this instance, none of the players besides Kaepernick paid a significant price for their unsanctioned acts.

Instead, the NFL suffered the economic burden emanating from the players' actions:

- Nearly 32 percent of adults said they were less likely to watch NFL game telecasts because of the Kaepernick-led player protests.[20]
- NFL ticket sales dropped 18 percent, the steepest decline since 2014. The slump in sales underscored the pressure facing the NFL over the anthem protests.[21]
- CBS, ESPN, Fox, and NBC suffered a substantial decline in NFL ratings, costing the four networks $500 million in lost revenue.[22]

Should highly paid employees be able to damage the business that pays their salary in the name of political protest with impunity?

- In 2016, American soccer player Megan Rapinoe knelt in solidarity with Colin Kaepernick during the national anthem before a game between the USA and Thailand.
- At ESPN, a sports television network, sportscasters frequently inject politics into its broadcasts. Is it appropriate for viewers of sports-related news to be subjected to ESPN commentators' political opinions?
- Megan Rapinoe expanded her protest at the Women's World Cup in 2019 when she declared that she is a "walking protest" when it comes to the Trump administration. Her decision to kneel during the national anthem is an "F you to the White House." She continues, "I'll probably never put my hand on my heart. I'll probably never sing the National Anthem again."[23]

---

[20] *Forbes: NFL Losing Millions of TV Viewers Because of National Anthem Protests*—October 2016

[21] CBS News—*NFL National Anthem Protests Denting Ticket Sales*—September 2017

[22] Out Kick the Coverage—NFL Partners set to lose up to $500 Million—November 2017

[23] *The Washington Examiner—Meghan Rapinoe: "I'm not going to the f… White House"*—June 2019

How did athletes refusing an invitation to the White House as a form of protest become an acceptable "thing"? It seems the epitome of disrespect.

In August 2019, Olympic gold medalist Race Imboden took a knee during the playing of the national anthem during the award ceremonies at the Pan American Games in Peru. He tweeted, "We must call for change. This week I am honored to represent Team USA at the Pan Am Games, taking home Gold and Bronze. My pride, however, has been cut short by the multiple shortcomings of the country I hold so dear to my heart. Racism, Gun Control, mistreatment of immigrants."[24] At the same games, Gwen Berry, gold medal winner in the hammer throw, raised a clenched-fist black-power salute during the national anthem. Berry told *USA Today*, "Somebody has to talk about the things that are too uncomfortable to talk about. Somebody has to stand for all of the injustices that are going on in America and a President who's making it worse."[25] Is it too cynical to suggest the motive of these most recent actions as directed more toward social media exposure and less toward political protest?

- In October 2016, the Beaumont Bulls, a youth football team in Beaumont, Texas, decided to take a knee. The reaction was swift—the game was canceled.[26]
- An eight-year-old St. Louis youth football team decided to kneel during the national anthem in September 2017 in protest of a white police officer being acquitted of murdering a black man in a car chase.[27]
- In September 2017, members of a girls' soccer team at Traip Academy in Kittery, Maine, knelt during the national

---

[24] NBC Sports—*Race Imboden, Olympic Fencer, takes knee at Pan Am Games*—August 2019
[25] *USA Today*—*US fencer hammer thrower show principles with podium protests*—August 2019
[26] *The Washington Post*—*These Youth Football Players Took a Knee*—October 2016
[27] *The Washington Post*—*Eight-Year Old Football Players kneel*—September 2017

anthem before their match. This was a day after Sunday NFL games were filled with players that took a knee.[28]
- In 2017, the high school band that played the national anthem before a Monday-night Oakland A's baseball game took a knee.
- Many school teams took a knee in 2016 when Kaepernick was active, and there are expectations that it will happen again.[29]

Are these "positive" influences? Can an eight-year-old understand the significance of their action? Shouldn't a coach be a better role model rather than simply use the children as political pawns?

In August 2019, the *Wall Street Journal* published an article suggesting that an athlete should be encouraged to be "a person in the world," using their platform to speak their voice on whatever policy or social event they feel passionately about.[30] I am in complete agreement with that sensibility. However, I prefer that their voice be expressed in *their* forum, not their employers', to *their audience*, rather than the fans at a sporting event, and be expressed without disrespect to things that are held dear by others.

There is a reason that these are called games. They are intended to allow recreation, not indoctrination. Why don't we insist that children be allowed to be children? Why do we steal their youth? Why do we insist on removing the fun from the games? Are the children and young adults protesting or parroting?

Title IX of the Education Amendments Act of 1972 is a federal law prohibiting gender discrimination in athletic programs at institutions that receive federal funds. The law was introduced by Senator Birch Bayh (D-IN) and Representative Edith Green (D-SD) and signed into law by Republican president Richard

---

[28] *Forbes: Young Athletes, Again, Take a Knee During National Anthem*—September 2017
[29] *The Washington Post*—*Eight -Year Old Football Players kneel*—September 2017
[30] *The Wall Street Journal*—*Sticking to Sports vs. Being a Person in the World*—August 2019

Nixon.[31] Senators Tower and Javits and Representative James O'Hara, all Republicans, attempted to dilute the bill in 1974 and 1975, introducing amendments that would restrict the distribution of funds away from income-generating college sports. All those attempts failed.[32]

Since it was enacted, the number of female high school and college athletes has increased tremendously. This was an appropriate action, intended to expand the opportunity for young women. While this may have created budget conflicts in the athletic departments of schools and colleges, it has also allowed generations of children to better enjoy sports, athletics, this "essential component to a complete education." The 2019 Women's World Soccer Cup was won by the Unites States team. This victory would not have been possible without Title IX.

Tim Delaney, sports author, wrote, "To ignore sport is to ignore a significant aspect of any society and its culture…sport is the opiate of the masses, due to the fact that we are in the age of the sport consumer, which is dissimilar to the age of the sport spectator."[33]

Title IX has proven to be good legislation; there was no unintended consequence.

It might be ultimately healthier for our children if parents allowed a realistic assessment of youthful athletic skill instead of insisting that it be masked with participation trophies and their misleading false parity, if parents resisted the temptation that their child must be the next "phenom" and let them simply enjoy the games, and if parents would stop trying to relive their own lives vicariously through their children. Then perhaps the pure enjoyment of athletics could return. It might be more productive if professional athletes would recognize that with their fame, fortune, and God-given talent comes an enormous responsibility as a role model for the young children that idolize and will emulate them. We might be better off if athletes remained silent regarding their political beliefs when

---

[31] United States Department of Justice—*Overview of Title IX of the Education Amendments of 1972*
[32] Women's Sports Foundation—*History of Title IX*
[33] *The Sociology of Sports: An Introduction*—Tim Delaney—2009

on the playing field. We might benefit if equipment manufacturers employed successful athletes to *market their products* rather than the *expression of a political perspective*. Perhaps Nike should sell their shoes, not their politics, and *ESPN* should report on sports and not politics.

Wouldn't we be better off if we let sports be games and allow children to be children, let the children enjoy and grow with sports?

Just askin'.

# Chapter II

# Economy

In order to understand the levers and gears, the brakes, the pumps and valves, and the fuel that drives our economy, we must retrace the evolution of currency, banking, and government agencies influencing, or influenced by, that economy. While I have taken the requisite undergraduate and graduate economics courses of a business major, I am hardly an economist. My purpose is to trace the way legislative decisions have affected, and might affect in the future, America's economic system.

Capitalism, socialism, or communism? In the "this is a football" introduction style of the legendary football coach Vince Lombardi, let us first express the actual definitions of *capitalism*, *socialism*, and *communism*.

Capitalism—an economic and political system in which a country's trade and industry are controlled by private owners for profit rather than by the state.

Socialism—a political and economic theory of social organization that advocates that the means of production, distribution, and exchange should be owned or regulated by the *community*.

Communism—a political theory derived from Karl Marx, advocating class war and leading to a society in which *all property* is *publicly owned* and each person works and is paid according to their abilities and needs.

Capitalism and socialism are opposing schools of thought rooted in the notions of economic equality and the role of government. On the one hand, capitalism is based upon privately owned business and is created with private capital and managed for profit, with the free market determining winners and losers. Success is rewarded; failure is punished. Capitalism encourages initiative, innovation, and ambition. Simply put, capitalists look for less government involvement—laissez-faire. On the other hand is socialism, where government is responsible for reducing perceived economic inequality through programs that benefit the poor. Free public education, free health care, social security programs for the elderly, and higher taxes for the wealthy. Simply put, socialists seek more government involvement—collectivization. No winners, no losers. Every developed country has some programs that are socialist in principle.

In capitalism, you reap your personal wealth and benefits based upon your personal efforts, whereas in socialism you derive those things from the government dole.

An extreme form of socialism is communism.

When contemporary polls show that almost 50 percent of Americans view "some form of socialism" as favorable, we seem at risk.

> I don't doubt the good intentions of the new identity politics, to expand the opportunities for people previously excluded, but what we have now is far more than the liberal project itself. Marxism with a patina of liberalism on top is still Marxism—and it's as hostile to the idea of a free society as white nationalism is. (Andrew Sullivan, British-born American author and editor)

I recently came across a piece written by Alyssa Ahlgren, a twentysomething student and writer from Middle America. According to the Foundation for Economic Education, Alyssa holds her bachelor's degree in business administration and currently works as an analyst in corporate finance. She is also pursuing her MBA through the University of Wisconsin. Alyssa spent most of her undergrad as a prelaw student until she decided to pursue her passion for current events and politics through writing and being an advocate for the conservative movement. I found Alyssa's thoughts to be profound and timely and offer them here:

## Thoughts from a Hipster Coffee Shop

I'm sitting in a small coffee shop near Nokomis trying to think of what to write about. I scroll through my newsfeed on my phone looking at the latest headlines of Democratic candidates calling for policies to "fix" the so-called injustices of capitalism.

I put my phone down and continue to look around. I see people talking freely, working on their MacBook's, ordering food they get in an instant, seeing cars go by outside, and it dawned on me. We live in the most privileged time in the most prosperous nation and we've become completely blind to it; vehicles, food, technology, freedom to associate with whom we choose.

These things are so ingrained in our American way of life we don't give them a second thought. We are so well off here in the United States that our poverty line begins 31 times above the global average. Thirty. One. Times.

Virtually no one in the United States is considered poor by global standards. Yet, in a time where we can order a product off Amazon with one click and have it at our doorstep the next day, we are unappreciative, unsatisfied, and ungrateful.

Our unappreciation is evident as the popularity of socialist policies among my generation continues to grow.

Democratic Congresswoman Alexandria Ocasio-Cortez recently said to Newsweek talking about the millennial generation, "An entire generation, which is now becoming one of the largest electorates in America, came of age and never saw American prosperity." Never saw American prosperity. Let that sink in. When I first read that statement, I thought to myself, that was quite literally the most entitled and factually illiterate thing I've ever heard in my 26 years on this earth. Now, I'm not attributing Miss Ocasio-Cortez's words to outright dishonesty. I do think she whole-heartedly believes the words she said to be true. Many young people agree with her, which is entirely misguided. My generation is being indoctrinated by a mainstream narrative to believe we have never seen prosperity. I know this firsthand, I went to college, let's just say I didn't have the popular opinion, but I digress.

Let me lay down some universal truths quick. The United States of America has lifted more people out of abject poverty, spread more freedom and democracy, and has created more innovation in technology and medicine than any other nation in human history. Not only that but our citizenry continually breaks world records with charitable donations, the rags to riches story is not only possible in America but not uncommon, we have the strongest purchasing power on earth, and we encompass 25 percent of the world's GDP. The list goes on. However, these universal truths don't matter. We are told that income inequality is an existential crisis (even though this is not an indicator of prosperity, some of the poorest countries in the world have low-income inequality), we are told that we are oppressed by capitalism (even though it's brought about more freedom and wealth to the most people than any other system in world history), we are told that the only way we will acquire the benefits of true prosperity is through socialism and centralization of federal power (even though history has proven time and again this only brings tyranny and suffering). Why then, with all the overwhelming evidence around us, evidence that I can even see sitting at a coffee shop, do we not view this as prosperity? We have people who are dying to get into our country. People around the world destitute and truly impoverished. Yet, we have a young generation convinced they've never seen prosperity, and as a result, elect politicians dead set on taking steps towards abolishing capitalism. Why? The answer is this, my generation has ONLY seen prosperity. We have no contrast. We didn't live in the great depression, or live through two world wars, or see the rise and fall of socialism and communism. We don't know what it's like not to live without the internet, without cars, without smartphones. We don't have a lack of prosperity problem. We have an entitlement problem, an ungratefulness problem, and it's spreading like a plague. With the current political climate giving rise to the misguided idea of a socialist utopia, will we see the light? Or will we have to lose it all to realize that what we have now is true prosperity? Destroying the free market will undo what millions of people have died to achieve. My generation is becoming the largest voting bloc in the country. We have an opportunity to continue to propel us forward with the gifts capitalism and democracy has given us. The other option is that we can fall into the trap of entitlement and relapse into restrictive socialist destitution. The choice doesn't seem too hard, does it?[34]

I believe that Alyssa has penned a perceptive, even brilliant, summary of our current national milieu. There is hope for the millennials.

We should be wary of where we have come and where we are going. We should learn from our experience and engage in our social engineering, giving more thought to a "longer view." Legislate with more trepidation regarding possible unintended consequences. Anticipate rather than react.

> When government—in pursuit of good intentions—tries to rearrange the economy, legislate morality, or help special interests, the cost come in inefficiency, lack of motivation, and loss of freedom. Government should be a referee, not an active player. (Milton Friedman, economist, Nobel laureate)

The industrial capacity of Europe and Asia had been destroyed in the Second World War, as had their economies. Much of the world was struggling to rebuild. After the war, the United Stated stood alone as the greatest industrial nation in the entire world and undertook the massive job of rebuilding Europe. America has always used its successful economy to assist the world.

Between 1947 and 1960, the United States enjoyed unfettered economic expansion, and its citizens reaped the harvest. As a nation, we shared that success with the rest of the world, both with the

---

[34] The Atlas Society—*Thoughts from a hipster coffee shop*—April 2019

Marshall Plan in Europe and with General MacArthur's stewardship in the rebuilding of Japan.

Again, today the US economy is the strongest in the world. Unemployment is at historic lows by every measure. Consumer confidence is high, wages are up, and the stock market is soaring. However, the economy is cyclical, and the future is not guaranteed.

Sadly, we seem to repeat the poor decisions that adversely affect our economy, most of which have been triggered by abandoning sound credit policy.

> America isn't Congress. America isn't Washington. America is the striving immigrant who starts a business, or the mom who works two low-wage jobs to give her kid a better life. America is the union leader and the CEO who put aside their differences to make the economy stronger. (Barack Obama, forty-fourth US president)

We must be better stewards.

## American Currency, the Treasury, Banking, and the Federal Reserve

Prior to 1690, the new American colonies relied upon coins as currency. This reliance changed when, with a shortage of coins, the Massachusetts Bay Company issued paper currency to meet the demands of trade.[35]

In July 1775, the Second Continental Congress assigned the responsibility for the administration of the revolutionary government's finances to joint Continental treasurers George Clymer and Michael Hillegas. The Congress stipulated that each of the colonies contribute to the Continental government's funds.[36]

---

[35] Daily Reckoning—*A Timeline of US Currency*—May 2015
[36] US Department of the Treasury—*History of the Treasury*

# UNINTENDED CONSEQUENCE

The Continental dollar, "Continentals," was the first currency printed in the United States, authorized by the Continental Congress in 1775 to fund the Revolutionary War. They were printed in such quantity that they resulted in inflation. People lost faith in the currency, and the expression "Not worth a Continental" came to mean "utterly worthless."[37]

This $65 Continental note was issued January 14, 1779. The Revolutionary money was printed in various denominations and signed by hand. (University Libraries of Notre Dame)

On September 2, 1789, Congress created a permanent institution for the management of government finances:

> Be it enacted by the Senate and House of Representatives of the United States of America in Congress assembled, that there shall be a Department of Treasury, in which shall be the following officers, namely: a Secretary of the

---
[37] Federal Reserve Education.Org—*History of the Federal Reserve*

> Treasury, to be deemed head of the department; a Comptroller, an Auditor, a Treasurer, a Register, and an Assistant to the Secretary of the Treasury, which assistant shall be appointed by the said Secretary.

Alexander Hamilton took the oath of office as the first secretary of the treasury on September 11, 1789, and his first official act was to submit a report to Congress in which he laid the foundation for the nation's financial health.[38] In January 1790, Hamilton presented his First Report on Public Credit to Congress, in which he insisted upon federal assumption and dollar-for-dollar repayment of the country's war debt of $75 million in order to revitalize the public credit: "There are arguments for it which rest on the immutable principles of moral obligation…This reflection derives additional strength from the nature of the debt of the United States. It was the price of liberty. The faith of America has been repeatedly pledged for it, and with solemnities that give peculiar force to the obligation."[39] Hamilton foresaw the development of industry and trade in the United States and suggested that government revenues be reliant upon customs duties.

The Treasury Department is responsible for promoting economic prosperity and ensuring the financial security of the United States. It advises the president on economic and financial issues, encouraging sustainable economic growth and fostering improved governance in financial institutions. The Department of the Treasury is responsible for the production of coin and currency, the disbursement of payments to the American public, revenue collection, and the borrowing of funds necessary to run the federal government.

For the first forty years after its independence, the US operated with gold and silver coins, with silver being the favored currency and purchases made with gold infrequent. By 1835, large amounts of silver were being exported; consequently, silver coins became less common and gold coins became the principal form of currency.[40]

---

[38] US Department of the Treasury—*History of the Treasury*
[39] Online Library of Liberty—*1790: Hamilton, First Report on Public Credit*
[40] US Department of the Treasury—*History of the Treasury*

# UNINTENDED CONSEQUENCE

In 1791, treasury secretary Alexander Hamilton established the First Bank of the United States, dominated by big banking and money interests, feared by the agrarian-minded Americans. When the bank's charter expired in 1811, Congress refused to renew it. In 1816, Congress chartered the Second Bank of the United States. President Andrew Jackson opposed the bank, and its charter was not renewed after 1828. During the "free bank period" of 1836 and 1865, state-chartered banks and unchartered "free banks" issued their own notes, purported to be redeemable in gold or silver.

In 1863, the National Banking Act was passed, providing for nationally chartered banks, whose circulating notes had to be backed by US government securities, effectively creating a uniform currency for the nation.

During the Civil War, the United States also issued its first fiat money, paper certificates without any convertibility into silver, gold, or any other precious metal. By 1879, Congress froze the amount of paper money allowed to be in circulation at $347 million, where it remained for almost a century.

A $1 "greenback," issued in 1862. It was the first time the U.S. issued paper money unbacked by physical gold or silver.

The government began issuing silver certificate dollars, referred to as "greenbacks," in 1878. The next year, the United States adopted the "classic" gold standard, where a standard amount of gold defined the value of a paper currency unit, which was then fully convertible into gold.

This lasted until World War I and is widely considered to be one of the most economically stable systems in American history.

In 1893, a banking panic triggered the worst depression the United States had ever seen, and the economy stabilized only after the intervention of financial mogul J. P. Morgan. It was clear that the nation's banking and financial system needed serious attention. There was a growing consensus among all Americans that a central banking authority was needed to ensure a healthy banking system and provide for an elastic currency.[41]

Congress passed the Gold Standard Act of 1900, making the gold dollar the official unit of currency. Silver certificates, "greenbacks," remained as legal tender but, for the first time, could be redeemed in gold.

President Woodrow Wilson signed the Federal Reserve Act of 1913 into law, creating a government agency with the responsibility of gaining control over the predominantly decentralized banking industry. The Federal Reserve System was created to provide the nation with a safer, more flexible, and more stable monetary and financial system. The responsibilities of the "Fed" are fivefold: to conduct monetary policy by influencing money and credit conditions in the economy in pursuit of full employment and stable prices, to supervise and regulate banks and other financial institutions to ensure the safety and soundness of the nation's banking and financial system, to protect the credit rights of consumers, to maintain the stability of the financial system and guard against systemic risk, and to provide certain financial services to the US government, US financial institutions, and foreign official institutions, by overseeing the nation's payments systems.

---

[41] Federal Reserve Education.Org—*History of the Federal Reserve*

In 1913, in response to periodic banking panics, when gold reserves fell short, the Federal Reserve was established as a "lender of last resort." The fed was charged with maintaining the gold standard but was also allowed to begin issuing Federal Reserve notes that were only 40 percent backed by gold. This was the first step in moving away from a strict gold standard.[42]

In 1933, four years after the Wall Street Crash of 1929, the feds removed the US from the gold standard to expand monetary policy. Convertibility of currency for precious metal was then ended. President Franklin Roosevelt told Congress, "The free circulation of gold coins is unnecessary," insisting that the transfer of gold "is essential only for the payment of international trade balances." Roosevelt nationalized gold by issuing an executive order requiring all gold coins, bullion, and certificates be turned over to the Federal Reserve Bank at $20.67 per ounce. Hoarding gold in coin or bullion would be punishable by a fine of up to $10,000 and/or imprisonment. These policies were reinforced in the Gold Reserve Act of 1934.

In 1944, representatives from the United States and forty-three other countries met in Bretton Woods, New Hampshire, to normalize international commercial and financial relations. They agreed upon a system whereby each country's currency, other than the US dollar, would have a fixed parity to the dollar, which was pegged to and could be exchanged for gold at $35 per ounce. (This did not apply to Americans, however, who were still prohibited from owning gold.) With this agreement, the dollar became the world's reserve currency.

In 1971, President Nixon announced that the US would no longer convert dollars into gold. By 1976, the US monetary system officially became one purely of fiat money. On December 31, 1974, President Gerald Ford permitted private gold ownership again in the United States. The value of gold rose 2,330 percent during the decade, from $35 per ounce to $850.[43]

---

[42] Board of Governors of the Federal Reserve System—*What is the Purpose of the Federal Reserve?*

[43] US Global Investors—*An Illustrated* Timeline *of the Gold Standard in the US*—December 2015

When a country adheres to a gold standard, the amount of its currency in existence is limited by their supply of gold. Since there is a finite amount of gold, a country's ability to print new currency is restricted. Conversely, without the gold standard guardrail, there is no limit to the volume of currency that can be printed and released into the economy.

As had been outlined earlier, for much of our country's existence, we have been on some level of the gold standard. However, in the early 1970s, the cost of the Vietnam War and President Johnson's "Great Society" escalated, which prompted President Nixon to completely abandon the gold standard. With the absence of the gold standard, American dollars were backed only by the "full faith and credit" of the US government. Fiat money. This allowed the government to print as many dollars as it wanted, as often as it wanted. The more it printed, the less value each dollar possessed. The most egregious result of the gold standard removal is that it allowed massive government overspending.[44]

The United States national debt in 1960 was $286 billion. In 2019, it is over $22 trillion.[45] Perhaps we should be guided by the lesson of the "continental."

As a nation, we have moved from fiat currency to a gold standard and returned to fiat currency again, backed by the "full faith and credit" of the United States. The danger of fiat currency is that it will certainly lead to the continued devaluation of the US dollar. As more billions, even trillions, are printed, we have all experienced the dwindling spending power of the dollar.

As if this fiscal irresponsibility weren't enough, we are now being faced with the advent of cryptocurrency, a digital currency in which encryption techniques are used to regulate the generation of units of currency and verify the transfer of funds, operating independently of a central bank. Read that as imaginary money. This is an illogical extension of eliminating the gold standard, yet it is estimated that

---

[44] *Forbes Magazine—Gold, the Dollar and Exploding Debt*—July 2012
[45] Polidiodic—*US National Debt by Year*

550,000 people currently participate in one cybercurrency known as Bitcoin.[46]

Are we really receding from the irresponsibility of fiat currency to the insanity of cryptocurrency? Is this really the future we want? Facebook seems to think so. According to recent news reports, Facebook is planning to launch its own version, called Libra. It will be a cryptocurrency available to the users of its array of platforms. Presumably, any merchant with an account on these platforms could transact in the cryptocurrency with customers who also have accounts for online purchases and physical-world purchases, such as groceries and restaurants.[47] While the Facebook entry to the market may give the concept some validity, in my view, cybercurrency may ultimately become a Ponzi scheme—beware!

Over time, our politicians have weakened our fiscal position and amassed enormous debt. "Free stuff" must be paid for. Before we decide what additional "free stuff" we might offer, we must first determine how we will pay for the "free stuff" already given.

As Alexander Hamilton advised, "The faith of America has been repeatedly pledged for it, and with solemnities that give peculiar force to the obligation."[48]

## Legislation that Shaped the Economy

In addition to legislation establishing and governing our country's banks, currency, treasury department, and the Federal Reserve, there have been a series of legislative initiatives that helped shape our national economy, some advantageous, others not so much. The furthest-reaching legislation falls under the category of income taxes, which affects every American. Our first secretary of the treasury, Alexander Hamilton, relied upon tariffs and customs duties to

---

[46] ICO Making—*How Many People Cryptocurrency*—July—2019
[47] *Forbes Magazine*—*What Facebook's Cryptocurrency Means*—June 2019
[48] Online Library of Liberty—*1790: Hamilton, First Report on Public Credit*

fund the US government, but there would come a time when those sources of revenue would fail to provide adequately.

The first income tax was imposed when Congress passed the Income Tax Act of 1894. The tax at that time was 2 percent on individual income in excess of $4,000, which meant that it reached only the wealthiest members of the population. The Supreme Court struck down the tax, holding that it violated the constitutional requirement that direct taxes be apportioned among the states by population.

This decision led to the Sixteenth Amendment to the Constitution, ratified in 1913, providing Congress with the power to lay and collect taxes on income without apportionment among the states. The objectives of the income tax were the equitable distribution of the tax burden and the raising of revenue.[49] Subsequent changes to the tax laws reflected the needs of the times. The tax of 1913 was later replaced with a graduated tax after America entered World War I.

The War Revenue Act of 1917 imposed a maximum tax rate for individuals of 67 percent, compared with a rate of 13 percent in 1916. After the war ended, the secretary of the treasury Andrew W. Mellon, speaking to Congress about the high level of taxation, stated, "The present system is a failure. It was an emergency measure, adopted under the pressure of war necessity and not to be counted upon as a permanent part of our revenue structure.... The high rates put pressure on taxpayers to reduce their taxable income, tend to destroy individual initiative and enterprise, and seriously impede the development of productive business.... Ways will always be found to avoid taxes so destructive in their nature, and the only way to save the situation is to put the taxes on a reasonable basis that will permit business to go on and industry to develop."

Consequently, the Revenue Act of 1924 reduced the maximum individual tax rate to 43 percent. In 1926, the rate was further reduced to 25 percent.[50] (The Trump administration shared Andrew Mellon's view of lower taxes being an economic stimulator.)

---

[49] Encyclopedia.com—*Income Tax*—September 2019
[50] Encyclopedia.com—*Income Tax*—September 2019

# UNINTENDED CONSEQUENCE

The Revenue Act of 1932 was the first tax law passed during the Great Depression; it increased the individual maximum rate from 25 percent to 63 percent and reduced personal exemptions. The repeal in 1933 of the Eighteenth Amendment, which had prohibited the manufacture and sale of alcohol, brought in an estimated $90 million in new liquor taxes in 1934.

The Social Security Act of 1935 provided for a wage tax, half to be paid by the employee and half by the employer, to establish a federal retirement fund.

A "wealth tax," also known as the Revenue Act of 1935, increased the maximum tax rate to 79 percent, the Revenue Acts of 1940 and 1941 increased it to 81 percent, the Revenue Act of 1942 raised it to 88 percent, and the Individual Income Tax Act of 1944 raised the individual maximum rate to 94 percent.[51]

The post-World War II Revenue Act of 1945 reduced the individual maximum tax from 94 percent to 91 percent. The Revenue Act of 1950, during the Korean Conflict, reduced it to 84.4 percent, but it was raised the next year to 92 percent. It remained at this level until 1964, when it was reduced to 70 percent.[52]

In 1974, the Employee Retirement Income Security Act (ERISA) created protections for employees whose employers promised specified pensions or other retirement contributions. ERISA required that for those contributions to be tax deductible, the employer's plan contribution must meet certain minimum standards as to employee participation and vesting and employer funding. ERISA also approved the use of individual retirement accounts (IRAs) to encourage tax-deferred retirement savings by individuals.

The Economic Recovery Tax Act of 1981 (ERTA) provided the largest tax cut up to that time, reducing the maximum individual rate from 70 percent to 50 percent. The most sweeping tax changes since World War II were enacted in the Tax Reform Act of 1986. This bill was signed into law by President Ronald Reagan and was designed to equalize the tax treatment of various assets, eliminate

---

[51] Encyclopedia.com—*Income Tax*—September 2019
[52] Encyclopedia.com—*Income Tax*—September 2019

tax shelters, and lower marginal rates. Tax rates were reduced to 15 percent on the first $17,850 of income for singles and $29,750 for married couples and set at 28 percent to 33 percent on remaining income. Many deductions were repealed.

The Omnibus Budget Reconciliation Act of 1993, the first budget and tax act enacted during President William J. Clinton's administration, provided for income tax rates of 15, 28, 31, 36, and 39.6 percent on varying levels of income. It also mandated the taxation of Social Security income if the taxpayer receives other income over a certain level.

In 2001, Congress enacted the Economic Growth and Tax Relief Reconciliation Act, a major income tax cut, at the urging of President George W. Bush. Over the course of eleven years, the law reduced marginal income tax rates across all levels of income. The 36 percent rate would be lowered to 33 percent, the 31 percent rate to 28 percent, the 28 percent rate to 25 percent. In addition, a new bottom 10 percent rate was created.[53]

In 2017, President Donald Trump signed the Tax Cuts and Jobs Act, which cut corporate tax rates permanently and individual tax rates until 2025, allowed immediate deductions for capital plant and equipment expenditures, permanently removed the "individual mandate" imposed by the Affordable Care Act, doubled the standard deduction to $24,000, and capped the federal deduction for state and local property taxes to $10,000.[54] Capping the state and local tax deduction at $10,000 was of significant concern to the mostly Democrat states of New York, New Jersey, and California, which had the highest property taxes in the country.

The tax plan enacted a deep and permanent cut for corporations, slashing the top rate from 35 percent to 21 percent. The bill also includes tax cuts for individuals and families of all income levels, with the largest breaks going to the wealthiest. The individual tax cuts were slated to expire in 2025, a move necessary to comply with

---

[53] Encyclopedia.com—*Income Tax*—September 2019
[54] Investopedia—*Explaining the Trump Tax Reform Plan*—August 2019

Senate budget rules, but Republicans said a future Congress would extend them.

Senator Chuck Schumer (D-NY) said, "Republicans would rue the day when they passed the Bill," which he blasted as a "disgrace." Representative Nancy Pelosi (D-CA) called it "the worst bill in history." She described it as "an all-out looting of America, a wholesale robbery of the middle class," and said, "The GOP tax scam will go down, again, as one of the worst, most scandalous acts of plutocracy in our history."

Results of the Trump tax cuts would prove them wrong.

Between 2017 and 2018, the real median earnings of all workers increased 3.4 percent, the median household income was $63,179 in 2018, and the number of full-time, year-round workers increased by 2.3 million between 2017 and 2018.

The official poverty rate in 2018 was 11.8 percent, a decrease of 0.5 percent from 2017. For the first time in eleven years, the official poverty rate was significantly lower than that of 2007. The Tax Cuts and Jobs Act re-energized the American economy, reducing unemployment to historic low levels and increasing employment in all communities, including black, Hispanic, and women.[55]

The Great Depression of 1929 rocked our economy. Individuals and businesses that had invested in the stock market beyond their means suffered greatly, and many were economically obliterated. By 1933, the unemployment rate reached almost 25 percent.[56] President Herbert Hoover tried unsuccessfully to wrest the country out of the economic crisis, which led to the overwhelming election of Franklin D. Roosevelt in 1932.

In that campaign, FDR promised a "New Deal" for Americans. In his inaugural address, President Roosevelt famously told the American people, "First of all, let me assert my firm belief that the only thing we have to fear is fear itself."

---

[55] US Census Bureau—*Income, Poverty and Health Insurance Coverage*—September 2019

[56] *United States History—Unemployment Statistics during the Great Depression*

Between 1933 and 1939, FDR enacted components of his New Deal program, targeting immediate economic relief as well as reforms in industry, agriculture, finance, waterpower, jobs, and housing. All of which vastly increased the scope of government involvement in each of these areas.[57] New Deal programs included the Tennessee Valley Authority Act, which enabled the federal government to build dams along the Tennessee River to control flooding and generate inexpensive hydroelectric power for the people in the region; the Agricultural Adjustment Act, which paid farmers who produced wheat, dairy products, tobacco, and corn to leave their fields fallow in order to end agricultural surpluses and boost prices; the National Industrial Recovery Act, which guaranteed workers would have the right to unionize and bargain collectively for higher wages and better working conditions; the Glass-Steagall Act, which effectively separated commercial banking from investment banking and created the Federal Deposit Insurance Corporation; and the Home Owners' Loan Act creating the Homeowners Loan Corporation, lending low-interest money to families in danger of losing their homes to foreclosure. Roosevelt created the Work's Progress Administration to provide jobs for unemployed people. WPA projects focused on building things like post offices, bridges, schools, highways, and parks. The WPA also gave work to artists, writers, theater directors, and musicians.[58]

In July 1935, the National Labor Relations Act, also known as the Wagner Act, created the National Labor Relations Board to supervise union elections and prevent businesses from treating their workers unfairly.[59]

The Social Security Act was signed into law by President Franklin Roosevelt in 1935. The original act provided only worker retirement benefits. In 1939, amendments made a fundamental change in the program, adding two new categories of benefits: dependent benefits, payments to the spouse and minor children of a retired worker, and survivors benefits paid to the family in the event of the prema-

---

[57] *Encyclopedia Britannica—New Deal*
[58] *Encyclopedia Britannica—New Deal*
[59] History.Com—*New Deal*

# UNINTENDED CONSEQUENCE

ture death of the worker. The amendments also increased benefit amounts and accelerated the start of monthly benefit payments. The act created the basic tenants of the modern welfare system in the United States, with its primary focus to provide aid for the elderly, the unemployed, and children.

A further amendment in 1950 raised benefits and placed the program on the road to the virtually universal coverage of today and introduced the cost-of-living adjustment (COLA). Since 1972, the COLA has only been denied three times, all under the Obama administrations.

In 1965, President Lyndon Johnson merged the Social Security's trust accounts into the general government budget, allowing LBJ to disguise the then-growing deficit caused primarily by the spending for the Vietnam War. This consolidation, or comingling, provided funds for future liberal administrations to support their social reengineering policies and weakened the Social Security Trust Fund.

An important development in social insurance occurred when President Johnson created the Medicare and Medicaid programs in 1965, providing health-care coverage to retired and indigent citizens.

Legislative actions of the 1970s had profound effects on the Social Security program and set the stage for much of the program's financial weakness today. Large benefit increases, a new benefit formula that was erroneously generous, and other changes created a situation in which annual program costs increased from 3 percent to 5 percent of our national gross domestic product. We can see how the basic component of the social safety net was expanded to eventually become economically unsustainable. According to the Social Security Administration, nearly sixty-four million Americans will receive Social Security benefits in 2019, totaling almost $1 trillion.[60]

In 1983, based upon a Democrat House bill signed by Republican president Ronald Reagan, the government began taxing Social Security benefits. It originally allowed taxation of up to 50 percent of benefits, primarily affecting only wealthy recipients.

---

[60] Social Security Administration—*Fact Sheet*

In 1993, under the Clinton administration, a second tier of taxing those benefits was added, allowing up to 85 percent of an individual's or couple's benefits to be taxed.

A recently released analysis from the Senior Citizens League finds that 51 percent of senior households today pay tax on their Social Security benefits, greatly reducing the disposable income of most senior citizens. Between 1984 and 2017, $474 billion in aggregate was collected by the taxation of benefits. But over the next decade (defined as 2018 through 2027 in the trustees' report), the taxation of benefits is expected to generate $561 billion.[61] Unfortunately, these taxes paid by our senior citizens were not reinvested to shore up the Social Security Trust Fund; instead, they were added to the general fund to underwrite additional government programs. It seems that our politicians have never seen a dollar that they do not want to tax or spend!

In 1964, Democrat president Lyndon Johnson's national War on Poverty intended "not only to relieve the symptoms of poverty, but to cure it and, above all, to prevent it."[62] The War on Poverty has cost over $50 trillion since its inception and created generations dependent upon the government dole, while having no measurable impact on our national poverty level. Some economists distort today's poverty level by including the value of government assistance as income, masking, to some degree, the actual poverty level.[63]

In September 2019, Fox Business News reported that "wealth inequality reached its highest level in over fifty years, according to the Census Bureau and the American Community Survey." This should not come as a surprise when we, as a nation, have been importing poverty at an accelerated level over the past decade.

Our welfare system seems to encourage irresponsibility. A single parent receives a stipend to support her child. If she has additional children, her stipend increases. In this age of contraception, isn't

---

[61] Social Security Administration
[62] President Johnson—*State of the Union Address*—January 1964
[63] *Encyclopedia Britannica—War on Poverty*

bringing children into the welfare state irresponsible? Yet our system seems to encourage it.

Democrat president Kennedy authorized the Food Stamp Program in 1964, intended to provide supplemental income to the working poor and the impoverished. Its original guideline aided families with monthly income under $30 and cost the government $70 million for each of the first three years. Through excess and abuse, the Food Stamp Program has steadily increased in payment and eligibility. Today, it has been replaced with the SNAP program.

Shamelessly, fraud continues to grow, increasing to $593 million in 2016, up 61 percent from 2012. In 2016, the number of fraud incidents was 963,965, up more than 30 percent from 2012. Almost half of those investigations were in New York.[64]

Our national War on Poverty has created generations dependent upon the government dole and has quelled individual ambition in many segments of our society. Have we lost sight of the notion that having a job gives a person a dignified place in our society? Has the generosity of our national welfare programs created a disincentive to pursue independence?

During the Obama years, SNAP participation reached forty-eight million Americans. That number was reduced to forty million by 2018. Still, the SNAP program is costing taxpayers $6.5 billion annually.[65]

Ironically, after spending $50 trillion on the war on poverty, with minimal success, Democrats now believe it would be a good idea to open our borders and import more poverty. We have arrived at a place where Liberals view success by the number of people that are put on food stamps, whereas conservatives view success by the number of people taken off.

The Community Reinvestment Act was signed into law by Democrat president Jimmy Carter in 1977. It was designed to assure that banks would respond to the needs of the communities that they

---

[64] *Forbs Magazine—The Facts About Food Stamp Fraud—April—2018*
[65] USDA—SNAP participation and Costs—1969 thru 2018

serve, intending to target "red-lining" practices, and allow "affordable housing" to minorities and low-income families.

In 1995, Democrat president William Clinton loosened the housing rules by rewriting the Community Reinvestment Act, which put added pressure on banks to provide mortgages in low-income neighborhoods. This led to the expansion of Fannie Mae and Freddie Mac, which are government-guaranteed lenders. They eventually assumed the debt on home mortgages from banks and mortgage brokers, eliminating the need for local banks to "partner" with new homeowners.

Foreseeable, but ignored, abuse of this program led to $5 trillion of Fannie Mae and Freddie Mac debt. In 2008, much of that debt was considered "subprime" toxic mortgages loaned to individuals that were not creditworthy.[66]

This encouraged the purchasing of homes larger than required, simply because they could. Many people speculated in real estate, purchasing a second home to "flip." This economic excess produced "McMansions," oversize homes on limited-size lots. The overextending of credit in the housing market led to the artificial increase in housing values, the economic crash of 2008, and its consequent rapid decline in real estate values.

In December 2003, Republican president George W. Bush signed the Medicare Prescription Drug, Improvement, and Modernization Act, which authorized Medicare coverage of outpatient prescription drugs. The new drug assistance program, known as Part D, represented a major new federal entitlement for Medicare beneficiaries. The drug assistance was "projected to cost taxpayers at least $395 billion, and possibly as much as $534 billion, over the next decade."[67] The cost to taxpayers was projected at $40 to $53 billion per year. In 2017, the actual cost of the program was $110 billion.[68]

---

[66] *Fortune Magazine*—July 2008

[67] medicarevotes. Org—*Medicare Prescription Drug Improvement and Modernization Act of 2003*

[68] HHS.gov—*HHS FY 2017 Budget—CMS—Medicare*

# UNINTENDED CONSEQUENCE

The Emergency Economic Stabilization Act of 2008 (TARP) was signed into law by Republican president George H. W. Bush, providing $700 billion dollars for toxic asset relief.

Ignoring the pork added to the act, its primary purpose, as I understood it, was to transfer "toxic" mortgage debt from the balance sheets of financial institutions to the Federal Reserve Bank. This would allow those institutions to reset their asset base and permit their ability to initiate new loans under the then-current asset-to-loan formulas.

The act was intended to provide capital to allow restructuring of nonperforming mortgages, funded by $700 billion of taxpayer money.

In my view, there was little to encourage optimism as to the potential success of this effort, given a variety of reasons:

- The government practice of throwing taxpayer money at a problem seldom produces a long-term solution.
- The actual extent of the "toxic" paper was unknown.
- There was no mandate to ensure that the financial institutions would in fact make credit more readily available to qualified borrowers after their toxic paper has been replaced with government cash.
- Under the *act*, financial institutions would enjoy a corporate income tax deduction via the sell-off of the toxic paper to the Fed.
- There was no immediate plan, or urgency, to address the underlying problem, which was nonperforming mortgages.
- The act forgave negligence, and perhaps illegality, with neither accountability nor consequence. The real effect of the act was for our government to underwrite the resolution of management negligence and imprudent behavior with taxpayer dollars.

To avoid the housing market crash of 2007, we could have considered an alternative program that might have achieved the objectives of the act while addressing most of the concerns cited above.

First, a comment: "Mark to market" is an accounting method that values an asset to its current market level. It shows how much a company would receive if it sold that asset *today*. I support the "mark to market" requirement because it helps illuminate the consequence of imprudent behavior and negligence. Further, it assists in identifying unforeseen market revisions, allowing those issues to be addressed, in whatever manner seemed appropriate, on a case-by-case basis. If this effort at transparency had been in place, the toxic-paper problem might have been avoided.

No one truly understood the extent, or limitation, of the toxic-paper crisis. While mortgage portfolios contained some transactions that had become "upside down" due to the realty market collapse, as well as others that are classified as nonperforming, ranging from delinquent to foreclosure, the largest percentage continued to perform under the terms of the mortgage.

An alternative strategy might have been this:

- Simply address this with a new accounting policy, limited to the mortgage portfolio question, with Internal Revenue Service and Federal Accounting Standards Board approval.
- Permit the financial institutions to adjust the balance sheet mortgage portfolio value using the "mark to market" strategy and amortize the write-down over the life of the underlying mortgages, then the balance sheet issue would have been resolved and taxpayer funds would not be required.
- Permit financial institutions to absorb the negative effect of their own misconduct over a period, as opposed to in one draconian instant.
- Require institutions that have elected to be protected by this program to evaluate their portfolios and identify specific nonperforming mortgages.
- This accounting technique would not have been without precedent.

As institutions identified specific nonperforming mortgages, they could have elected to have them purchased by the Federal

Reserve Bank in some discounted manner, reflecting current market value of the underlying real estate.

The "qualifying" mortgages would be as follows:

- Primary residence mortgages only.
- Qualifiers would be means tested.
- Mortgaged property would be "reasonable to the requirements" of the mortgagee.

The government could have refinanced the mortgages at current market value, over an extended period, dependent upon the actual ability of the mortgagee to pay, at a rate of 4 percent. The mortgagee would be required to demonstrate the ability to perform under the new terms. The IRS had already agreed to forgive any imputed income from such principal forgiveness to the mortgagee.

The US Treasury could have funded this mortgage assumption program by issuing "rescue bonds" consistent with the following:

- Bonds would have a thirty-year maturity and pay 8 percent interest annually, exempt from federal tax.
- The sale of rescue bonds would be primarily targeted toward senior citizens, allowing them to establish a predictable fixed income.
- The bonds would not be available to foreign entities, to limit foreign control over US debt.
- The Treasury would establish a limit on individual purchases of rescue bonds.

Additional funding for the mortgage refinance program could have been gleaned from a bill allowing the government to recoup excessive compensation and bonuses paid to the executives of failed and failing corporations during 2005, 2006, and 2007.

Under this alternative, financial institutions would not enjoy a corporate income tax deduction via the sell-off of the toxic paper to the Federal Reserve until after the institution has specifically defined their scope and current value. Rather than receiving cash from the

US Treasury, financial institutions would be motivated to issue new loans to compensate for the lost profit caused by the toxic-paper amortization.

This creative thinking "outside the box" might have been more productive than throwing US taxpayer money at the problem.

In 2009, a $787 billion Economic Stimulus Program was passed by the Nancy Pelosi and Harry Reid Democrat Congress "to ensure that unemployment would never exceed 8%." The plan did not achieve its desired effect; in fact, it failed miserably. In 2010, unemployment exceeded 10 percent, wasting $787 billion of taxpayer money.[69]

Its primary objective was to fund shovel-ready infrastructure projects, creating jobs; however, progress was hampered by increasing EPA and permitting regulations.[70],[71]

The primary benefit of the Stimulus Program, beyond the political pork and its contribution of $45 billion in extra education funding, was to create an undisclosed number of new government jobs. One of the most egregious, self-serving pork items included in the package was Representative John P. Murtha's (D-PA) $800,000 earmarked to repave a backup runway in his private Pennsylvania airport.

The administration did nothing to offer financial relief to seniors during this continuing financial crisis. Most seniors living on fixed incomes were burdened by the Federal Reserve Board's zero-discount-rate policy and received a pittance in interest on their savings accounts.

At that time, I had submitted a proposal to the White House: allow the Treasury to issue "patriot bonds," yielding 7.5 percent interest annually, free of federal, state, or local tax liability. The bonds would only be available to American citizens aged sixty-five and older.

Senior citizen savings rates would have received relief and an improvement in their cash flow that was neither afforded nor addressed by the Obama administration. This program could have produced $97 billion in immediate economic stimulus.

---

[69] *CNS News—Obama's Stimulus: A Documented Failure*—May 2012
[70] NPR—*Stimulus Bill Gives Shovel Ready Projects Priority*—February 2009
[71] *Forbes: The Reason that Shovel Ready Stimulus Did Not Work*—November 2013

# UNINTENDED CONSEQUENCE

At the time China held more than $1.3 trillion of American debt, the Treasury could have used the proceeds of the bond sale to retire the China debt. Under this approach, Americans, rather than the Chinese government, would be investing in the future of our country.

In 2009, the Obama administration passed a bill allowing the government takeover of the student loan program and mandated direct government lending to replace the federally subsidized loans made by private banks and creating an economic disaster. The *Wall Street Journal* judged this as thus:

> His administration cut out the middlemen by killing off the Guaranteed Student Loan Program created under Presidents Johnson and Nixon, that relied on banks, in favor of a direct loan program, in which money came from the Treasury. But the government's loose lending policy, with few questions asked, remained in place.
>
> The Obama administration also heavily promoted income-based repayment programs, which set borrowers' monthly payments at 10% of their discretionary income and then forgave a portion of their debt after 20 to 25 years of payments. This severed the link between the value of students' education and how much they could borrow, providing a huge incentive for schools to raise tuition, since taxpayers would pick up more of the tab. Enrollment in these programs is one big reason that the government's costs for student loans are exploding. With easy student loan approval college became available, even to students that were neither academically prepared nor qualified.[72]

---

[72] *Wall Street Journal: Government Takeover of Student Loan Market Fails Miserably*—March 2013

There was no test to determine if the borrowers were creditworthy. The parents of the students were no longer required to guarantee repayment; they would have no "skin in the game." Clearly, our politicians did not learn a lesson from the economic crash of 2008, which was caused by a similar strategy regarding home mortgage creditworthiness. Student application rates soared, and based upon the laws of supply and demand, college tuition increased faster than previously, close to doubling in a decade.

*The Wall Street Journal* reported, "Americans are increasingly dissatisfied with College tuition rates that have soared 1,375% since 1978, more than four times the rate of overall inflation."[73] Today the average undergraduate leaves school with $50,000 in debt, up from about $17,000 when President Obama first announced the program. Facing a weak job market and burdened with significant debt, many graduates are forced to return to their parents' home.

This well-intended program was abused by online college programs offering worthless degrees to unsuspecting students and veterans, causing them to incur debt.

According to a recent *Wall Street Journal* article, over "two million students have defaulted on their loans in just the past six years, and the number grows by 1,400 a day. After years of projecting big profits from student lending, the federal government now acknowledges that taxpayers stand to lose $31.5 billion on the program over the next decade, and the losses are growing rapidly. The combination of open access to schools and open access to loans turned the higher education market into a version of the Wild West."[74]

The program would be further injured by the Obama administration, when it increased the program's student interest rate, to offset some of the cost of the Affordable Care Act. Today we are facing a student loan crisis, where students have been encouraged to incur substantial debt, totaling close to $1.6 trillion at this writing. This is affecting their future creditworthiness and hampering their ability

---

[73] *Wall Street Journal: Government Takeover of Student Loan Market Fails Miserably*—March 2013

[74] *Wall Street Journal: Government Takeover of Student Loan Market Fails Miserably*—March 2013

to obtain a home mortgage or car loan. This was nothing less than self-serving partisan politics with little regard to its consequence on American citizens. Where was government oversight?

Two 2020 Democrat presidential contenders have proposed a new "wealth tax" on "millionaires and businesses" to repay these loans. How is it the responsibility of millionaires and businesses to pay for the poor decisions of others? Why should successful people and businesses be responsible for the ill-conceived student loan program? This is a typical liberal response—my mistake…oops, let the wealthy bail us out.

Another government social program was President Barack Obama's Affordable Care Act of 2010. After investing more than $2 billion in a failed website, the ongoing cost of the ACA could reach $100 billion each year, leaving the majority of the uninsured still uninsured and all those previously insured with higher premiums and deductibles.[75] The ACA, a noble effort, clearly could not deliver as advertised, and its architect, Professor Jonathan Gruber, knew it.

During a panel discussion at the University of Pennsylvania in October 2013, Gruber, a professor of economics at the Massachusetts Institute of Technology, said that "the stupidity of the American voter" made it important for Democrats to hide Obamacare's true costs from the public. Professor Gruber told the panel, "Lack of transparency is a huge political advantage. And basically, call it the stupidity of the American voter or whatever, but basically that was really, really critical for the thing to pass." Gruber pointed out that if Democrats had been honest about these facts and that the law's individual mandate is, in effect, a major tax hike, Obamacare could never have passed Congress.[76]

Had the Obama administration had the counsel of any practical, rather than academic, economist, it would have understood that the goal of providing health care for all, removing any restriction on preexisting conditions, while reducing premiums simultane-

---

[75] *The Washington Examiner* and The Congressional Budget Office—April 2014
[76] *Forbes Magazine—The Stupidity of the American Voter Led Us to Hide…*—November 2014

ously, was an economic fantasy. The following was expressed in *The Bloomberg Report*:

> It will cost the U.S. government almost $700 billion in subsidies this year to help provide Americans under age 65 with health insurance through their jobs or in government-sponsored health programs, according to a report from the nonpartisan Congressional Budget Office. The subsidies come from four main categories. About $296 billion is federal spending on programs like Medicaid and the Children's Health Insurance Program, which help insure low-income people. Almost as big are the tax write-offs that employers take for providing coverage to their workers. Medicare-eligible people, such as the disabled, account for $82 billion. Subsidies for Obamacare and for other individual coverage are the smallest segment, at $55 billion.[77]

If we assume that the ACA added twelve million citizens to the health insurance rolls, the expense to taxpayers is about $15,000 each, per year. Wasn't there a simpler, less expensive way?

President Obama was faced with the enormous task of rebuilding the collapsed economy that he had inherited.

Given that, why did his administration invest their unique position of controlling all three branches of government, which they had won in the 2008 election, and choose to invest that enormous political capital in a liberal philosophical imperative, restructuring health care, rather than apply that dominant advantage to the national imperative of creating jobs?

In 2016, the voters chose Donald Trump as our new president. Using his proven business experience, he filled his Cabinet and chose

---

[77] Bloomberg Report: *It Costs $685 Billion a Year to Subsidize US Healthcare—* May 2018

his advisers from the most accomplished, successful people in their field and brought his business acumen and strategies to government. The results have been nothing less than remarkable.

Through eliminating burdensome regulations, encouraging fossil fuel production in the United States, and passing the pro-growth Tax Cuts and Jobs Act of 2017, the Trump administration invigorated the US economy. No Democrat voted for the bill in either the House (224–201) or the Senate (51–48).

"According to the Tax Policy Center, 65% of Americans did receive a tax cut thanks to the new code. H&R Block reports that the average tax cut was approximately $1,200 based on the returns the company processed, as of early 2019."[78]

"The Treasury Department reported this week that individual income tax collections for FY 2018 totaled $1.7 trillion. That's up $14 billion from fiscal 2017, and an all-time high. And that's even though individual income tax rates got a significant cut this year as part of President Donald Trump's tax reform plan."[79]

Unemployment is at a record low. Employment of black, Hispanic, and women are at record highs, and wages are steadily improving.[80] In January 2018, CNBC reported that "pay gains during Trump's first year in office were the best since the Great Recession."

The United States has reduced its reliance of Far Eastern and Russian oil and has, in fact, become a petroleum and gas exporter. Manufacturing is moving back into the United States. These bold measures have resulted in tremendous improvements to our economy.

Tariffs are a blunt but effective weapon, and the Trump administration is utilizing them to great effect. Tariffs can lead to trade wars or can be a useful tool in negotiating new trade deals.

While President Trump did walk away from the Transpacific Partnership (TPP), he has embarked on a series of trade deals, replacing the job killing North American Free Trade Act with the United States Mexico and Canada Agreement, signed by Mexico and

---

[78] Investopedia—*Explaining the Trump Tax Reform Plan*—August 2019
[79] *Investor's Business Daily—Federal Revenues Hit All-Time High Under Trump…*—October 2018
[80] *Newsmax—Under Trump, Wages and Jobs have improved*—September 2019

Canada and awaiting a vote in the Democrat-controlled House of Representatives. The administration has signed unilateral trade deals with South Korea and Japan, and it is in continuing negotiations with the United Kingdom and China, attempting to reverse the decades-old imbalance. Well-structured business strategies applied to the economic problems of our country yielded impressive results, despite Democrat resistance. This demonstrates what can happen when policy is given priority over partisan politics. President Trump plays the long game, a concept that is alien to the "win the next election" mind-set of our politicians.

Our politicians have a penchant for pulling the trigger on legislation before they have taken adequate aim to consider its actual implications. The economic uncertainty created by the reckless expansion of the Social Security and Medicare programs has led to an unsustainable level of expense.

The Affordable Care Act has disrupted our national medical delivery system. It has saddled most Americans with burdensome expense incurred due to higher deductibles, higher co-pays, and extended wait times for medical service. The student loan program has burdened a generation with impossible debt and skyrocketed college tuition rates. History tells us that few, if any, government programs have stayed within budget or economic projection; in fact, most have egregiously exceeded them.

What result can we expect from the programs that are being offered by the 2020 presidential candidates for the Democrat Party nomination? They are touting free Medicare for all, including illegal immigrants; government repayment of medical debt; government repayment of student tuition debt; decriminalizing illegal immigration; the Green New Deal; and assessing a "wealth tax" to pay for it all. What could possibly go wrong?

What is predictable is that if America continues to pursue the same shortsighted, feel-good legislation, we can expect the same unintended consequence.

We should be seeking commonsense solutions, pursue limited government, and strive for fiscal responsibility.

The 2020 election should not be about a political party winning or losing; it should be about America winning or losing.

## Stock Market: Security and Exchange Commission

In October of 1929, the stock market crashed, leading us into America's Great Depression of the 1930s. The decade known as the Roaring Twenties was a period of exuberant and substantial political, economic, and social growth in the United States, but that era came to a dramatic and abrupt end.

Experts conclude that the crash occurred because the stock market was overbought, overvalued, and excessively bullish, rising despite deteriorating national and international economic conditions. It was a period of pure speculation rather than investing.[81]

> The Great Depression, like most other periods of severe unemployment, was produced by government mismanagement rather than by any inherent instability of the private economy. (Milton Friedman, economist, Nobel laureate)

At that time, individuals purchased stock on "margin," which meant that the buyer would only have to put down a small percentage of the actual stock price (10 percent) and the broker would cover the rest. The brokers loaned the investors the largest amount of the cash required to purchase stock. People used this device in the 1920s to acquire more stock than they could otherwise afford.

If the stock price dropped too low, the broker could issue a "margin call," which meant the buyer would be required to repay all the money that the broker had loaned. The massive margin call of 1929 collapsed the stock market and contributed to the Depression.[82]

---

[81] *Encyclopedia Britannica—Stock Market Crash of 1929*
[82] *Encyclopedia Britannica—Stock Market Crash of 1929*

A positive that resulted from the economic calamity was the creation of the Securities and Exchange Commission by Democrat president Franklin Roosevelt in 1934. The primary responsibility of the SEC was to enforce the federal securities laws; propose securities rules and regulate the securities industry, the nation's stock and options exchanges; and regulate other activities and organizations, including electronic securities markets.

The SEC has a three-part mission: to protect investors; maintain fair, orderly, and efficient markets; and facilitate capital formation. The commission oversees securities exchanges, securities brokers and dealers, investment advisers, and mutual funds. It ensures the disclosure of important market information and works to prevent fraud. Joseph P. Kennedy Sr. was the first chairman of the Securities and Exchange Commission.[83]

Unfortunately, the pain of the Depression was lost on future generations and liberal policy makers, as we would repeat the same mistakes in 2000 and 2007. In the future, our government's policies of overextending credit, where the recipients were not "creditworthy," would become a recurring theme and would repeatedly result in economic disaster. It is unfathomable to me how government failed to head off those market collapses. Clearly, Congress has been a poor steward of our economy, failing to learn from history. Instead, politicians seem to prefer to rewrite history, allowing them to ignore it.

The Dot-Com Crash of 2000 was caused by traders speculating in stocks of companies that had produced neither sales nor profits, effectively creating a Ponzi scheme. This, as well as the advent of "day traders," would have the same market effect as the margin purchases of the 1920s. The result was another market crash where investment portfolios and retirement savings accounts were wiped out. Where was the Securities and Exchange Commission?

The Housing Market Crash of 2007 was instigated by easy mortgage money being provided to individuals with neither the prospect nor the ability to repay. Subprime mortgages were readily approved. Liberal congressman Barney Frank (D-MA) was a major

---

[83] USA.gov—*The Securities and Exchange Commission*

champion of this program, despite its continued losses. Frank blamed Republicans for the failure of Fannie and Freddie, yet he spent years blocking GOP lawmakers from imposing tougher regulations on the mortgage giants. In 1991, Frank pushed the agency to loosen regulations on mortgages for two-family and three-family homes, even though they were defaulting at several times the rate of single-family homes. Three years later, President William Clinton's Department of Housing and Urban Development tried to impose a new regulation on Fannie, but that effort to reign in the excess was thwarted by Frank.[84]

The Federal Reserve Board ignored the danger of this program; that lack of government responsibility and control ultimately led to the housing market, and economic, crash of 2007.

A reckless, "designer" financial instrument, the credit default swap (CDS), was invented by J. P. Morgan & Co. in 1994. They were a credit derivative that provided the buyer with protection against default and other risks. In theory, the buyer of a CDS made periodic payments to the seller until the credit maturity date. In the agreement, the seller commits that if the debt issuer defaults, the seller will pay the buyer all premiums and interests that would've been paid up to the date of maturity. Just like an insurance policy, a CDS allowed purchasers to buy protection against an unlikely event that may affect the investment.

Default swaps became popular in the early 2000s, and by 2007, the outstanding credit default swaps value stood at $62.2 trillion. There was no legal framework to regulate swaps, and the lack of transparency in the market became a concern among regulators, but no effective action was taken. Before the financial crisis of 2008, there was more money invested in credit default swaps than there was in the stock market, mortgages, or treasury notes, contributing to the 2008 market collapse. The biggest casualty was the Lehman Brothers investment bank, which owed $600 billion in debt, out of which $400 billion was covered by CDS. The bank's insurer, American

---

[84] *The Atlantic—Hey, Barney Frank: The Government Did Cause the Housing Crisis*—December 2011

Insurance Group, lacked enough funds to clear the debt, and the Federal Reserve of the United States needed to intervene to bail it out. AIG was severely weakened as well.[85]

The Credit Crunch of 2007 grew into a full-blown crisis by mid-2008. The prestigious investment services company Lehman Brothers was forced to file for chapter 11 bankruptcy protection.[86] Business leaders and politicians, led by Treasury secretary Henry Paulson, mobilized to contain the crisis.[87]

The Dodd-Frank Wall Street Report Act of 2009 was introduced to regulate the credit default swap market, tantamount to closing the barn door after the horses had escaped.[88]

While *Fannie Mae* was at the epicenter of the 2008 financial meltdown, Herb Moses (Representative Frank's life partner) was Fannie Mae's assistant director for product marketing, at the same time Frank was on the powerful House Banking Committee. A case might be made that Representative Frank ignored warnings of the failing policy to protect the career of his life partner. Five trillion dollars of debt—conflict of interest? You decide.

When personal or political interests are placed ahead of our national purpose, such as they were with Fannie Mae and Freddie Mac, Americans suffer. When government agencies, charged with guarding our financial systems, fail to exercise their responsibility, as the SEC failed to do in 2000 and 2007, American citizens are compelled to foot the bill.

Values and institutions that we grew up with are disappearing, and we have allowed it, even encouraged it, to happen. I believe that, through our vote, we have the power to regain them.

The stock market has become a family wealth builder, enjoyed by most Americans. Recent studies have found that 55 percent of adults in the United States invested in the stock market during 2018; 52 percent participated at the end of the Obama administration. While that is an increase from the last two years, it remains below

---

[85] Corporate Finance Institute—*Credit Default Swap*
[86] University of California—Berkley—*Slaying the Dragon of Debt*
[87] University of California—Berkley—*Slaying the Dragon of Debt*
[88] Corporate Finance Institute—*Credit Default Swap*

the levels before the financial crisis of 2008, when those invested in the market peaked at 65 percent in 2007.[89]

The 2020 election should not be about a political party winning or losing; it should be about America winning or losing.

## The National Debt

In 1960, the US federal debt was $290 billion; today's national debt now exceeds $23 trillion. How did we get here?[90]

First, an explanation of the distinction between *debt* and *deficit*. *Debt* is the amount our country owes; *deficit* is the amount our government overspends in a single fiscal year. Debt is the aggregate of annual deficits.

If we examine the change in our total national debt over the last century by administration, we can see several remarkable things. First, that most of our debt has been incurred since the elimination of the *gold standard* by Republican president Richard Nixon, which gave our politicians unfettered access to cash. Second, the willingness to overspend was not limited to a political party as both Democrats and Republicans spent wantonly. Third, that the most egregious spender was the two Obama administrations, during which the national debt surged at the rate of almost $1.2 trillion *each year*, for *eight years*, totaling almost $10 trillion.

As a historical note, only one administration in the past one hundred years reduced the national debt; that was Calvin Coolidge, a Republican, under which the debt was reduced by $5.3 billion over six years.[91]

Our international largesse, the funds we disperse in aid to foreign governments or to assist in disaster relief, accounts for a small portion of the national debt. The debt surge has been the result of

---

[89] Statista—*Share of adults investing money in the stock market*—September 2019
[90] Polidiodic—*US National Debt by Year*
[91] Polidiodic—*US National Debt by Year*

funding wars and mostly ineffective liberal efforts to reengineer our society.[92]

Huge national debt blunts prospects for growth. (Heffx, Singapore)

This cartoon published in *Heffx* alongside an editorial piece written by Paul Ebeling in September 2016 hit the nail on the head. America is chained to its unmanageable debt. Economic growth and stability are being weighted down.

Today's debt rapidly approaches twenty-three trillion dollars, yet there has been no evidence of our Congress being concerned with this circumstance.

> We cannot defer this responsibility to posterity.
> Time will not wait. (Walter Cronkite)

Our elected politicians have no appetite for trimming our federal expense: that would require a sense of fiscal responsibility and cutting "free stuff," which would jeopardize votes and reelection. Their political survival instinct seems stronger than their commitment to do what is best for our country—again, self over service. While we are burdening future generations with resolving this dilemma, Congress

---

[92] Polidiodic—*US National Debt by Year*

continues to spend in total disregard, and trillion-dollar deficits have become the new normal.[93]

We have spent trillions on wars and social reengineering, with some positive but mostly unintended results. One of the most measurable results is the increase to our national debt, now exceeding twenty-two trillion dollars; that's a hell of a legacy to leave our children and grandchildren.

After World War II, the United Stated stood alone as the greatest industrial nation in the entire world and we undertook the massive job of rebuilding Europe and Japan.

Today, we again have achieved that enviable dominant economic position. Shouldn't we use that advantage to rebuild America?

The Trump administration sought to reset the economic table with policies rooted in eliminating burdensome regulations both by providing tax relief to middle-class America and business and by negotiating strategic trade deals, tariffs, and energy independence. Trade deals may require short-term pain to yield longer-term gain.

The US Department of Commerce reported, "The Trump administration is fulfilling its promise to create good jobs for American workers. Over the next five years, millions of American workers will be equipped with the skills they need to grow and thrive in the modern economy. Through our work, and that of the Trump administration, all Americans will benefit from the country's economic success."[94]

As a nation, we have been "eating our seed corn." Debt matters, and we should not enslave our children and grandchildren with it. I would propose a national sales tax of 3 percent on *all* purchases, with the proceeds being *legally committed* to repaying the national debt. The funds cannot be available to politicians to squander. The wealthiest among us would contribute the larger share, but *every* American would be required to contribute.

---

[93] *Forbes*: *Trump Trillion-Dollar Budget Deficits Officially Begin*—April 2018
[94] U.S. Department of Commerce—*White House creating good jobs for workers*—July 2019

It would take decades to repay the debt. We should also require a constitutional amendment that mandates a balanced federal budget. We have been deficit spending for far too long. We must stop the annual hemorrhaging of our national interest.

> A billion here, a billion there, pretty soon you're talking about real money. (Senator Everett Dirksen, R-IL)

In 2020, we should not be voting for a political party; we will be voting for fiscal responsibility.

# Chapter III

# Education

*Education is the most powerful weapon that you can use to change the world.*
—Nelson Mandela,
president of South Africa

*Live as if you were to die tomorrow. Learn as if you were to live forever.*
—Mahatma Gandhi,
political activist, India

While writing this chapter, I have sought the counsel, advice, and opinion of thirteen educators: six retired teachers, four actively teaching; one regional superintendent of schools; one principal; and one PhD school administrator. While a relatively small sample, it covers a wide range of demographics encompassing teaching experience in California, Florida, Massachusetts, North Carolina, New Jersey, and New York, ranged in age from thirty-two to seventy-nine; male and female; black and white; Independents, Democrats, and Republicans; liberals, conservatives, and moderates. While they provided critical input, all opinions expressed herein are mine, unless otherwise specifically indicated.

As a point of curiosity, only two of the thirteen educators contacted chose not to engage, each an acknowledged liberal, one an active teacher from California, the other an active PhD administrator from Florida. This might give credence to my premise that many liberals tend to avoid intellectual debate that challenges their political views.

We have migrated from a country where achievement was recognized and rewarded to one of helicopter moms and an obsession that no child should suffer failure. In our march toward "sameness," we have created a society of "participation trophies," "mercy rules," and bubble-wrapped, sanitized "snowflakes." The "helicopter moms" have evolved into "lawn mower" and "bulldozer" parents. Essentially plowing any negative or challenging obstacles out of the way so that their children can "succeed" without effort, frustration, difficulty, or emotional distress.[95]

We are failing to adequately prepare our youth for the reality of the world that they will encounter, which can be a bruising journey at times. Some degree of failure awaits in everyone's future. Are we failing to prepare our youth to deal with it? By eliminating valedictorians, we discourage the pursuit of excellence, which seems counterintuitive to the notion that competition brings out the best in us.

In the mid-1950s, the Advanced Placement Program was initiated. It is directed by the nonprofit college board, makers and monitors of the college SAT exams, and was designed to give students the experience of introductory-level college classes while they were still in high school. This program identified and "fast-tracked" the brightest high school students.

In 2011, Congress and the Department of Education passed Title I—Improving the Academic Achievement of the Disadvantaged Act, substantially refocusing education goals toward achieving better state testing scores.

The US Department of Education has said, "The purpose of this title is to ensure that all children have a fair, equal, and significant opportunity to obtain a high-quality education and reach, at a

---

[95] USA Today—*Meet the Lawnmower Parent, the New Helicopter Parents of 2018*—September 2018

minimum, proficiency on challenging State academic achievement standards and state academic assessments."[96]

In the first instance, the Advanced Placement Program isolates the brightest students to accelerate their education experience; in the latter case, Title I, the education process for the better-prepared students seems impaired to allow those less prepared to "catch up." These two methods appear to be in conflict—dumb them down while young, only to accelerate the brightest later. When our testable grades K-through-12 curricula is primarily targeting successful test-taking rather than preparation for a successful life, we have failed. "Teaching to the test" may allow an arbitrary statistical advantage in evaluating a school's performance, but it limits, even curtails, the education of our children.

When our institutions of higher learning exhibit liberal bias, inside and outside the classroom, the minds of young adults are cheated and freedom dies by a thousand cuts. When college campuses, once the bastion of free speech and exchange of ideas, become the most intellectually intolerant institutions in our country, we should be very concerned.

Zappa seems to make a valid point:

> If you want to get laid, go to college. If you want an education, go to the library. (Frank Zappa, American musician)

Education and the public school system in the United States evolved from its beginning when the Boston Latin School, first in the original thirteen colonies, opened in 1635. In that era, schools taught the virtues of family, religion, and community.[97] In early rural and agrarian America, education of the masses was provided in single-room schoolhouses, with schoolmarms. Children of all ages sat in a single room with a single teacher and a curriculum devoted to the three r's of "readin', ritin', n' 'rithmatic." Older students assisted in

---

[96] *Title I—Improving the Academic Achievement of The Disadvantaged—USDOE*
[97] Boston Latin School—*Wikipedia*

teaching the younger ones. The school day and school year schedules were a function of time available before and after farm and family chores.[98] Parents typically paid "tuition" by providing housing for the schoolteacher or contributing other commodities.

In the midnineteenth century, academics became the responsibility of public schools, which were slower to develop in the Southern states. Affluent families paid private tutors to educate their children. Education of black Americans was prohibited until after the Reconstruction Era, when the Freedmen's Bureau opened schools across the South for black children. Freedmen were eager for schooling, both adult and children, and the enrollments were high and enthusiastic. The bureau spent $5 million to set up schools for blacks, with more than ninety thousand freedmen enrolled by the end of 1865, with curriculum resembling that of schools in the North.[99]

An important new technique was introduced by Horace Mann, secretary of education in Massachusetts, which he had learned in Prussia and introduced in 1848. The concept was to place students in classes by age, assigning them to different grades as they progressed through them, regardless of differences of aptitude. This "lecture method" common in European universities allowed students to receive instruction rather than being required to take an active role in instructing one another, as had been the case in America's early ninety-century schools.[100]

With the introduction of age grading, multiaged classrooms all but disappeared, and when students progressed with their grade and completed all courses the secondary school had to offer, they were "graduated" and awarded a certificate of completion, a diploma.

By 1900 thirty-one states had compulsory school attendance for children between ages eight and fourteen.[101]

The Industrial Revolution in America began in the latter part of the nineteenth century, bringing with it many important inven-

---

[98] *Education News: American Public Education: An Origin Story*—April 2013
[99] Wikipedia—*Freedmen's Bureau*
[100] *Encyclopedia Britannica—Horace Mann: American Educator*
[101] *Education News: American Public Education: An Origin Story*—April 2013

tions and techniques, making work easier and cheaper. These inventions created new manufacturing and industry opportunities, and in response, citizens moved from their farms to the cities, seeking better employment and wage prospects.

With the advent of industrialization in America, the titans of industry (Ford, Rockefeller, Carnegie, Morgan, Vanderbilt, and Pullman) recognized the need for better-educated workers in their factories, plants, refineries, mills, business offices, and railroads. Understanding the value of laborers who were able to read and write, they vigorously supported the expansion of America's public school system.

By 1918, every state required students to complete elementary school. According to *The Wall Street Journal*, "At the start of the (twentieth) century, less than a tenth of American workers had a high school diploma, let alone a college degree. But by the 1960s, high school was universally required, and college attendance was growing rapidly."

In the 1920s, John Dewey, an American philosopher, psychologist, and educational reformer, influenced education and social reform. He believed that learning should be active and that contemporary schooling was unnecessarily long and restrictive and that children came to school to do things and live in a community, all of which gave them real, guided experiences that fostered their capacity to contribute to society. The common theme underlying Dewey's philosophy was his belief that a democratic society of informed and engaged inquirers was the best means of promoting human interests. He believed that students should be involved in real-life tasks and challenges: math could be learned through learning proportions in cooking or figuring out how long it would take to get from one place by mule to another; history could be learned by experiencing how people lived, their geography, what the climate was like, and how plants and animals grew.

Dewey had a gift for suggesting activities that captured the center of what his classes were studying. His education philosophy helped promote the "progressive education" movement and gave birth to the development of "experimental education" programs.[102]

During the first one hundred years of public schools in America, teachers had no collective bargaining rights, though many had civil service protection. During this period, the public schools made steady progress; however, teachers were underpaid. In 1961, the United Federation of Teachers was formed; teachers went on strike, and they won the right to bargain for all New York City teachers. The contract the UFT signed with the New York City Board of Education paralleled the traditional industrial model: set up uniform pay scales and seniority rights for teachers, limited their classroom hours, and required new teachers to be automatically enrolled in the union and have their dues deducted from their paychecks. Following this example, the more conservative National Education Association also veered toward aggressive trade unionism.[103]

The American Federation of Teachers distinguishes itself from the NEA by its exclusion of school administrators from membership. According to Wikipedia, the AFT membership approached 1.6 million with dues income of $35 million in 2017.

In the mid-1960s, legislation influencing public schools erupted. The Elementary and Secondary Education Act was signed into law by President Lyndon Johnson in 1965 as part of Johnson's War on Poverty. The act proposed major reforms of federal education policy and provided federal funding to both primary and secondary education, with funds authorized for professional development and instructional materials. The act also emphasized equal access to education, providing federal funding to support schools with children from impoverished families.

The United States Department of Education was created by an unpopular president Jimmy Carter in 1979. He wanted the nation's largest union on his side before an election, and his acknowledged

---

[102] *Encyclopedia Britannica—John Dewey—American Philosopher and Educator*
[103] American Federation of Teachers.com—History

political motivation was to curry favor with the American Federation of Teachers.[104]

Since its inception, the Department of Education expanded its focus to be more inclusive and pursued its mission to provide a more uniform education nationwide. As a result, it has moved our public schools to a more liberally biased curriculum.

By 1997, the NEA, UFT, and AFT had most of the nation's teachers covered by collective bargaining agreements, representing more than three million school employees, including 80 percent of the nation's public school teachers. They collected $1.3 billion each year from dues and employed over six thousand full-time staff members. The NEA spent only half of its income on activities related to collective bargaining and used the other half for electoral politics, lobbying, and general advocacy for social, educational, and political causes. Nationally, in the 1996 election, the teachers' unions contributed more than $9 million directly to William Clinton and other Democratic candidates through political action committees.[105]

In 1976, the Republican Congress was on the verge of passing legislation to rescue a few thousand poor students from the broken public school system of Washington, DC, by offering them private school scholarships. The NEA, fearful that these vouchers might encourage similar legislation in areas beyond Washington, DC, furiously lobbied the White House. President Ford, who had first indicated that he would sign the bill, backtracked and said he would veto it. The unions' political investments seem to have paid off.

While teachers' unions were beneficial to teachers and school employees, they also retarded the education process to retain their influence over the education system.

Based upon my conversations with educators over the years, it is my belief that many, if not most, younger teachers are conflicted regarding union representation. I would suspect that most have no actual interaction with the union other than on the local level. However, the union can create social issues, such as pro-union versus

---

[104] *Reason—Why Do We Have a Department of Education*—February 2017
[105] *Education Week—Teachers Allege Improper Use of Union Dues*

less-committed advocates, during contentious contract negotiations. Peer pressure could make some uncomfortable, and opposing the union might be career suicide.

Common Core (Common Core State Standards, CCSS), initiated by the Obama administration in 2010, provided guidelines for public schools, concentrating on English language arts (ELA) and mathematics. While not a federal mandate, receiving federal funds for education was tied directly to states implementing the CCSS program.

Did you follow that sequence of events? In the mid-1960s, the federal government passed a law to provide funding to public schools; in 1979, the federal government created the Department of Education; then in 2010, the D of E announced Common Core, and while participation was *elective*, your federal school subsidies were held hostage, tied to your compliance.

The curriculum concentration was intended to better prepare students for state testing, anticipating the weight that they would carry in evaluating schools and teachers. It refocused the primary objective of education to make better student "test-takers" rather than providing a comprehensive education. It seems to be missing its mark.

School districts supporting Common Core allocate a substantial amount of class time to the ELA and math instruction, because they are tested subjects, resulting in less time being invested in history, civics, and writing.

There is a growing trend of states opting out of Common Core, due to disappointing results.[106]

There is an increasing push from both the federal government and parents in the community voicing discontent about students not being adequately prepared to enter the workforce. Professionals at the collegiate level and in the workforce are voicing concerns about students and employees not being adequately prepared with basic skills.

---

[106] *The Washington Post—Why the movement to opt out of Common Core*—June 2015

# UNINTENDED CONSEQUENCE

Not without politically correct bias, liberal authors and publishers pushed to require that all-time references in world history instruction replace the BC (Before Christ) and AD (Anno Domini) with BCE (Before the Common Era) and CE (Common Era), ostensibly further disconnecting Christian religion from education.[107]

It appears that our education systems, both public and private, have been assailed by a liberal curriculum. Our youth is no longer educated sufficiently in history and civics. Cursive writing seems to be a lost art. CBS News reported, "More than half of all companies (60%) said new…(college)…grads lacked critical thinking skills and attention to detail (56%), while 44% found fault with their writing proficiency, and 39% were critical of their public speaking ability."[108]

The competition for curriculum time in the classroom is further heightened by the requirement that schools teach "good character," which seems lost on many home fronts, due to a variety of causes, such as single-parent families.

When young children arrive at kindergarten knowing how to use their iPad but not knowing how to use their imagination, or how to interact with other children, education suffers. Teachers are then required to "teach the basic" rather than build *it*.

One current teacher that I consulted acknowledged this circumstance, indicating that the condition is compounded by children at the other end of the spectrum, where "the children are entitled, and it is scary."

It is my belief that when our primary school curriculum masks history with contemporary bias, if taught at all, when civics is skewed or absent, when achievement and excellence go unrecognized or discouraged, then the minds of our youth are unfairly molded and we fail our children and our society. America is an idea; that idea needs to be taught and understood. It needs to be nurtured and expanded, not neglected and distorted. Our history should be taught in our schools and understood and accepted by our citizens, warts and all.

---

[107] *Los Angeles Times—Some Find Removing BC, AD from History to Be too PC—* April 2005

[108] *CBS News—New College Grads are not Ready for the Workplace—*May 2016

Our public school system seems to be in disrepair. Teachers are rarely judged on performance, the unions support the expansion of a liberally biased curriculum, and they worship at the altar of "tenure," making longevity more important than quality performance. Of primary concern today should be the excellence of American education. Study after study documents the poor performance of students in every subject area.

It would appear that while our nation's teachers might be better compensated, our nations students are being underserved.

Parents need to be teachers as well. They are a child's "first teacher." A child should arrive at the classroom with basic values, ethics about learning, working hard, and treating others with respect.[109] Wouldn't it be wonderful if all parents embodied the same emphasis and insistence on education that is commonly seen in Asian, Jewish, and Eastern European cultures? The results can be witnessed in the performance of most students from those ethnic groups.

Higher education evolved differently than the public school system. Prior to 1800, colleges were largely oriented toward training men as ministers. Doctors and lawyers were trained in local apprentice systems.

Harvard College was founded by the colonial legislature in 1636 and focused on training young Caucasian Protestant men for the ministry, but many alumni went into law, medicine, government, or business. Harvard was a leader in bringing Newtonian science to its curriculum. This philosophical and scientific doctrine, inspired by the beliefs of Isaac Newton, suggested that the universe was governed by rational and understandable laws. This doctrine laid both the foundation for enlightened thought and the groundwork for modern science. This study also influenced philosophy, political thought, and theology in the colonies.

Yale College was founded by the Puritans in 1701. The *conservative* Puritan ministers of Connecticut had grown dissatisfied with the more *liberal* theology of Harvard and wanted their own school to train Orthodox ministers. Yale strengthened the curricu-

---

[109] *US News—Don't Give Parents a Pass on Education*—June 2017

lum in the natural sciences and made Yale a stronghold of revivalist New Light theology. The stated mission of the college was to ensure that Caucasian, Protestant men "may be instructed in the Arts and Sciences who through the blessing of God may be fitted for Publick employment both in Church and Civil State."[110]

Isn't it a bit ironic that, over time, they have become equal, as fortresses of liberal thought?

Over the next three hundred years, the number of colleges, variety of curriculum, and expanse of educational opportunities would explode, achieving the consensus that there was a college in our country for anyone who chose, and could afford, to pursue higher education.

It would be quite some time before women attended college. The first woman to earn her degree was Catherine Elizabeth Benson Brewer, who received it in July 1840 at the Georgia Female College, now known as Wesleyan.[111]

For most of the next 120 years, a woman's curriculum choice was predominantly limited to teaching or nursing. An interesting depiction of the woman's college experience in the 1950s was captured in the 2003 film *Mona Lisa Smile*, starring Julia Roberts.

As an example of how our education system might be failing our youth, let me recount a topical, real-life experience. Recently, I had a discussion with a first-year college student who was unable to identify the three branches of government and wasn't certain who won the Second World War. In her freshman English composition class, she was tasked to write a paper on "the zombie apocalypse." Would it not have been more productive to assign a topic of intellectual value? Perhaps explaining the three branches of government?

Our higher education students seem to be immersed in progressivism and socialism. Dartmouth professor Mark Bray authored a book titled *Antifa: The Anti-Fascist Handbook*, which addresses the history of the Antifa movement as well as the ideologies and tactics behind it. Bray penned an op-ed in *The Washington Post* that read,

---

[110] Yale College—*Traditions and History*
[111] Wesleyan College—*First for Women*

"Physical violence against white supremacists is both ethically justifiable and strategically effective." When the school administration criticized the book, over one hundred Dartmouth faculty members signed a letter addressed to President Hanlon and Dean of Faculty Elizabeth Smith criticizing the college's statement on Bray.[112]

A passage from William F. Buckley Jr.'s book *Four Reforms*, published in 1973, offered an interesting prognostication: "Perhaps in due course we shall face a lumpenbaccalaureate [I had to access the dictionary on that one] class that disdains the jobs for which its members consider themselves unfit, in virtue of the exalted testimonials to their achievement as rendered in their diplomas. But that is in the future." Upon reflection, I realize "the future" might be now.[113]

- UC-Berkley, once the bastion of free speech in the 1960s, has violently suppressed conservative thought on campus. Far Left groups, such as Antifa, resort to physical force, intimidation, and destruction to quell speech.
- In response to some student protests, Rutgers University canceled a speech to be given by former secretary of state Condoleezza Rice due to her conservative views. How is our education process enhanced by suppressing the thoughts of such an accomplished minority woman?
- In a quest to achieve today's academic penchant for political correctness, the University of Kansas offered a course called "Angry White Male Studies," Yale University offered a course called "Constructions of Whiteness," and Florida Gulf Coast University offered a course titled "White Racism," where students would learn how to challenge white supremacy. How do such studies promote anything but racism?
- The height of insanity may have been achieved in August 2019, when a New York New School professor, Richard

---

[112] *The Dartmouth*—Dartmouth and lecturer Mark Bray at center of Antifa…—September 2017

[113] *FOUR REFORMS*—William F. Buckley, Jr.—1973 (Page 79)

> Wolff, known for his outspoken views against capitalism, declared that student grading in education was "capitalism in action," and recommended their elimination. "Wolff has been known to promote Marxism and condemn capitalism, even going so far as to blame capitalism for American homelessness. More recently, he made headlines by comparing President Trump to Adolf Hitler," posted on Twitter.[114]
> - Another example of this madness was reported in October 2019 by Education News, equating mathematics to racism: "An Ethnic Studies Advisory Committee, under the Seattle Public Schools Superintendent, published a preliminary Math Ethnic Studies document that explains math as a racist study used to oppress students—and if you correct a student's faulty math logic, you're guilty."

None of this has anything to do with the math children would be taught in K-12 classes; these are topics left for a progressive college course pondering the questions "Where does Power and Oppression show up in our math experiences?" and "Who gets to say if an answer is right?"[115]

This is simply foolishness.

Is political correctness destroying the college experience, the quality of a college education, and the value of a college degree?

The students seem more intrigued with the concept of protesting than with the content of the actual protest. Or perhaps this intrigue is just the result of the drumbeat of their liberally influenced education and socialist themes.

Robert Charles, assistant secretary of state for President George W. Bush, spoke at Dartmouth College in May 2019 and addressed the liberal bias on campus with this sage advice: "If you start with respect and you end with respect, you can reach the truth."

---

[114] *Education News—Prof. moves to eliminate grades…"capitalism in action"*— August 2019

[115] Education News—Seattle Schools document say math is oppressive, US government racist—October 2019

With the increasing number of millennials in the workforce, I am told that they are coming in with such a sense of entitlement that they can be difficult to work with. I suspect that this is the cumulative effect of the liberal higher education, helicopter parents, and the "everyone wants to be a Kardashian" syndrome.

At some level, something or someone in our society has failed these individuals. A recent *Forbes* magazine article ranked the public school systems by state:

| Overall Rank (1 = Best) | State | Total Score | Quality Rank | Safety Rank |
|---|---|---|---|---|
| 1 | Massachusetts | 74.16 | 1 | 1 |
| 2 | New Jersey | 67.09 | 3 | 9 |
| 3 | Connecticut | 66.93 | 2 | 11 |
| 4 | New Hampshire | 65.11 | 4 | 7 |
| 5 | Vermont | 63.18 | 5 | 4 |
| 6 | Virginia | 63.03 | 7 | 2 |
| 7 | Minnesota | 60.34 | 6 | 27 |
| 8 | Maryland | 57.82 | 10 | 20 |
| 9 | Wisconsin | 57.59 | 9 | 26 |
| 10 | Colorado | 57.45 | 14 | 8 |
| 11 | North Dakota | 57.03 | 11 | 29 |
| 12 | Wyoming | 57.02 | 8 | 37 |
| 13 | Maine | 56.82 | 16 | 5 |
| 14 | Nebraska | 56.42 | 12 | 28 |
| 15 | Kansas | 55.55 | 21 | 6 |
| 16 | Iowa | 55.33 | 13 | 35 |
| 17 | Rhode Island | 54.78 | 19 | 14 |
| 18 | Washington | 54.58 | 17 | 10 |
| 19 | Delaware | 54.36 | 31 | 3 |
| 20 | Kentucky | 54.34 | 20 | 19 |
| 21 | Illinois | 54.20 | 15 | 40 |
| 22 | New York | 53.36 | 24 | 12 |
| 23 | Montana | 52.78 | 18 | 37 |

| 24 | Indiana | 52.69 | 22 | 23 |
| 25 | South Dakota | 52.27 | 23 | 24 |
| 26 | Florida | 52.10 | 25 | 22 |
| 27 | Ohio | 51.93 | 29 | 18 |
| 28 | Pennsylvania | 51.36 | 30 | 17 |
| 29 | Missouri | 51.20 | 26 | 34 |
| 30 | Utah | 50.99 | 28 | 32 |
| 31 | Michigan | 50.07 | 27 | 44 |
| 32 | North Carolina | 48.91 | 32 | 25 |
| 33 | Oklahoma | 48.79 | 36 | 16 |
| 34 | Idaho | 47.84 | 33 | 39 |
| 35 | Tennessee | 46.90 | 39 | 15 |
| 36 | Texas | 46.90 | 35 | 41 |
| 37 | California | 46.33 | 38 | 21 |
| 38 | Georgia | 45.67 | 37 | 42 |
| 39 | Hawaii | 45.09 | 41 | 13 |
| 40 | South Carolina | 42.24 | 40 | 46 |
| 41 | Arkansas | 42.18 | 34 | 50 |
| 42 | West Virginia | 39.91 | 44 | 31 |
| 43 | Oregon | 39.79 | 42 | 49 |
| 44 | Alabama | 38.98 | 43 | 45 |
| 45 | Mississippi | 38.87 | 45 | 43 |
| 46 | Nevada | 38.54 | 47 | 36 |
| 47 | Arizona | 37.53 | 48 | 30 |
| 48 | Alaska | 35.87 | 50 | 33 |
| 49 | District of Columbia | 33.62 | 49 | 48 |
| 50 | Louisiana | 32.50 | 46 | 51 |
| 51 | New Mexico | 31.53 | 51 | 47 |

Budget cuts surely have an impact on the quality of public school education, with funds declining over the past decades. "Educators are asked to do more—federal and state mandates—with less funding," says Barbara Jeanne Erwin, clinical associate professor at Indiana University Bloomington.[116]

While previewing this chapter prior to publication, a retired principal from Staten Island, New York, offered the following: "The Department of Education has done more to hurt the education system than any group I know. The constantly changing mandates [Title 1, 2, 3, Common Core, etc.] have placed a tremendous burden on the local system. There is never enough money from the federal government to pay for all the changes."

In summary, once again, big government has hindered more than improved the process. There were unintended consequences.

While many Americans are content to wrongly blame the declining efficacy of our public school system on teachers, the actual cause seems to be attributed to three elements: *parents* that have failed to prepare their children properly for the education experience and are willing to abdicate that responsibility to teachers; *government* that tinkers with education rules, laws, and mandates in its effort to reengineer our society; and *educators* that allow the curriculum to become biased toward their own political philosophy.

> In a completely rational society, the best of us would aspire to be teachers and the rest of us would have to settle for something less, because passing civilization along from one generation to the next ought to be the highest honor and the highest responsibility anyone could have. (Lee Iacocca, business executive)

By 2019, the Department of Education had almost four thousand employees and an annual budget of $81 billion.[117]

In addition to federal spending, on a nationwide basis, states spent an average of $11,000 per student in the 2011–2012 school year, a 2.8 percent drop from 2010–2011. In Florida, Texas, and

---

[116] *Forbs Magazine—States with The Best Public-School Systems*—July 2018
[117] US Department of Education

Wisconsin, the decrease was more than 8 percent. Just seven states (Alaska, Connecticut, Delaware, Indiana, New Jersey, North Dakota, and Vermont) increased per-student spending. The increases ranged from 0.2 percent in North Dakota to 10 percent in Vermont.[118]

Yet with this massive investment, many teachers find it necessary to purchase required school supplies out of their own pockets or supplement their incomes with a second job. We currently see television ads bemoaning that teachers are underpaid. How can this be? Where does that massive investment go?

One of the New Jersey educators that I consulted in preparing this chapter, holding a master's degree in education as well as an additional degree in supervision and curriculum, spoke to the issue of teacher compensation: "After teaching for twenty-five years…the pay is terrible. I will retire in seven years, with thirty-two years' experience. We are no longer getting raises, and I am paying more for insurance and dues. I will never make $100,000."

The enormous financial support that we provide our education system in the United States is squandered if the system fails to prepare our children, intellectually and emotionally, for the voyage of life.

We seem to have restructured our education system to prepare students for state testing rather than for providing them instruction to prepare them for a productive life.

Demonstrating amazing prescience, William F. Buckley Jr. postulated in his 1951 book *God & Man at Yale*, "If impartiality is desirable in classroom treatment of conflicting ideologies…all sides should be presented impartially, that the student should be encouraged to select the side that pleases him most."[119]

When curriculum is biased, either toward liberalism or conservatism, rather than balanced, the educational process is undermined and students are done a disservice. Such a curriculum becomes more indoctrination and less education.

---

[118] National Center for Education Statistics
[119] *God & Man at Yale*—William F. Buckley, Jr.

In my own humble effort to encourage some degree of "balance" to young people I know who are about to embark on the college experience, I give them a present, a copy of Charles Krauthammer's book *Things That Matter*, together with a personal note:

> I offer you this book, *Things That Matter*, written by Charles Krauthammer.
>
> Prior to his death, he was the most steadfast apostle of conservative thought, since the passing of William F. Buckley Jr.
>
> The book is a primer in moderate conservative thought.
>
> I am hopeful that it will prepare you with some perspective to contrast the liberal bias that you will surely be exposed to as you pursue your college years.
>
> I encourage you to challenge what is presented with an open mind; consider both sides of every argument and have the intellectual strength to formulate your own decisions and beliefs.
>
> As you voyage through life, you will accumulate things that could be taken from you, but no one can take your education or intelligence. Education is a blessing; savor it and immerse yourself into it. The process never ends.
>
> Opportunity and fortune await you. Prepare yourself. Enjoy the journey! Carpe diem!
> —WLK

Dennis Prager, conservative radio host, made an interesting observation that I will paraphrase: sending our children to college and exposing them to intensive liberal bias might be like playing Russian roulette with their values.

I believe that we are shortchanging our youth by denying them the opportunity to obtain an education that would allow them to become something greater than themselves. Will it ever be possible to move our young Americans closer to a "service before self" philosophy?

The introduction of technology seems to be a two-edged sword. On the one hand, technology offers easy access to information, powerful math tools, and instant communication capabilities. Conversely, relying upon technology has compromised individual research techniques, sacrificed the need for basic math skills, and essentially eliminated the requirement of writing and interpersonal proficiencies.

*Parents* need to accept the responsibility for preparing their children with the basic skills required for those children to succeed in the education experience. Failing that, perhaps a solution could be found in pre-K training. Identify those children that are unprepared linguistically, academically, and socially for kindergarten and provide them with the fundamental training in those areas.

*Government* should not dictate curriculum based upon what is currently deemed politically correct; it seems to focus on the minority while depriving the majority.

*Educators* should be evaluated based upon their success with the students rather than their longevity and protection by the union.

> Children must be taught how to think, not what to think. (Margaret Mead, anthropologist and author)

Perhaps we should revert to the "three r's" again.

> No other investment yields as great a return as the investment in education. An educated workforce is the foundation of every community and the future of every economy. (Brad Henry, Oklahoma governor)

# Chapter IV

# Environment

*Earth provides enough to satisfy every man's needs, but not every man's greed.*

—Mahatma Gandhi,
political activist, India

*Global warming,* now referred to as climate change, is decreed as "settled science" and is one of today's liberal mantras. Ironically, in the 1970s, the fear was *global cooling,* and then, as today, it was the considered settled science, the then-prevailing concern of the science community. Is it possible that they were correct both times? They might not have been correct in the 1970s, and they are likely incorrect now. Let us explore the notion of *settled science.*

For centuries, physicians relied heavily on bloodletting for hysteria, heart disease, and just about every other illness. "The theory behind the practice changed often over time, but the practice itself remained much the same—with doctors often bleeding patients until they were weak, pale and, sometimes, unconscious." For thousands of years, bloodletting was "settled science."[120] Karl Landsteiner, an Austrian American immunologist and pathologist, discovered the major blood groups and developed the ABO system of blood typing at the beginning of the twentieth century. This allowed for the first

---

[120] *Los Angeles Times—When bleeding was a treatment*—June 2006

successful transfusion in 1907. He received the 1930 Nobel Prize for Physiology or Medicine.[121] Blood transfusions are a life-sustaining and lifesaving treatment. Transfusions are administered for acute trauma, blood loss, compromised blood-cell production, and disease. Transfusions became the new "settled science."[122] Today medical researchers are exploring the use of stem cells and blood spinning, perhaps tomorrow's "settled science." My point is that today's settled science awaits tomorrow's new revelation.

While we cannot deny that the world's climate changes and evolves, we can reasonably dispute the "doomsday" scenarios that have been offered. Representative Alexandria Ocasio-Cortez (D-NY) warned, "The world is going to end in 12 years if we don't address climate change….it is our World War II."[123] While I cannot accept the prediction being made by Representative Cortez, I recognize it for what it is, hyperbole; these alarmist statements do not help the climate change argument.

The United States has been long aware of the damage that we do to our planet. In 1970, when world events became less tumultuous, attempts began in earnest to increase the recycling effort within our country and, in fact, the world.

Each president from Ricard Nixon to George W. Bush, and all in between, initiated some action or legislation in pursuit of a cleaner country and a cleaner planet.

In his ongoing commitment to reduce or eliminate the use of fossil fuel, President Obama committed the United States to the Paris Climate Agreement in 2017, along with over 190 other countries. While the objective was both noble and necessary to aid our planet, the strategy was just another example of liberal philosophical prattle, doomed to failure.

The agreement was more altruistic and aspirational than practical. Two of the top three polluters in the world, China and India, were excluded. India would not participate until it first received $2.5

---

[121] *Encyclopedia Britannica—Karl Landsteiner*
[122] *American Nurse Today—The Rules of Transfusion*—April 2010
[123] *Newsweek—A.O.C. Warns "World is going to end in 12 years"*—January 2019

trillion in aid, and China will not join in until 2035.[124] In June 2017, President Donald Trump announced that the US would withdraw from the agreement.

The "settled science" and political grappling will continue. The yin and yang of environmental concerns and economic progress will continue to conflict. We will continue to evolve.

Environmental concern has been a growing issue in the United States over the past century. We have come to understand that our planet requires protection and conservation, oftentimes protection from ourselves.

In 1906, Theodore Roosevelt, the noted conservation president, signed legislation establishing the National Park Service. Initially, five national parks were designated: Crater Lake, Oregon; Wind Cave, South Dakota; Sullys Hill, North Dakota; Mesa Verde, Colorado; and Platt, Oklahoma.[125] Later that year, he signed the Antiquities Act of 1906. While not creating a single park itself, the Antiquities Act enabled Roosevelt and his successors to proclaim and protect "historic landmarks, historic or prehistoric structures, and other objects of historic or scientific interest" in federal ownership as national monuments.[126]

Our nation's interest in conservation and the well-being of our planet waned during World War I, the Great Depression, World War II, the Korean Conflict, the Vietnam War, and the 1969–1970 economic recession. Public concern rekindled political action in 1970, when President Nixon created the Environmental Protection Agency, merging antipollution programs of the Department of Agriculture and the Department of Interior. Over the years, legislation increased the influence of this agency, with bills like the Clean Water Act and the Resource and Conservation and Recovery Act.

In its first year, the EPA had a budget of $1.4 billion and 5,800 employees. It was primarily a technical assistance agency that set goals and standards. Soon, new acts and amendments passed by

---

[124] Ballotpedia—*China, India and the Paris Climate Agreement*—June 2017
[125] History.com—*National Park Service*
[126] Theodore Roosevelt Center—*Antiquities Act of 1906*

Congress gave the agency more regulatory authority. By President Obama's second term, the EPA had 17,106 employees, with a budget of $8.5 billion.[127]

During an interview with Steven Kroft on the *60 Minutes* television opinion program in 2015, President Obama declared, "My definition of leadership is leading on climate change."

Consciousness of conservation and recycling increased in popularity with a receptive American population in 1970. The recycling discipline and its advantages were being taught to our children in public school, and the students, in turn, were bringing the new awareness home to their parents.

The first Earth Day brought national and international attention to the problem of increasing waste and the importance of recycling. Earth Day, founded by Senator Gaylord Nelson (D-WI) in 1970, is now supported by over 192 countries on April 22. Over a billion people, including almost every school-aged child, take part in annual celebrations to promote conserving our environment by protecting and recycling.[128]

There is no national law in the United States that mandates recycling; state and local governments regulate that activity. In 2014, the recycling rate for municipal solid waste in the United States was 34.6 percent.[129]

Surprisingly, the United States, at less than 35 percent, falls far behind other countries in its recycling effort. Austria sits with the highest recycling rate of any country in the world at 63 percent, followed by Germany (62 percent), Taiwan (60 percent), Singapore (59 percent), South Korea (49 percent), United Kingdom (39 percent), Italy (36 percent), and France (35 percent). The worst recycling performers are Turkey and Chile, which each having recycled an abysmal 1 percent of total waste.[130] China is the world's largest municipal solid waste generator. In 2004, the urban areas of China generated

---

[127] US Environmental Protection Agency
[128] Resource Center—*A Brief Timeline of the History of Recycling*—May 2017
[129] EPA—*Materials and Waste Management in the United States*—May 2018
[130] General Kinematics—*Top 10 Recycling Countries Around the World*—September 2016

about 190 million metric tons, and by 2030, this amount is projected to be at least 480 million. No country has ever experienced as large, or as rapid, an increase in waste generation.[131]

In 1986, when the Chernobyl nuclear disaster occurred in the Soviet Union, the EPA was tasked with identifying its impact on the United States and keeping the public informed. The same year, Congress passed the Emergency Planning and Community Right to Know Act, which authorized the EPA to gather data on toxic chemicals and share this information with the public.

Between 1970 and 2008, the Environmental Protection Agency targeted reasonable issues of public safety.

The Federal Resource Conservation and Recovery Act was passed in 1976 both to close open dumps and to create standards for landfills, incinerators, and hazardous waste disposal.[132]

During the Obama administration, the EPA was weaponized and accounted for over 4,000 of the administration's 20,642 new regulations that generally restricted commerce and industry and specifically restricted exploration and drilling of fossil fuels.[133, 134]

The agency became an arm of the politically biased liberal agenda. I provide two such examples.

In May 2015, by executive order, the Obama administration moved to expand antipollution regulations over *smaller bodies of water*, which drew cheers from environmentalists and jeers from Republicans. The EPA, which already regulated large rivers and bays under President Nixon's 1972 Clean Water Act, issued a rule extending that authority to include smaller rivers and wetlands. President Obama said, "One in three Americans now gets drinking water from streams lacking clear protection, and businesses and industries that depend on clean water face uncertainty and delay, which costs our economy every day, too many of our waters have been left vulnerable to pollution."

---

[131] World Bank—*Waste Management in China*—May 2005
[132] *Federal Register*—*Resource Conservation and Recovery Act*
[133] Americans for Tax Reform—*Nearly 4,000 EPA Regulations Passed Under Obama*—July 2016
[134] *THE Daily Signal*—*20,642 Regulations Passed Under President Obama*—May 2016

The National Federation of Independent Businesses said the new requirements mean higher permit fees for their members and that the increased regulations affect "puddles, ponds, and even streambeds" that are dry most of the year.[135] The "Waters of the United States" rule, enacted by Obama's executive order, was revoked by the Trump administration because it too broadly defined which waterways are subject to federal regulation.

Since enactment of the Clean Water Act in 1972, the federal government has gone beyond protection of navigable waterways and their major tributaries. The Environmental Protection Agency now wants to assert jurisdiction over "isolated ponds and channels that flow only after it rains. As the definition expanded, so too has Washington's power over private property and the states' traditional authority to regulate their land and water resources, this action officially ends an egregious power grab and sets the stage for a new rule that will provide much-needed regulatory certainty for farmers, home builders and property owners nationwide," EPA chief Andrew Wheeler said.[136]

The *light bulb* regulation enacted by the Obama administration, to be effective in January 2020, redefined four categories of incandescent and halogen bulbs that would be subject to existing energy efficiency rules from which they were previously exempt. It would have applied to about half of the six billion light bulbs used in the US. The revised rules require the replacement of common light bulbs, including three-way incandescent, candle-shaped chandelier, and recessed reflector bulbs, with energy-efficient versions, such as LEDs.[137] The "light bulb" executive order was rescinded by the Trump administration.

EPA spokeswoman Shaylyn Hynes said the Obama-era rules "would increase the price…by almost 300 percent, leaving the cost burden on American consumers and businesses, this action will

---

[135] *USA Today—Obama team ramps up water regulations—*May 2015

[136] *Los Angeles Times—Trump Administration to finalize rollback of Obama…—September 2019*

[137] *NBC News—Trump Administration rolls back Obama-era light bulb Reg—September 2019*

ensure that the choice of how to light homes and businesses is left to the American people, not the federal government."[138]

Micromanaging of our environment by the government can often result in overbearing regulation with little thought or regard given to its risk-reward relationship.

The Obama-era EPA regulations contributed to stifling economic growth in the nation.

In 2010, the administration's investment in *renewable energy* subsidized solar and other renewal energy projects in the United States with taxpayer money costing $39 billion per year, on average, for each of five years.

According to *The Washington Times*, "Taxpayers are on the hook for more than $2.2 Billion in expected costs from the federal government's energy loan guarantee program, according to a new audit... that suggests the controversial projects may not pay for themselves, as officials had promised. Nearly $1 Billion in loans have already defaulted under the program, which included the infamous Solyndra project and dozens of other green technology programs that the Obama Administration has approved, totaling about $30 Billion in taxpayer backing."[139]

Public opinion at that time showed 58 percent of Americans preferred more gas and drilling.

"Obama has spent billions of taxpayer dollars subsidizing windmills and solar plants as part of his vision of a 'clean energy' future. But despite his repeated claims about a huge increase in renewable energy production, renewables today make up just 11% of the nation's total energy production, according to the Energy Information Administration. In mid-1983, the share of energy production comprised of renewables was...11%. The biggest shift in energy under Obama came not from a government program, but from fracking, which vastly expanded the supply of domestic oil and natural gas."[140]

---

[138] WGNO—ABC News—*Administration flips switch on light bulb regulations*—September 2019

[139] *The Washington Times: Obama clean energy...leaves taxpayers in $2.2 billion hole*—April 2015

[140] *Time*—The Press: *I'll Furnish the War*—October 1947

The massive subsidies have done little to increase the contributions of solar power to the electricity generation mix. Solar accounts for less than 1 percent of electricity generation. The colossal failure of Solyndra and others demonstrates the cost difference between what liberals wish for and what can be practically achieved. It is better to let the free marketplace innovate as demand dictates.

EPA regulations restricted the mining and consumption of coal and critically damaged the coal industry in West Virginia and Pennsylvania. Hillary Clinton, in a presidential campaign speech of 2016, promised to "put the coal industry out of business."[141] EPA regulations restricted the exploration for oil, particularly in Alaska's Arctic National Wildlife Refuge Region (ANWAR), which holds identified oil reserves third only to Venezuela and Saudi Arabia. United States Geological Survey reports revealed that there is somewhere between 4.3 and 11.8 *billion* barrels of oil in the coastal plain of the ANWAR.[142]

Regulations and liberal bias impeded construction of the XL Pipeline, which could provide a steady, non-railcar-dependent source of crude oil from Canada to the US refineries in Texas and Louisiana.

These regulations denied America the opportunity to become energy independent. Imagine, for a moment, the foreign relations and economic impact of the United States becoming the major exporter rather than importer of oil. Middle East nations relying upon oil revenue to foment terrorism might be neutered. Russia's ability to expand its international presence and aggressive acquisition of territory could be unfunded. Where is the advantage in reducing environmental risk when the greater risk is terrorism, Russian aggression, and a weakened US economy? The Trump administration's reversal of these impeding regulations overturned these disadvantages.

In the 1967 film *The Graduate*, Dustin Hoffman's character was famously advised by family friend Mr. McGuire, "I want to say one word to you. Just one word…plastics." Mr. McGuire was correct in 1967, and the plastics industry boomed and provided a great career

---

[141] *CNN* Townhall—March 2016
[142] USGS—*Arctic National Wildlife Reserve—Petroleum Assessment*—November 2017

opportunity. In 2019, plastics have created an environmental nightmare. Plastics have been with us for more than a century, and by now they're everywhere, for good and for ill. Plastic containers and coatings help keep food fresh. PVC is used for everything from pipes and flooring to furniture and clothes. But plastic contains toxins.

To reduce plastic waste and its negative effects, recycling programs have been implemented in many parts of the United States but remain underutilized. Much is due to the nature of plastic itself, which often can only be "downcycled" rather than recycled; a torn plastic bag might eventually be transformed into a lunch tray, but it will never be a plastic bag again. Many cities and states have begun more serious efforts to restrict their use, but the subject remains a matter of considerable debate. The vast majority ends up in landfills. Immense quantities of plastic are also sent to the developing world, where "recycling" frequently involves open-air burning.[143]

It is estimated that 1.1 to 2.4 million tons of plastic are entering the ocean each year. More than half of this plastic is less dense than water and will not sink once it enters the sea. This has created an area known as the Great Pacific Garbage Patch.[144]

In September 2016, as party to the Paris Climate Agreement, President Barack Obama committed the United States to join more than 190 countries in reducing greenhouse gas emissions, in hopes of preventing the global average temperature from increasing by 3.6 degrees Fahrenheit.[145] The Paris Agreement laid out a framework for countries to adopt clean energy and phase out fossil fuels. The United States' plan set the goal of reducing greenhouse gas emissions by 26 percent to 28 percent by 2025.[146] At the signing of the agreement, the world's largest annual greenhouse gas emission polluters, in

---

[143] Harvard University—Shorenstein Center: *Plastics, human health and environmental impacts*
[144] The Ocean Cleanup—*The Great Pacific Garbage Patch*
[145] *Business Insider—Here's what the US agreed to in the Paris climate deal*—June 2017
[146] *Washington Examiner—The Paris climate agreement was a terrible deal for the U.S.*—June 2017

metric tons, were China, 10,360; United Sates, 5,410; India, 2,270; Russia, 1,620; and Japan, 1,240.[147]

*Forbes* magazine concluded, "Claims that carbon cuts will be free or even generate economic growth don't stack up given today's technology. Every economic model shows real costs. If not, we wouldn't need the Paris treaty: every nation would stampede to voluntarily cut $CO_2$ and get rich."[148]

In June 2017, EPA administrator Scott Pruitt said that the Paris Climate Agreement "did not hold China and India accountable" and that "India didn't have to take any steps in the agreement to reduce $CO_2$ emissions until they received $2.5 trillion in aid. China didn't have to take any steps until the year 2035." Each signatory to the Paris Climate Agreement was required to submit a plan detailing emissions reduction. Pruitt added, "There is no penalty if China, India, or any other signatory does not achieve those targets."[149] China is the world's largest generator of greenhouse gas emissions and solid waste, yet they were excluded from being an active player in the agreement. How could the plan possibly succeed? In June 2017, President Donald Trump announced the US withdrawal from the agreement.

After the 2018, midterm elections, new members of Congress began touting the Green New Deal (GND), panned by most economists as foolhardy and wishful thinking. Announced in February 2019 by Representative Alexandria Ocasio-Cortez (D-NY) and Senator Edward Markey (D-MA), it has already been endorsed by six of the Democrat presidential contenders for 2020.

The plan's authors warn us that this "massive transformation of our society" needs some "clear goals and a timeline." Their timeline is ten years, and their goals are the following: eliminating all fossil fuel energy production; eliminating all nuclear power; replacing every "combustion-engine vehicle," trucks, airplanes, boats, and 99 percent cars "within ten years"; retrofitting "every building in America" with

---

[147] *Reuter's -Who are the world's biggest polluters?*—June 2017
[148] *Forbes Magazine—We Have A Climate Treaty—But at What Cost?*—December 2015
[149] Ballotpedia—*China, India and the Paris Climate Agreement*—June 2017

"state-of-the-art energy efficiency"; and building out "high-speed rail at a scale where air travel stops become necessary."

The GND promises that the United States government will provide every American with a job that includes a "family-sustaining wage, family and medical leave, vacations, and a pension" and free college or trade schools. The government will provide "healthy food" to every American; the government will provide, "safe, affordable, adequate housing" for every citizen and provide "economic security" for all who are "unable or unwilling" to work. The deal also promises to ban the consumption of beef.[150]

The Green New Deal did not address whether these handouts would be available to illegal immigrants, but then neither did the Affordable Care Act.

Beyond the elimination of the several industries that would result, the loss of 1.4 million jobs, and the consequent additional cost to taxpayers and consumers, *Forbes* magazine has predicted "the resolution's ambitious promises will add trillions of dollars to the nation's debt."[151] The New Green Deal proposal is beyond frivolous—it is insanity. If enacted, its expense would bankrupt our nation.

The fact remains that the United States, with all its economic and political power, is not listed among the top ten in the world in either clean air or clean water, as ranked in 2017 by the Purlife, an air and water purification company, based in Singapore.

In the final analysis, the Paris Climate Agreement and the New Green Deal are purely political "feel good" exercises, embracing some of the philosophies of good planet stewardship but designed to accomplish very little in a positive perspective.

As a nation, we must protect our planet, and we need to do better. However, government and leadership require a balance between theory and what is realistically achievable. Conservation and economic progress ought not be mutually exclusive.

---

[150] *The Federalist—The 10 Most Insane Requirements of the Green New Deal—*February 2019

[151] *Forbes Magazine—The Green New Deal Would Cost A Lot of Green—*February 2019

Here is your country. Cherish these natural wonders, cherish the natural resources, cherish the history and romance as a sacred heritage, for your children and your children's children. Do not let selfish men or greedy interests skin your country of its beauty, its riches or its romance. (Theodore Roosevelt, twenty-sixth US president)

# Chapter V

# Health Care

When the Affordable Care Act was proposed, 60 percent of Americans polled voiced opposition against the liberal legislation. Ergo, while most Americans were unhappy with some aspects of America's health-care system, they were not in favor of a wholesale overhaul.[152]

The US Census Bureau reported that 45.7 million Americans were without health insurance in 2007. That number fell to 28.5 million in 2017, when employer-based insurance accounted for 56 percent of the coverage, followed by Medicaid (19 percent) and Medicare (17 percent).[153], [154]

The significant increase in coverage over the decade was in the category of "employer-provided coverage," which was the result of a dramatic decrease in unemployment, as well as a surge in Medicaid coverage, which was the result of federal government subsidies. It appears that the actual influence of the health insurance plans offered by the Affordable Care Act on the government website was minimal. Much was promised; little was delivered.

Since passage of the ACA, our national health-care delivery system has been turned on its head: wait time to see a physician has been greatly extended; co-pays and deductibles have skyrocketed,

---

[152] *Politifact—Obamacare has never been favored by most Americans*—September 2013
[153] U S Census Bureau—*Income, Poverty and Health Insurance Coverage 2007*—August 2008
[154] U S Census Bureau—*Health Insurance Coverage 2017*—September 2018

making most policies economically ineffective; and prescription costs have ballooned. American health insurance policies have been transformed into protection against catastrophic expense coverage only. Today, America's health-care system covers 90 percent of our citizens. Independent experts estimate that more than 50 percent of the roughly twenty-eight million uninsured people are *eligible* for health insurance through *existing programs* but have *elected not to enroll.*

When Democrats passed the Affordable Care Act in 2010, it was intended to address the 18 percent of uninsured Americans at that time. Now, the bigger issue for 100 percent of the people with health insurance is struggling to pay their deductibles and copays.

A new word has entered the lexicon of the health insurance industry, *underinsured.* It is a term that describes policyholders exposed to high out-of-pocket costs when compared with their individual incomes. A recent report estimated forty-four million Americans were underinsured in 2018, compared with twenty-nine million in 2010, when the ACA was passed. That's about a 50 percent increase, with the greatest jump among people with *employer coverage.* Employers have been forced to increase deductibles and co-pays in order to manage employee health insurance premium expense.[155]

"When you have 90% of the American people covered and they are drowning in their health care bills, what they want to hear from politicians are plans that will address their health care costs, more than plans that will cover the remaining 10%," said Drew Altman, president of the Kaiser Family Foundation, a nonpartisan research organization that tracks the health-care system. "When Democrats talk about universal coverage more than health care costs, they are playing to the dreams of activists and progressives…much less to the actual concerns of the 90% who have coverage today."[156]

Polls conducted in anticipation of the 2020 presidential race revealed *spiraling* health-care cost to be the number one concern of the electorate. An unintended consequence.[157]

---

[155] NBC News—*32 Million Underinsured in the US*—March 2014
[156] Associated Press—*Despite calls to start over, US health system covers 90%*—July 2019
[157] Fox Business News—*Health care tops Americas' 2020 election priorities*—September 2019

First, in the interest of transparency, I should disclose that I have no experience in the health-care industry or medicine other than as a patient. In research for this chapter, I have discovered that the evolution of medicine and health care in the United States was slow, messy, and until the twentieth century, the product of a largely poorly informed society.

Before modern medicine, the understanding of disease and illness was based upon ideas that were two thousand years old and lacked any scientific basis. It was assumed that disease was caused by an imbalance or disturbance within the body, an evil spirit or a contagious disease. Conventional wisdom suggested that the cure would be through the elimination of those elements, by removing the offending substance through the mouth, nose, rectum, or skin. This was primarily accomplished by removing blood through "bleeding" or "leeching" or performing enemas. There was no understanding of germs invading the body or of mosquitos, fleas, or rodents carrying disease.

During the colonial era, most American doctors were trained in Europe or had been apprenticed to those who had. Few people consulted doctors because of the high fees charged; instead, most relied upon home remedies, midwives, and folk healers.

After our independence was won, the character of the physician changed—fewer came from the educated population. Standards of medical education declined dramatically. Medical schools eliminated most academic requirements that had been traditional and seldom offered any laboratory experience. Few taught anatomy or even required literacy for admission. There was neither licensing requirements for medical personnel nor professional oversight of any kind.[158] In the face of declining respectability, Benjamin Rush, an esteemed physician and professor of medicine at the University of Pennsylvania, was anxious to re-establish the credentials of his pro-

---

[158] George Washington University—*What Was Healthcare Like in the 1800's*—December 2012

fession and began teaching the use of more extreme bleeding and purging.[159]

I suspect that many might be surprised to learn that George Washington died from excessive purging administered in response to flu-like symptoms and throat discomfort. As was the practice of the day, doctors administered four bloodletting sessions and an enema within twenty-four hours, attempting to cure his maladies. He died on December 14, 1799.[160]

During the late eighteenth century, there was a proliferation of competing health initiatives: homeopaths, hydropaths, and new botanical theorists. What followed in the nineteenth century was an age of fitness gurus, elixirs, pills, and potions. Only the shape of the bottle required a patent. There was no control over their ingredients. The medical scene was a chaotic free-for-all.[161]

As American doctors continued to conduct bloodletting therapies, European doctors were moving in the opposite direction, drawing on scientific methods and laboratory studies. They had begun to extract key ingredients of herbal remedies, such as quinine, one of the very few curative remedies available for malaria. In France, doctors were using autopsies and concluded that the time-honored therapies did not work and could, in fact, cause harm. The European studies were putting science to use to evaluate their traditional remedies and found them wanting.[162] Americans rejected both the science and the idea of moderation, choosing instead to continue with the purge therapies. Even the most forward-looking physician in America, Oliver Wendell Holmes Sr., a proponent of clean hands, ridiculed the idea that science could have any practical value for the medical profession. When the idea of germs causing disease was introduced in Europe by Pasteur and Koch in the second half of the nineteenth

---

[159] *Encyclopedia Britannica -Benjamin Rush*
[160] George Washington's Mount Vernon—*The Death of George Washington*
[161] George Washington University—*What Was Healthcare Like in the 1800's*—December 2012
[162] George Washington University—*What Was Healthcare Like in the 1800's*—December 2012

century, American doctors vigorously denied such a notion. Science did not apply to American medicine.[163]

It wasn't until the beginning of the twentieth century that attitudes toward medicine and the notion of organized medicine began. Physicians started to band together and created the American Medical Association. US lawmakers elected not to make health policy a legislative issue.

In 1912, Theodore Roosevelt campaigned on the issue of mandatory health insurance and was supported by many progressive groups; however, their efforts were set aside with the beginning of World War I.[164]

As was the case with America's progress regarding environmental protection being interrupted by other pressing calamities of the period, so would our advancement in health care be delayed.

The cost of health care rose during the 1920s, making it increasingly more difficult for the middle class to afford.

The first venture into providing health insurance to employees was initiated in 1929, when a group of Dallas, Texas, schoolteachers contracted with Baylor Hospital to provide room, board, and medical services for a set monthly fee.[165]

The aftermath of the Great Depression compelled the government to provide some degree of government-based benefits. When the Social Security Act was passed in 1935, it did not include health insurance because of opposition from the American Medical Association. The AMA felt that "a health insurance program would increase bureaucracy and limit doctors' freedom."[166]

Life insurance companies entered the health insurance field during the 1930s and 1940s as its popularity increased. In 1932, Blue Cross and Blue Shield was first to offer group health plans, successful because they incorporated discounted contracts negotiated

---

[163] George Washington University—*What Was Healthcare Like in the 1800's*—December 2012
[164] MidlevelU.com—*Timeline: History of the U.S. Health Care System*—January 2013
[165] *Neurosurgical.com—The History of Health Insurance in The United States*
[166] MidlevelU.com—*Timeline: History of the U.S. Health Care System*—January 2013

with doctors and hospitals, in return for promises of increased volume and prompt payment.[167]

During World War II, employers began to offer health insurance coverage to their employees to compensate them for the government-imposed wage controls enacted. This was the genesis of the employer-based system we have today.

Democrat president Harry Truman proposed a nationalized health-care system in 1949 that would have included mandatory coverage; however, it was again opposed by the American Medical Association, whose members deemed Truman's plan "socialized medicine."[168]

Few legislative changes were made to health care, as America's legislative attention was diverted to the Korean conflict. Government programs to cover health-care costs did not begin to reemerge until the 1950s and 1960s, accelerated by strong unions bargaining for better benefit packages.[169]

Disability benefits were included in Social Security coverage for the first time in 1954 by Republican president Dwight Eisenhower.

Democrat president Lyndon Johnson created the Medicare and Medicaid programs in 1965, providing health-care coverage to retired and indigent citizens. The cost of health care exponentially increased after the passage of Medicare and Medicaid. President Richard Nixon signed the Health Maintenance Organization Act of 1973 to help reduce costs.

In December 2003, Republican president George W. Bush expanded Medicare coverage by signing the Medicare Prescription Drug, Improvement, and Modernization Act, which authorizes coverage of outpatient prescription drugs. The new drug assistance program, known as Part D, represented a major new federal entitlement. The drug assistance was "projected to cost taxpayers at least $395 billion, and possibly as much as $534 billion, over the next decade."[170]

---

[167] *Neurosurgical.com—The History of Health Insurance in The United States*
[168] MidlevelU.com—*Timeline: History of the U.S. Health Care System*—January 2013
[169] *Neurosurgical.com—The History of Health Insurance in The United States*
[170] medicarevotes. Org—*Medicare Prescription Drug Improvement and Modernization Act of 2003*

The cost of the prescription program to taxpayers, projected at $40 to $53 billion per year, reached $110 billion in 2017.[171]

Democrat president William Clinton signed the Children's Health Insurance Program (CHIP) of 1997, providing matching funds to states for health insurance to families with uninsured children and incomes that were modest but high enough to make them ineligible for Medicaid.

When created, CHIP was the largest expansion of taxpayer-funded health insurance coverage for children in the country. States were given flexibility in designing CHIP eligibility requirements and policies within broad federal guidelines.

The original intent of the law was to aid "working-poor" families, but it has now been expanded to provide coverage, dependent upon the state that you live in, to families with an annual family income of $70,000. The CHIP program covered 7.6 million children during federal fiscal year 2010. This availability of coverage has led to improvements in access to health care.[172]

In 2009, President Barack Obama signed the Children's Health Insurance Reauthorization Act, expanding the program to an additional four million children and pregnant women, including "lawfully residing" immigrants, without a waiting period. In 2017, this program cost the taxpayers $17.5 billion.[173]

In 2010, the Obama administration, in defiance of more than 60 percent public opinion against the bill and without a single Republican vote, passed the Affordable Care Act. It has proven to be anything but "affordable."[174]

In order to sell this program to the American people, the president made promises that were untrue and could never be delivered:

---

[171] HHS.gov—*HHS FY 2017 Budget—CMS—Medicare*

[172] National Conference of State Legislators—*Children's Health Insurance Program Overview*—January 2017

[173] Kaiser Family Foundation—*Children's Health Insurance Reauthorization Act*—February 2009

[174] *Politifact—Obamacare has never been favored by most Americans*—September 2013

# UNINTENDED CONSEQUENCE

"If you like your doctor, you can keep your doctor" and "It will reduce your annual medical expense by $2,800." Neither was achieved.[175]

Success is more likely achieved through the implementation of change in digestible steps rather than blanket overhaul, which generally leads to confusion and failure, as it had with the Affordable Care Act.

President Barack Obama, Speaker Nancy Pelosi, and Majority Leader Harry Reid could have learned a valuable lesson from Machiavelli. It might have been useful if they heeded the sage strategy contained within *The Prince*, wherein Machiavelli suggested that the most successful path to implementing change is to enlist your detractors as coauthors, thereby denying them the opportunity to be critic.[176] Pelosi and Reid violated this counsel and denied Republicans any honest participation in the process. During the House and Senate Committee meetings, almost every suggestion offered by Republicans was voted down by the majority Democrat members. As a result, Republicans, recognizing the destructive economic consequence and wounded by being shut out of the ACA legislative process, vehemently opposed the bill.

The ACA had zero Republican support. Therefore, the Senate bribed, or bought, a series of votes from Democrats in order to secure the liberal votes needed to pass the bill. They might not have supported the legislation without the following inducements:

- *Cornhusker Kickback.* Senator Ben Nelson (D-NE) ensured that Nebraska would be the only state to have the full $100 million amount of its increased Medicaid costs paid for by the federal government.[177]
- *The Louisiana Purchase.* The Senate bill provided extra Medicaid funding for "any state in which every county has been declared a disaster area." Because of hurricane Katrina, Louisiana was the only state that would qualify—an obvi-

---

[175] *Forbes Magazine—Obamacare's Five Biggest Broken Promises*—October 2016
[176] *The Prince*—Machiavelli
[177] Americans for Tax Reform—*A Full List of Backroom Deals in Healthcare Bill*

ous sham. The $300 million provision for Louisiana was slipped in late in the process to persuade Senator Mary Landrieu (D-LA) to support the health-care takeover.[178]

- *Gator Aid.* At the request of Senator Bill Nelson (D-Fl), the Senate bill included a formula for protecting certain Medicare Advantage enrollees from billions of dollars in cuts. The formula would only apply to five states, most notably Florida, in which eight hundred thousand of the state's Medicare Advantage enrollees would be exempt from cuts.[179]
- *New England Handouts.* The Senate bill contained $600 million in extra Medicaid cash to Vermont and $500 million in additional money to Massachusetts.[180]
- *The Dodd Clinic.* The bill provided $100 million for construction at an unnamed "health-care facility" affiliated with an academic health center. Senator Chris Dodd (D-CT) later sent a press release saying that he was securing the money for the University of Connecticut.[181]
- *Montana Medicare Earmark.* A provision in the Senate bill for Senator Max Baucus (D-MT) expanded Medicare coverage for individuals who reside "in or around the geographic area subject to an emergency declaration made as of June 17, 2009." Senator Baucus referred to the asbestos-contaminated area near Libby, Montana. Another sham.[182]

Without these votes from fellow Democrats, the ACA could never have become law. Sausage making can be messy, and so can politics. What measure of corruption did this demonstrate?

The Affordable Care Act contained controversial provisions: requiring insurance providers to cover preexisting conditions and

---

[178] Americans for Tax Reform—*A Full List of Backroom Deals in Healthcare Bill*
[179] Americans for Tax Reform—*A Full List of Backroom Deals in Healthcare Bill*
[180] Americans for Tax Reform—*A Full List of Backroom Deals in Healthcare Bill*
[181] Americans for Tax Reform—*A Full List of Backroom Deals in Healthcare Bill*
[182] Americans for Tax Reform—*A Full List of Backroom Deals in Healthcare Bill*

mandatory reimbursement for birth control pills, requiring every American to purchase health insurance or be subject to a penalty fee, and exempting members of Congress from the plan.

> The airheads of Congress will keep their own plush health care plan—it's the rest of us guinea pigs who will be thrown to the wolves. (Camille Paglia, professor, American writer)

The ACA provided 100 percent funding for states agreeing to expand the Medicaid roles, for the first three years, after which the additional cost was to be borne by the state's taxpayers, creating a future financial burden. In the end, it will be the state taxpayers that will be required to carry the burden for that segment of this liberal largess.

The Democrats fully understood that they were perpetrating a fraud upon the American people. During a panel discussion at the University of Pennsylvania in October 2013, Jonathan Gruber, professor of economics at the Massachusetts Institute of Technology, said that "the stupidity of the American voter" made it important for Democrats to hide Obamacare's true costs from the public. Professor Gruber told the panel, "Lack of transparency is a huge political advantage. And basically, call it the stupidity of the American voter or whatever, but basically that was really, really critical for the thing to pass."[183] Gruber pointed out that if Democrats had been honest about these facts and had disclosed that the law's individual mandate was, in effect, a major tax hike, Obamacare would never have passed Congress.[184]

While the program is widely touted as having provided health care to an additional twelve million people, the unintended consequence was that it has prevented many insureds from seeking medical help, due to the exploding deductibles and co-pay require-

---

[183] *Forbes Magazine—The Stupidity of the American Voter Led Us to Hide…*—November 2014
[184] *Forbes Magazine—The Stupidity of the American Voter Led Us to Hide…*—November 2014

ments. Wait times required to schedule a doctor's appointment have increased dramatically. Is this because there are twelve million additional insureds, because new regulations and restrictions are encouraging doctors to leave the field, or because the medical doctor population is aging and retiring?

The uninsured dropped from 18 percent in 2011 to 12 percent in 2015. Most of the "newly" insureds were covered under Medicaid, which might already have been available, prior to the ACA bill passing, had the states chosen to fund it, as they are now required to do. The real cost of the ACA is being borne by the 82 percent of Americans who had pre-ACA coverage, through increased premiums, deductibles, and escalated prescription costs. According to the *Los Angeles Times* in 2019, soaring deductibles and medical bills are burdening American families and creating an affordability crisis. Since ACA's inception, annual deductibles in employer-based health plans have nearly *quadrupled*. Approximately 20 percent of Americans said that health-care costs have depleted their savings.[185]

The Affordable Care Act was impractical and unsustainable; it has been detrimental to our society and our economy. Our politicians have been unwilling or unable to correct it. Our legislators seem to choose politics over our national well-being.

At the time the ACA was being deliberated in Congress, Warren Buffett offered a sage advice: "Bend the cost curve, and then look to expand the health care system for more inclusion." Buffet's theory was, if we were successful in reducing medical costs, thereby reducing health premiums, then our system would be more affordable and allow expanded coverage.

The feel-good ACA ignored the fundamental issues that continue to drive medical costs up and, consequently, failed to bend the cost curve:

- *Tort reform.* Malpractice insurance premiums compel physicians to increase medical fees. Defensive medicine com-

---

[185] HealthLeaders—*Health Deductibles Soar Leaving Americans with Unaffordable Bills*—May 2019

pels physicians to prescribe tests that are intended primarily to protect the physician from a negligence legal action. Most malpractice cases are "settled" in the interest of expediency. Revising our legal system to compel a plaintiff to reimburse the defendant physician for litigation expense, in an instance where the plaintiff does not prevail, would significantly reduce the number of litigation actions, eliminate the necessity for defensive medical testing, reduce the "expedient" settlements, and cut malpractice insurance premiums.

- *Medicare and Medicaid waste and abuse.* This has been cited as $200 billion in waste annually. Many legislators rely upon this figure and its intended elimination as a method to fund new liberal programs. However, the reduction in waste and abuse never occurs. A simple solution to reduce the propensity to commit such fraud would be to revise our justice system, ascribing substantial penalties for conviction: a fine equal to one thousand times the financial gain, a minimum three years in prison, and the revocation of any medical, or other licenses, for life.

- *Establish a medical price board.* Medicine is the only area where Americans are indifferent to the cost of service, which can vary substantially from one physician to another. A medical price board would be responsible to set reasonable price controls on medical services, establishing pricing norms. This would eliminate the surprise expense that hospitals bill to patients for services provided that were "not covered by your health plan."

- *Purchase health insurance across state lines.* Health care is a *national* problem and requires a *national* solution. Let the marketplace determine the cost of health insurance. Increased competition should lead to lower premiums.

- *Medical expense of undocumented aliens.* The cost of any illegal immigrant receiving medical care in our emergency rooms could be invoiced to their parent government or contra the expense to whatever aid the United States might be providing their homelands. This might offer a double incentive, recoup the medical expense to our Treasury, and encourage the foreign government to better control the flow of emigres from their country to ours.

Is it simply curious, or profoundly instructional, that 60 percent of Americans were satisfied with their health-care insurance in 2010 and yet, in 2020, the number one issue polled among potential presidential voters is the cost of health care?[186]

The Republicans are not without blame. In 2017, with control of the House, Senate, and White House, the Republicans foolishly attempted to repeal the Affordable Care Act without first proposing a cogent replacement for the plan. They almost succeeded, save a "nay" vote from Senator John McCain (R-AZ), who cited a "procedural objection." McCain placed his hatred for President Trump above his sense of duty as a senator. Politics over policy.

In the summer of 2019, the editorial board of *USA Today* convened a "Q&A" with health insurance executives and trade groups representing the health insurance industry. The most illuminating question posed was, "What is the biggest challenge facing the US health care system?" The consensus answer was, "Cost and affordability. That's really the biggest driver of a lot of the change and dissatisfaction with the health-care system, in addition to some of the complexity that we see. I think we are at a tipping point in terms of what we can afford both at a sort of systemic level and at an individual level."[187]

Health expenditures increased from 17.2 percent of gross domestic product in 2013 to 18 percent of GDP in 2016.[188]

With no clear end in sight.

Tipping point, indeed. The ACA is a textbook example of a noble idea being sacrificed by insufficient planning and thoughtless implementation in the interest of a political agenda. *Feel good* doesn't

---

[186] Fox Business News—*Health care tops Americas' 2020 election priorities*—September 2019

[187] *USA Today—Q&A with America's Health Insurance Plans CEO—July 2019*

[188] Statista—*US National Health Expense Expenditure; 1960 to 2019*—August 2019

necessarily do good. Good intentions gone awry, thus hampering our economy.

The unintended consequence of the Affordable Care Act has been a greatly hampered national medical delivery system and an economic disaster. The new health law has disrupted coverage for millions and driven up costs for millions more.

The outcome of the ACA may have been unforeseen, but the deception of the American people was fully recognized and constituted a fraud upon them.

We can see that, except for Medicare, Part D prescription drug coverage signed into law by President Bush, every other government health-care legislation was enacted by a Democrat president. Without exception, each of these programs grossly exceeded their anticipated cost to the American taxpayers. This fact is irrefutable: the cost consequence of these programs was either unintended or of no concern. I have seen no evidence that, at any time, the health care of our national economy was considered.

Sardonically, it has only required a century for us to "advance" from bloodletting as a cure for illness to economic hemorrhaging as a cure for our perceived social ills.

So what might our national health-care future look like?

Erin Tolbert, a certified family nurse practitioner and founder of Midlevel U, an organization for nurse practitioners (NPs) and others in the health-care community, assesses the future of health care in the United States this way:

> I feel a change of attitudes and a transitioning of roles is in the air. You can feel it. People are looking more and more to the internet to solve their medical dilemmas. Nurse practitioners are pushing to expand their roles. The complexities and often injustices of medical payment systems are being exposed. These changes strike fear in many providers—no one likes change.[189]

---

[189] MidlevelU.com—*Timeline: History of the U.S. Health Care System*—January 2013

# Chapter VI

# Immigration

*In the first place, we should insist that if the immigrant who comes here in good faith becomes an American and assimilates himself to us, he shall be treated on an exact equality with everyone else, for it is an outrage to discriminate against any such man because of creed, or birthplace, or origin. But this is predicated upon the person's becoming in every facet an American, and nothing but an American. There can be no divided allegiance here. Any man who says he is an American, but something else also, isn't an American at all. We have room for but one flag, the American flag… We have room for but one language here, and that is the English language…and we have room for but one sole loyalty and that is a loyalty to the American people.*

—Theodore Roosevelt,
twenty-sixth US president

*Remember, remember always, that all of us, and you and I especially, are descended from immigrants and revolutionists.*

—Franklin D. Roosevelt,
thirty-second US president

# UNINTENDED CONSEQUENCE

*We have become not a melting pot but a beautiful mosaic. Different people, different beliefs, different yearnings, different hopes, different dreams.*

—Jimmy Carter,
thirty-ninth US president

And so our current national dilemma was born and defined.

It is important to recognize the distinction between *legal* immigration and *illegal* immigration. *Legal* immigration is a benefit, whereas *illegal* immigration is a crime.

The patchwork of immigration legislation over the past 150 years, each act directed toward some then-parochial concern, lacked the broader vision of significant, longer-term issues. While they might have been successful in addressing the problem of the era, they sowed the seeds of today's chaos. Our southern border is in chaos because our immigration laws are porous and ineffective. Those laws and our public largesse have created incentives for people to illegally cross our borders. The cost of this border intrusion is unsustainable.

A June 2018 poll conducted by CBS, no bastion of pro-Trump sympathy, concluded, "A majority (54%) of Americans tend to believe illegal immigrants should be treated well, but they would also prefer for them to stay out of the country…a majority (51%) also thought the border wall was a good idea."[190]

In control of all three branches of government during the 2009–2010 congressional session, the Congress, led Pelosi (D-NY) and Reid (D-NV), failed to address this issue. Their negligence is beyond understanding.

In control of all three branches of government during the 2017–2018 congressional session, the Republican Congress, led by Ryan (R-WI) and McConnell (R-KY), failed to address this issue. Their delinquency is incomprehensible.

In April and May of 2019, 110,000 illegal immigrants were caught crossing the southern border each month. Immigration Customs Enforcement has publicly estimated that the number will

---

[190] *Town Hall: CBS Poll: 51% of Americans think a Border Wall is a Good Idea*—June 2018

exceed one million in 2019. We have no measure of those that have crossed the border illegally and were not apprehended, while many others are overstaying visas with impunity.

When President Donald Trump advised America of the crisis at the southern border, Democrat Pelosi and Schumer called it a manufactured crisis, while most Republicans viewed it as a national emergency. The motives of each were clear. Speaker Nancy Pelosi (D-CA), Minority Leader Chuck Schumer (D-NY), and most of the Democrats in Congress chose to ignore rather than address this crisis. Their sole motivation seemed to be refusing to allow President Donald Trump a "win" on immigration.

Democrats seem convinced that the border chaos will be a winning argument for them in the 2020 election with Latin voters and seem willing to allow it to continue unimpeded to protect that perceived advantage. Politics rather than purpose. Do they believe that the American electorate is that ignorant?

In June 2019, the president gave Congress three weeks to address the millions of illegal immigrants in the United States that had already been processed through our legal system and ordered to be deported. Congress failed. In July 2019, the president ordered ICE to arrest and deport those individuals; in reaction, Speaker Nancy Pelosi, former secretary of state Hillary Clinton, and a slew of mayors across the country, all Democrats, publicly advised the illegals to flout, abuse, and evade the law and resist ICE, advising them of their rights and techniques to avoid deportation. Is this not approaching anarchy?

Given the senseless resistance from Congress, President Donald Trump chose to successfully negotiate with the Mexican government for border assistance. Isn't it disappointing, even shocking, that our president finds it easier to negotiate with a foreign government than with our own Congress? The agreement with Mexico rapidly improved conditions and circumstances on our southern border, yet the Democrats panned it. How can our legislature be so feckless?

The insanity continued to expand in 2017 with the notion of "sanctuary cities," in which liberally governed cities and states welcomed illegal immigrants and increased financial support to them.

# UNINTENDED CONSEQUENCE

At the same time, they instructed their local law enforcement to outright defy our federal law and the enforcement agencies.

- Democrat governors in New Jersey,[191], New York,[192], and California[193] have each proposed a fund of $2.1, $10, and $10 million, respectively, to provide legal aid to illegal immigrants.
- Governor Gavin Newsom (D) and Democrats in the California state legislature have passed a bill that will provide low-income young adults between the ages of nineteen and twenty-five living in California *illegally* full access to California's Medicaid program, known as Medi-Cal. The deal will cost $98 million each year, according to *The New York Times*.[194]
- San Diego recently announced plans to spend $11 million to provide shelters for the homeless. Isn't California already plagued with homelessness and high taxes?
- In 2017, FAIR (Federation for Immigrant Reform) released a report, "The Fiscal Burden of Illegal Immigration on United States Taxpayers," which put the total cost of illegal immigration at $135 billion each year, while claiming undocumented immigrants paid $19 billion in taxes. That leaves an annual net cost to the US taxpayers of $116 billion.

When will taxpayers say, "Enough"? Today's national debt now exceeds $23 trillion, is it wise for America to import more poverty?

Indentured servants first arrived in America in the decade following the settlement of Jamestown by the Virginia Company in 1607. The concept was born in the need for cheap labor. Settlers realized that they had lots of land to care for but no one to care for

---

[191] Immigration Reform—3/26/18
[192] *Canyon News*—December 2016
[193] *Conservative Daily Post*—April 2017
[194] *USA Today*—June 2019

it.[195] Passage to the colonies was expensive, so the Virginia Company developed the system of indentured servitude to attract workers. Europe's economy was depressed, and life in the New World offered hope to those unemployed. Servants worked between four to seven years to repay the cost of passage, room, and board. The life of an indentured servant was harsh, but it was not slavery. One-half to two-thirds of immigrants that came to the colonies arrived as indentured servants.[196]

By the mid-1600s, communities of European immigrants gathered on the Eastern Seaboard—the Spanish in Florida, the British in New England and Virginia, the Dutch in New York, and the Swedes in Delaware. Some came for religious freedom, while others sought greater economic opportunities. Still others, including hundreds of thousands of enslaved Africans, arrived in America against their will.[197]

American immigration history can be viewed as four periods: the colonial period, the midnineteenth century, the twentieth century, and the post-1965. Each period brought distinct national groups, races, and ethnicities to the United States.

*The colonial period.* In 1790, through the Naturalization Act, Congress passed its first law, defining who would be qualified for US citizenship. It allowed any free white person of "good character" living in the United States for two years or longer to apply for citizenship. Those without citizenship and nonwhite residents were denied basic constitutional protections, including the right to vote, own property, or testify in court.[198] This might be considered the original "white privilege."

Between the end of the revolution and the War of 1812, immigration to the United States was slow, steady, and primarily from Europe.

---

[195] The Statue of Liberty—Ellis Island Foundation
[196] The Statue of Liberty—Ellis Island Foundation
[197] The Statue of Liberty—Ellis Island Foundation
[198] The Statue of Liberty—Ellis Island Foundation

The United States began westward expansion and required manpower of great fortitude, self-reliance, and ambition to execute the venture.

After the War of 1812, with peace having been established with Britain, immigration experienced a significant surge. An estimated one-third of the immigrants came from Ireland, locating in New York, with significant numbers from Germany locating in the Midwest.[199]

At that time, many immigrants arrived ill or dying. In response, Congress passed the Steerage Act in 1819. The act required better conditions on ships arriving to this country and compelled ship captains to submit demographic information on passengers, creating the first federal records on the ethnic composition of immigrants to the United States.[200]

*Midnineteenth century period.* After the Civil War, in response to continued economic growth, the need for unskilled labor, and a vast westward expansion, another immigration surge developed.

The Citizenship Clause is the first sentence of Section 1 of the Fourteenth Amendment to the United States Constitution and was adopted on July 9, 1868. It states, "All persons born or naturalized in the United States, and subject to the jurisdiction thereof, are citizens of the United States and of the State wherein they reside." In its original writing, the Constitution did not recognize slaves to be citizens.[201]

The United States traditionally viewed the American immigration process as a "melting pot" where, over time, generations of immigrants melted together, abandoned their original cultures, and became totally assimilated into American society. America has always been a nation of immigrants.

America began a period of rapid industrialization and urbanization between 1880 and 1920, during which more than twenty million immigrants arrived. The majority were from Southern, Eastern,

---

[199] The Statue of Liberty—Ellis Island Foundation
[200] The Statue of Liberty—Ellis Island Foundation
[201] National Constitution Website

and Central Europe, including four million Italians and two million Jews. Most settled in major US cities, providing necessary labor for their new factories.[202]

Democrat "bosses" met immigrants at the water's edge, bribed them with cash "gifts" funded by the Party, and recruited them into their political ranks. Immigrants moved from the docks, through tenements, learned the language, became self-sufficient, and assimilated into American society.

Chinese immigrants began entering the US in the 1850s, working in the gold mines and garment factories, building railroads, and taking agricultural jobs. Anti-Chinese sentiment grew as Chinese laborers became successful in America. White workers, without any factual basis, blamed them for low wages. In response, Congress passed the Chinese Exclusion Act of 1882, the first in American history to place broad restrictions on a specific immigrant group.

The Mexican-American War ended with the 1848 signing of the Treaty of Guadalupe Hidalgo, giving vast expanses of the Southwestern territory to the United States and setting the southern US boundary at the *middle* of the Rio Grande River.[203]

This would create significant problems in the twenty-first century, when the United States would be besieged by tens of thousands of immigrants illegally crossing the southern border. One remedy that would be considered would be the building of a wall, impractical in the middle of the Rio Grande.

The Statue of Liberty, a colossal copper statue, was dedicated in October 1886. It was a gift to the United States from the people of France and is recognized around the world as a universal symbol of freedom and democracy.[204] Erected on a pedestal in New York Harbor, it bears a plaque at the entrance engraved with a sonnet titled "The New Colossus," written in 1883 by Emma Lazarus. What follows is its most famous passage:

---

[202] The Statue of Liberty—Ellis Island Foundation
[203] *Encyclopedia Britannica—The Mexican American War*
[204] National Park Service—*Statue of Liberty*

# UNINTENDED CONSEQUENCE

> Give me your tired, your poor
> Your huddled masses yearning to breathe free
> The wretched refuse of your teeming shore
> Send these, the homeless, tempest-tost to me
> I lift my lamp beside the golden door![205]

In 1892, the United States opened its first immigration station, Ellis Island, in New York Harbor. The first immigrant processed was a teenager from Ireland. More than twelve million immigrants entered the United States through Ellis Island, underneath the shadow of the statue, between 1892 and 1954. Ellis Island was formally closed in June 1954.[206]

The Immigration Act of 1891 further restricted those who could enter the United States, barring the immigration of polygamists, people convicted of certain crimes, and the sick or diseased. The act created a federal office of immigration and a corps of immigration inspectors, stationed at principal ports of entry.

*Twentieth-century period.* By 1910, 75 percent of New York residents were immigrants or first-generation Americans. The Immigration Act of 1917 established a literacy requirement for immigrants entering the country and halted immigration from most Asian countries. This Asian restriction would remain in place until repealed in 1952 by Democrat president Harry Truman.

The Immigration Act of 1924 strictly limited the number of immigrants allowed through nationality quotas. Under the quota system, the United States issued immigration visas to 2 percent of the total number of people of each nationality in the United States at the 1890 census. The law favored immigration from Northern and Western European countries. The act completely excluded immigrants from Asia, aside from the Philippines, then an American colony.[207] In reaction to the numerical limits established by the 1924 law, illegal immigration increased and the US Border Patrol was estab-

---

[205] History.com—*Statue of Liberty*
[206] The Statue of Liberty—Ellis Island Foundation
[207] The Statue of Liberty—Ellis Island Foundation

lished to crack down on illegals crossing the Mexican and Canadian borders into the United States.[208]

The Immigration and Nationality Act of 1952 upheld and reinforced the controversial national origins quota system of immigrant selection and maintained the literacy requirement. It ended the exclusion of Asians from immigrating to the United States and introduced a system of preferences based on skill sets and family reunification (chain migration). Representative Emanuel Celler (D-NY) favored the liberalization of immigration laws, expressing concerns that the restrictive quota system heavily favored immigration from Northern and Western Europe and, therefore, created resentment against the United States in other parts of the world.[209]

The Immigration and Nationality Act of 1965 overhauled the American immigration system, ending the national origin quotas enacted in the 1920s. That quota system was replaced with a preference system, emphasizing family reunification and skilled immigrants. Upon signing the new bill, President Johnson called the old immigration system "un-American" and said the new bill would correct a "cruel and enduring wrong in the conduct of the American Nation."[210] The act of 1965 continued the requirement of successful completion of an English test that immigrants would be required to take to become a citizen.[211] However, there were exceptions in which some immigrants could bypass that test.[212]

During the 1960s, almost 125,000 Cuban refugees made a sea-crossing in overcrowded boats to arrive on the Florida shore, seeking political asylum. A Cuban apprehended in the waters between Cuba and the United States would be granted asylum.

---

[208] The Statue of Liberty—Ellis Island Foundation
[209] US Department of State—Office of the Historian
[210] President Johnson Speech upon signing the Immigration bill of 1965—October 3, 1965
[211] President Johnson Speech upon signing the Immigration bill of 1965—October 3, 1965
[212] *US Dept of Homeland Security—US Citizenship and I. S.—Exceptions and Accommodations*

Between 1960 and 1962, approximately fourteen thousand unaccompanied children were brought to the United States from Cuba during Operation Peter Pan, a covert program that helped school-age kids escape repression in Cuba. The program was designed to both protect Cuban children whose parents were being targeted by Fidel Castro's new regime and to shield them from the communist ideologies feared by the US.[213]

*Post-1965 period.* The Cuban Adjustment Act of 1966 was signed into law by President Lyndon Johnson. The law applied to any native or citizen of Cuba who had been inspected and admitted or paroled into the United States after January 1, 1959, and had been physically present in our country for at least one year. The act determined that anyone qualified under these conditions shall be considered a permanent resident.

In April 1980, the Castro regime announced that all Cubans wishing to immigrate to the US are free to board boats at the port of Mariel west of Havana, launching the Mariel boatlift. The first of 125,000 Cuban refugees reached Florida the next day. In perfect gamesmanship over President Jimmy Carter, Fidel Castro ordered the release of occupants from Cuban jails and mental health facilities and shipped them to the United States.[214]

In 1985, a class action lawsuit was filed on behalf of immigrant children detained by the Immigration and Naturalization Service (INS) challenging procedures regarding the detention, treatment, and release of immigrant children. The agreement was named for Jenny Lisette Flores, a fifteen-year-old girl from El Salvador. She fled her country in 1985 and tried to enter the United States to be with her aunt. The INS arrested her at the border, and she was placed in a juvenile detention center, where she was handcuffed and strip-searched. It was not until 1997, after years of litigation, that the parties reached the Flores Settlement Agreement mandating that the government shall be required to release children from detention "without unnecessary delay," they must not detain a child for more

---

[213] History.com—*The Secret Cold War Program That Airlifted Cuban Kids to the US*
[214] History.com—*Castro Announces Mariel Boatlift*

than twenty days, and the government shall be required to implement standards relating to the care and treatment of children in immigration detention.[215]

In 1978, the Democrat Jimmy Carter's administration redirected our immigration policy away from the "melting pot" philosophy, toward one of multiculturalism, where cultural diversity would be considered a positive thing and immigrants would be encouraged to maintain their own traditions and their native language. This model of racial integration was described as a "salad bowl," "American quilt," or "mosaic," with people of different cultures living in harmony, like the lettuce, tomatoes, and carrots in a salad. This dramatic redirection of policy had serious unintended consequences to our culture, economy, and education system. It encouraged new immigrants to form neighborhoods by culture, thus fragmenting American society, and it created increased federal and state welfare burdens; it overtaxed our public school systems, requiring an English as a second language curriculum.

In 1986, President Ronald Reagan signed the Immigration Reform and Control Act. The act granted amnesty to more than three million immigrants living illegally in the United States, made it illegal to knowingly hire illegal aliens, and established financial and other penalties for companies that employed them. In return, Congress had promised tighter border security, but Congress never delivered.

The Immigration Act of 1990 was signed by President George W. Bush as a national reform of the Immigration and Nationality Act of 1965: it increased the total immigration, allowing 700,000 immigrants to come to the US per year for the fiscal years 1992–1994, and 675,000 per year after that. It expanded the family-based immigration visa (chain migration), it created five distinct employment-based visas, categorized by occupation, and it added a diversity visa (visa lottery) program that targeted immigrants from "low-ad-

---

[215] CNN—*What is the Flores Settlement*—July 2018

mittance" countries where their citizenry was underrepresented in the United States.[216]

All seemingly designed to expand the "salad bowl."

Prior to 1995, the US government allowed all Cubans who reached US territorial *waters* to remain in the US. The Clinton administration came to an agreement with Cuba that would stop admitting people intercepted in US waters. In what became known as the "wet foot, dry foot" policy, a Cuban caught on the waters between the two nations ("wet feet") would summarily be sent home or to a third country. One who made it to shore ("dry feet") would be allowed to remain in the United States and would later qualify for expedited "legal permanent resident" status.

In response to the Democrat-controlled Congress's inability to pass comprehensive immigration legislation, in 2012, Democrat president Barack Obama signed an executive order, Deferred Action for Childhood Arrivals (DACA), which temporarily shielded some illegal immigrants from deportation but did not provide a path to citizenship. In January 2017, President Obama announced the immediate end of the "wet foot, dry foot" policy. As he was renewing political dialogue with the Castro government, Obama issued a statement saying the US is working to normalize relations with its onetime foe, and ending this policy was the next logical step. He said, "Effective immediately, Cuban nationals who attempt to enter the United States illegally and do not qualify for humanitarian relief will be subject to removal. By taking this step, we are treating Cuban migrants the same way we treat migrants from other countries."

In 2017, President Donald Trump issued two executive orders, each titled "Protecting the Nation from Foreign Terrorist Entry into the United States," aimed at curtailing travel and immigration from six majority Muslim countries suffering in terrorism turmoil, as well as North Korea and Venezuela. Both executive orders were challenged in state and federal courts. In June 2018, the US Supreme Court upheld a third version of the ban.

---

[216] Congress.Gov—Immigration Act of 1990—S.358

In 2017, counties and states, typically governed by Democrat administrations, established the concept of sanctuary cities. In a sinister plot intended less to improve the quality of life and more to cultivate the electorate, liberal cities and states initiated the concept of "sanctuary cities." Each of these jurisdictions had laws or ordinances that obstruct immigration enforcement and shield criminals from Immigration and Customs Enforcement (ICE), by refusing to, or prohibiting agencies from, complying with ICE detainers.

A *detainer* is the primary tool used by ICE to gain custody of criminal aliens for deportation. It is a notice to another law enforcement agency that ICE intends to assume custody of an alien and includes information on the alien's previous criminal history, immigration violations, and potential threat to public safety or security.

In July 2019, federal prosecutors in San Francisco indicted twenty-two MS-13 gang members linked to a series of grisly killings in Los Angeles. Nineteen of those indicted were illegal immigrants from Central America. All but two were under the age of twenty-four.[217]

Sanctuary cities represented a serious threat to the well-being and safety of American citizens. A study performed by Statista suggests that sanctuary cities are a magnet for homelessness.[218]

I am certain that the outrageous expense of real estate factors into California's homelessness. However, with statistically full employment in our nation, the inability to obtain a job should not be an issue, unless you are an undocumented illegal alien.

There has been consistent reporting of crimes committed by illegal aliens, including rape and murder, which might have been prevented if the offenders had been deported.

The following chart confirms that, except for Las Vegas, cities deemed "sanctuary" have the highest degree of homelessness. Many of these states also have legalized recreational marijuana; some might attract migrants because of favorable weather.

---

[217] *USA Today—MS-13 Gang members indicted in Los Angeles*
[218] Statistica—*The US Cities with The Most Homeless People*

UNINTENDED CONSEQUENCE

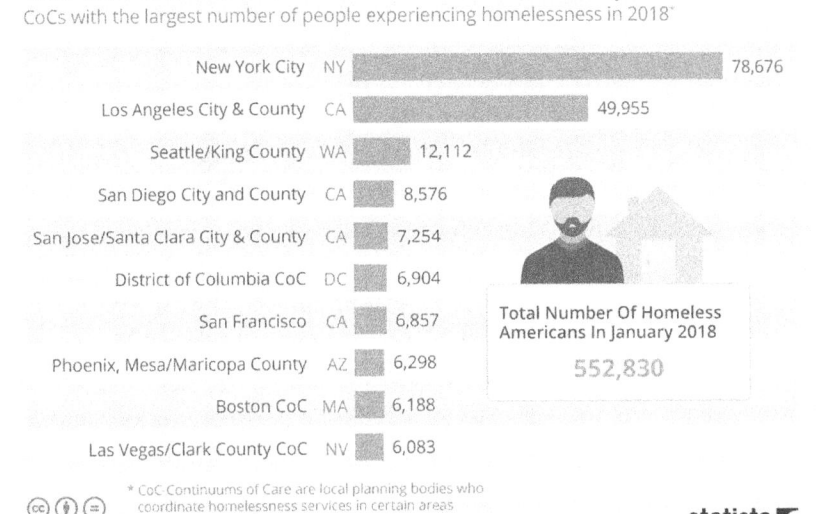

**The U.S. Cities With The Most Homeless People**
CoCs with the largest number of people experiencing homelessness in 2018*

|  |  |  |
|---|---|---|
| New York City | NY | 78,676 |
| Los Angeles City & County | CA | 49,955 |
| Seattle/King County | WA | 12,112 |
| San Diego City and County | CA | 8,576 |
| San Jose/Santa Clara City & County | CA | 7,254 |
| District of Columbia CoC | DC | 6,904 |
| San Francisco | CA | 6,857 |
| Phoenix, Mesa/Maricopa County | AZ | 6,298 |
| Boston CoC | MA | 6,188 |
| Las Vegas/Clark County CoC | NV | 6,083 |

Total Number Of Homeless Americans In January 2018
**552,830**

* CoC Continuums of Care are local planning bodies who coordinate homelessness services in certain areas
@StatistaCharts Source: U.S. Department of Housing and Urban Development

statista

The motive of these liberally governed cities and states is clear. The political advantages of an increased population are thus:

- It affects the number of members in the House of Representatives, which is determined by the ratio of the state's population to the combined population of all the states at the time of the last official census. Multiplying that ratio by 435, the total number of representatives currently fixed by the Reapportionment Act of 1929.
- It affects the number of Electoral College votes in each state, which are allocated among the states based on the most current census. Every state is allocated Electoral College votes equal to the number of senators and representatives in its US congressional delegation, two votes for its senators in the US Senate plus votes equal to the number of its members in the US House of Representatives.
- It affects the calculation for the distribution of billions of dollars in federal aid, which is generally based upon population count.

The upsurge of illegal immigration in recent years has inspired a spirited debate regarding construction of a wall on our southern border. While some find the notion morally repugnant, others find it as a national security imperative.

In the 1990s, the first sections of fencing were built in El Paso and near San Diego, on the US-Mexico border, supported by deployments of Border Patrol agents. In the weeks that followed, crossings in those sectors dropped to almost zero. However, fortified walls did not prevent crossings into the United States; instead, they shifted flows to other locations that were more remote or less fortified.

The Berlin Wall, the wall between North and South Korea, and the walls in Israel, while constructed for military reasons, worked. In 1995, Spain built a fence to keep immigrants out, and it has worked. Fewer migrants make it into Spain, but several continue to come in by swimming around the border.[219]

A "wall" is not the sole answer to controlling illegal immigration along our southern border, but it represents an essential component in an overall strategy.

Our society, our economy, and our country cannot sustain the continued illegal influx. Look at the existing homeless population in the United States. We are saturated. Why has it become so wrong for immigrants to be asked to assimilate into American society and American culture?

Were we not better off when we sought those things that united us, were common among and within us? Wouldn't life be more harmonious, public schools be more effective, and societal differences be minimized if we all strove to be Americans? Why should English be a "second language" in America? Immigrants come to America for refuge, opportunity, and freedom; why can't the price of those things be becoming American? Isn't it time to shed the "salad bowl" and return to the "melting pot"?

We need not ask immigrants to abandon their individual culture or traditions; we simply should expect them to embrace America's. Our country has a history of Irish Americans, Italian Americans,

---

[219] Migration Policy Institute—*Borders and Walls*—October 2016

# UNINTENDED CONSEQUENCE

Polish Americans, Chinese Americans, etc.—the common thread is Americans, through which we have become the most powerful, most successful, most envied people on this planet. Why change it? Immigrant parents should insist that their children embrace the American language and culture; it will only enhance their future success in achieving the American dream.

> A simple way to take measure of a country is to look at how many want in…and how many want out. (Tony Blair, British prime minister)

So what are the unintended consequences of our ineffective immigration policies?

Immigration legislation has been reactionary; yesterday's legislative crafters had been narrow-minded, today's legislators are at an impasse, and our southern border appears to be not much more than a line on a map. Our southern border is in chaos, our national and state welfare systems are overburdened and economically unsustainable, our public school system is overtaxed financially, and our educators are overtasked with students not fluent in English and have generally regressed in their ability to teach effectively. Our society is strained and conflicted by multicultural and intercultural pressures and priorities.

In 1886, when the Statue of Liberty was dedicated, the population of the United States, according to *the Census Bureau,* was just over 50 million, westward expansion continued, open land was in great abundance, and we needed immigrants to expand.[220] Today, the population is over 329 million,[221] and the boundaries of the United States are clearly defined. Additional population requires room to expand, but we have exhausted that.

Our societal requirements have changed over the decades. Economic conditions and innovation increase our need for immigrant talents. America now requires skilled labor. Our geographical

---

[220] Unites States Census—*Statistical Abstract of the United States: 1885*
[221] Unites States Census—*U.S. and World Population Clock*

expansion has ended: we can no longer absorb unlimited numbers. We are a nation of laws, and they must be obeyed.

The Democrat legislators today continue the strategy that the "ward bosses" employed during the immigration surge of 1880 through 1920, providing "free stuff" to encourage loyalty to their cause. However, today they are funded not by the party but by the American taxpayer.

President Obama issued a series of executive orders implementing an immigration policy opposed by Congress and 60 percent of the American people, who preferred to first secure the borders. Illegal immigration spiraled during the Obama administrations, estimated by the Department of Homeland Security at ten million. Liberals proclaim that restricting immigration is somehow un-American or immoral, and advocate for "open borders."

The lack of congressional foresight was again demonstrated in June 2019, when the Democrat-controlled House of Representative passed a $4.6 billion humanitarian aid package for our southern border. Typically treating the "snakebite" rather than "killing the snake."[222]

It is time for the Washington politicians to stop their antagonistic, party-prejudiced bickering and do the job they were sent there to do. It is time to refocus upon country rather than party. It makes perfect sense for Congress to enact a comprehensive immigration bill, secure our borders, absorb the law-abiding illegal immigrants that are already here, and rigorously control the flow of new immigrants into our country.

Our first order of business should be to secure our southern border. Stop the hemorrhaging of illegal immigrants into our country, so to speak. This will require us to deploy all the strategies and technologies available to us—drones, sensors, border agents, and barriers, including building a wall in those places deemed necessary by the Immigration and Customs Enforcement Agency.

A comprehensive bill needs to address all the unfinished issues, as well as the ill-designed facets of existing law. It must address the

---

[222] CNBC—*House passes Senate's $4.6 billion emergency border aid bill*—June 2019

theory of "birthright citizenship" to the children of illegals, creating anchor children; green card and visa control and enforcement; asylum reform; DACA status; resolution of the twelve to twenty-five million illegals already here; and the insanity of applying the "dry foot" policy to the middle of the Rio Grande River.

> A nation that cannot control its borders is not a nation. (Ronald Reagan, fortieth US president)

# Chapter VII

# Media

*The ethic of the journalist is to recognize one's prejudices, biases, and avoid getting them into print.*

*The profession of journalism ought to be about telling people what they need to know—not what they want to know.*

—Walter Cronkite,
American journalist

I cannot recall a point where the trust in the mainstream media has been as low as it is today. Our democracy requires a free and honest press, but sadly, it has become openly biased, often incorrect, sensational, and unprofessional. To witness media bias, one needs to look no further than the *New York Times* on August 6, 2019, following a speech by President Donald Trump. The first edition of the *Times* headline read, "Trump Urges Unity Vs. Racism." After criticism by prominent Democrats, the *Times* changed the second edition headline to read, "Assailing Hate but Not Guns."[223]

> The media's the most powerful entity on earth.
> They have the power to make the innocent guilty

---

[223] *The New York Times—A Times Headline About Trump Stoked Anger—*August 2019

> and to make the guilty innocent, and that's power. Because they control the minds of the masses. (Malcolm X, American human rights activist)

Historically, media was predominantly local. In the 1920s, radio expanded the news outreach to be national. By the 1950s, most people had a television, with news coming into our homes every evening. After the year 2000, we had seemingly limitless choices, with cable TV, the internet, and the blogosphere. Media now provides an endless source of bias confirmation. These platforms no longer "speak to the middle"; instead, they target their own splintered audiences, often absent responsibility and accountability. This continual stream of biased reporting serves as an accelerant to our national division. When the media "filters" news to support their bias, they sacrifice veracity. Misinformation has become pervasive, and lazy citizens accept what they are presented as truth, failing to question or validate content. One person's expressed position, right or wrong, seems to become another person's truth.

> I am dumbfounded that there hasn't been a crackdown with the libel and slander laws on some of those would-be writers and reporters on the internet. (Walter Cronkite)

The media, particularly newspapers, have contributed dramatically to the development of the United States.

From the revolution, following independence, through the crafting of the Declaration of Independence and the Constitution, newspapers played a pivotal role in informing citizens of current affairs and advancement. They enlightened our citizens as to the nature, reason, and purpose behind the US Constitution while it was being drafted. Eighty-five essays or editorials, written by Alexander Hamilton, James Madison, and John Jay, known as *The Federalist Papers*, helped explain the Constitution and promote its ratification. The essays were published serially in the *Independent Journal*, the

*New York Packet*, and *The Daily Advertiser* between October 1787 and April 1788.

The Constitution was ratified eleven years after the signing of the Declaration of Independence, and its first article guaranteed—along with freedom of speech, assembly, protest, and religion—freedom of the press.

Between the ratification of the Constitution and the Civil War, the press played an essential role, sometimes biased, but seldom dishonest, in reporting the events of the day.

In 1898, the USS *Maine* was destroyed in the harbor of Havana, Cuba. New York City newspaper publishers William Randolph Hearst and Joseph Pulitzer decided that the Spanish were to blame, and they publicized that theory *as fact* in their newspapers. They used sensationalistic accounts of atrocities committed by the Spanish in Cuba by using headlines in their newspapers, such as "Spanish Murderers" and "Remember the Maine." When Hearst artist Frederic Remington cabled from Cuba in 1897 that "there will be no war," William Randolph Hearst cabled back, "You furnish the pictures and I'll furnish the war."[224] The press exaggerated what was happening; their stories were based on factual accounts, but the articles that were published were embellished and written with incendiary language, causing heated responses among readers.

This new "yellow journalism," uncommon outside New York City, with dramatic headlines, was targeting the larger audiences in the cities where multiple newspapers were published. Its purpose was to sell more newspapers than their competitors.

Later, a bit ironically, it was Joseph Pulitzer that founded the Pulitzer Prize. "Pulitzer was the first to call for the training of journalists at the university level in a school of journalism. And certainly, the lasting influence of the Pulitzer Prizes on journalism, literature, music, and drama is to be attributed to his visionary acumen."[225]

By 1900 major newspapers, which had become objective powerhouses of advocacy, turned to their lesser angels and participated in

---

[224] *Time*—The Press: *I'll Furnish the War-TIME*—October 1947
[225] The Pulitzer Prizes—*History of the Pulitzer Prize*

muckraking and sensationalism, along with their serious newsgathering. According to Wikipedia, during the early twentieth century, the average educated American read several newspapers every day.

In June of 1919, a new type of tabloid newspaper hit New York City. *The Daily News* was different in format, size, and content. Characterized by large headlines on the first page, with large pictures, it targeted the masses.

Beginning in the 1920s, changes in technology morphed the nature of American journalism as radio and, later, television began to play increasingly important competitive roles.

In my youth and young adulthood, Walter Cronkite was the gold standard of news anchors. He reported the truth as he knew and verified it, without bias, plainspoken. We watched, listened, and were informed. He was "the most trusted man in America," signing off his broadcasts with a single sentence: "And that's the way it is."

Walter Cronkite did not spin the news, as many seem to do today: he simply and honestly reported it.

Television became an important player in media coverage in 1951 during the Army-McCarthy Hearings in Washington, DC. The hearings were convened by Senator Joseph McCarthy (R-WI) to investigate suspected members of the Communist Party being employed by the Department of the Army and the US State Department.

ABC and the Dumont television networks carried gavel-to-gavel live coverage. The television media coverage greatly contributed to McCarthy's decline in popularity and his eventual censure by the Senate. McCarthy was also undermined significantly by the incisive and skillful criticism of Edward R. Morrow, the premier journalist of that time, with his devastating television editorial about McCarthy, broadcast on his television show *See It Now*.[226]

The essence of journalism changed dramatically in 1972 with the Watergate investigation. The scandal relaunched, and made popular, an era of sensational journalism, both making Bob Woodward and Carl Bernstein stars and media darlings, and brought down the presidency of Richard Nixon.

---

[226] *Encyclopedia Britannica—McCarthyism*

"Watergate" opened the door for Daniel Ellsberg's leaking of the Pentagon Papers to *The Washington Post* in 1971, disclosing the secret Department of Defense report "History of the United States Political and Military Involvement in Vietnam, between 1945 and 1967."

William F. Buckley Jr., a conservative syndicated columnist and publisher, was so incensed by the *Times* leaking of these documents that he published *fabricated* "Pentagon Papers" in his *National Review* magazine. It was Buckley's way of cautioning Americans not to believe everything they read.

Some might question whether the 1971 Ellsberg leak helped end the Vietnam War, but clearly this was not the case. The decision to end the conflict was made in February 1968, when Walter Cronkite reported that, at best, the war would end in a "stalemate," and President Lyndon Johnson acknowledged that he "had lost Middle America." Had the Pentagon Papers been released earlier, could it have influenced the timing? One can only speculate. It seems that the only purpose Ellsberg served with the leak was to embarrass the Nixon administration, which was very much in vogue with the media at that time.

As in the 1920s, with the advent of radio, and later television, additional modes of "publishing" affected the mainstream media as the twenty-first century approached.

Cable news was initiated by CNN in 1980, followed by MSNBC in 1996. Each offered a liberal-leaning format. Later in 1996, FOX Cable News was launched to offer an *alternative* conservative venue, countering CNN and MSNBC.

At the beginning of the new millennium, the nature of journalism changed dramatically. CNN and MSNBC unabashedly pilloried President George W. Bush, then unreservedly supported President Barack Obama. Any pretext was gone. News anchors willingly endorsed this mandate. FOX, in turn, became a pro-Trump platform. Bill O'Reilly lost his number one rated cable show over a sex scandal; Sean Hannity became the extreme right-wing counter to MSNBC's uber-Left Joe Scarborough and Mika Brzezinski. Some "fair and balanced" reporting continued with FOX anchors Brett Baier, Britt

## UNINTENDED CONSEQUENCE

Hume, Chris Wallace, Harris Faulkner, Dana Perino, Shannon Bream, and Martha MacCallum. Other FOX anchors like Hannity became more extreme right wing, providing an "all-Trump" venue.

From this point forward, political reporters, having chosen sensationalism over hard-nosed investigative reporting, would no longer be trusted as responsible, unbiased reporters of American life. Others would violate their national trust in pursuit of their own "fifteen minutes of fame," their own journalism "me too" movement.

- Brian Williams, NBC news anchor, whose credibility plummeted after acknowledging that he exaggerated his role in a helicopter episode in Iraq, was suspended and taken off the air.[227]
- Dan Rather ended his nearly twenty-four-year reign as CBS news anchor after his rushed and admittedly flawed story on President George W. Bush's National Guard service.[228]

By the turn of the twenty-first century, newspaper formats were challenged, and often being replaced, by instant, 24-7 social media, Facebook, Twitter, and Instagram, as well as cable TV and WikiLeaks, each competing for clicks and eyeballs. The anonymity of social media enabled someone to be cruel, inflammatory, libelous, and criminal without accountability or personal consequence.

> Social media websites are no longer performing an envisaged function of creating a positive communication link among friends, family and professionals. It is a veritable battleground, where insults fly from the human quiver, damaging lives, destroying self-esteem and a person's sense of self-worth. (Anthony Carmona, president of Trinidad)

---

[227] *New York Times: Brian Williams Suspended from NBC*—February 2015
[228] *The Washington Post: Dan Rather Steps Down at CBS*—November 2004

In January 2010, Army specialist Bradley Manning (later to become known as Chelsey Manning) downloaded four hundred thousand documents known as the Iraq War Logs and ninety-one thousand documents known as the Afghan War Logs from classified US government records. He saved the material on a compact disc.[229] (44) Manning contacted *The Washington Post* and *The New York Times* to ask if they were interested in the material; the *Post* expressed no interest, and the *Times* did not return his call.[230] Kudos to *The Washington Post* and *The New York Times* for not accepting this leak of classified information. Manning instead provided the stolen classified information to Julian Assange at WikiLeaks in February 2010. Absent sensibility and concern regarding classified information potentially harmful to the United States, WikiLeaks published the secret information pertaining to US intelligence and spy craft.[231] Manning had his fifteen minutes of fame and went to prison.

In 2012, Edward Snowden, working as an analyst for the National Security Agency in Hawaii, contacted a journalist working at the British daily newspaper *The Guardian* and disclosed that he had sensitive documents that he would like to share. Snowden then contacted *The Washington Post* in May 2013. The *Post* declined to guarantee publication within seventy-two hours of all the stolen material that Snowden had leaked, exposing the US government's electronic data mining program. Snowden wrote, "I understand that I will be made to suffer for my actions, and that the return of this information to the public marks my end." After disclosing the copied documents, Snowden promised that nothing would stop subsequent disclosures. He said, "All I can say right now is the US government is not going to be able to cover this up by jailing or murdering me. Truth is coming, and it cannot be stopped."[232] Snowden, too, had his fifteen minutes of fame and sought asylum in Russia.

---

[229] *The Guardian: Bradley Manning Trial*
[230] *The Guardian: Bradley Manning Trial*
[231] *The Guardian: Bradley Manning Trial*
[232] *Business Insider: This is Everything Eric Snowden Revealed*

# UNINTENDED CONSEQUENCE

In the Manning and Snowden examples, *The Wall Street Journal* and *The New York Times* exercised prudent discretion and restraint, presumably in consideration of US national security.

During 2017, the government leaks to the media reached an apocalyptic level. Seemingly, every day there were leaks relating to the Trump administration. The tenets of good journalism seem violated when news articles rely solely upon "anonymous sources." Whether motivated by politics or an irrational hatred of President Donald Trump, the leakers, as well as the irresponsible press, were subverting national security.

On December 15, 2016, FBI agent Peter Strzok texted bureau colleague Lisa Page, "Think our sisters have begun leaking like mad. Scorned and worried and political, they're kicking into overdrive." Later, on June 6, 2017, Strzok texted, "Think there will be a crescendo of leaks/articles."[233] For those that might be dubious regarding the existence of a "deep state," I believe that this revelation certainly supports the idea.

During that time, British prime minister Theresa May indicated that the United Kingdom would no longer share intelligence information with the United States until the US government could ensure its security. The prime minister's concern was in response to anonymous source information being leaked and published in *The New York Times*, jeopardizing the British investigation of terrorist attacks in Manchester.

I believe these leakers, in addition to Manning and Snowden, to be cowards, not patriots. Surely, patriots would be proud to be revealed, not shroud their identity behind anonymity.

Should media be constrained? We have experienced a recent period of journalistic abuse of their privilege and protection. Hopefully, it can be stemmed. Freedom of speech does not allow shouting "Fire!" in a crowded theater, nor should it allow the publication of unsourced or unverified classified information. Which is the "greater good," freedom of an irresponsible press or national

---

[233] *Business Insider: This is Everything Eric Snowden Revealed*

security? Should there be some measure of accountability, integrity, and the establishment of acceptable, "best practice" standards?

Lord Acton, the British politician and historian of the late nineteenth century, warned, "All power tends to corrupt and absolute power corrupts absolutely."[234]

The quality and accuracy of media content has continued to decline through this day. With the resurgence of yellow journalism and muckraking, newspaper circulation per capita declined from 35 percent in the mid-1940s to under 15 percent today. The number of newspaper journalists has decreased from forty-three thousand in 1978 to thirty-three thousand in 2015. Other news media have also suffered. Since 1980, the television networks have lost half their audience for evening newscasts; the audience for radio news has shrunk by 40 percent.[235] Mainstream media seems to have violated its public trust and should be cautious when spewing its bias, perhaps offending half of the population. Social media is growing exponentially, while print and TV audiences are declining.

Today, a great majority of our electorate does not pay attention, is uninformed, and relies upon the media to form opinions. The danger in this is that the media have become so openly biased, either conservative or liberal, and offers only predominantly prejudiced opinions.

Media has become disingenuous. It is beyond slanted; it is venomous. Cable news programs have become echo chambers for those, either liberal or conservative, that share their view.

During 2017, in research for a letter to the editor I was drafting, I examined the circulation departments of two major US newspapers to determine their audience. I also researched the internet to determine the size of President Donald Trump's Twitter audience. The combined circulation of *The New York Times* and *Wall Street Journal*, both print and electronic, was 4 million, whereas President Trump had 6.3 million Twitter followers. I suspect that, in 2019, both the

---

[234] McGraw-Hill—*Dictionary of American Idioms and Phrasal Verbs*—2002
[235] Wikipedia—Network and media audience

circulation numbers of the *Times* and *Journal* have dwindled, and Trump's Twitter audience has grown.

It is believed that Representative Charles Brownson (R-IN) coined the phrase "One ought not pick a fight with someone that buys ink by the barrel."[236] Today, the "ink" is electronic media, *Twitter* and the internet.

I always welcome and encourage informed debate on political and social topics; however, I am often confronted with those who have little or no understanding of the issues and simply parrot the views of media "talking heads" with belligerent certitude.

> Rarely do we find men who willingly engage in hard, solid thinking. There is an almost universal quest for easy answers and half-baked solutions. Nothing pains some people more than having to think. (Martin Luther King Jr.)

A blatant example of media bias was demonstrated in a May 2018 *USA Today* column authored by Fredreka Schouten, with the headline "Lobbyists with Trump, Pence Ties Rake in Millions." In the article, Schouten contended that "lobbying firms managed by former campaign aides, fundraisers and others with ties to President Donald Trump and Vice President Mike Pence have collected at least $28 million in federal lobbying fees since Trump assumed the Presidency." Her report might have appeared less biased had she included any of the blatant, obscene, and disturbing revelations in Peter Schweizer's book *Secret Empires*. Schweizer revealed the exploitation of family privilege by then vice president Joe Biden's son Hunter and then secretary of state John Kerry's stepson Christopher Heinz. Schweizer disclosed that while Biden and Kerry were negotiating with China and the Ukraine, their children were amassing hundreds of millions in private equity ventures with both countries.

The "smash and grab" tactics, exposed by Schweizer, based upon apparent insider regulation information throughout the

---

[236] QuoteInvestigator.com

Obama administration, made billions for Obama cronies; damaged American coal, energy, student loan, and financial service companies; and sacrificed national security with the A123 battery sale to China.

A123 Systems was an American-owned battery manufacturer that had received $375 million in grants from the Bush and Obama administrations. The cash-strapped battery maker, with contracts to provide lithium batteries to the US military, reached an agreement with the auto-parts division of Wanxiang that gave the Chinese company a controlling interest.

China's purchase of a United States high-technology battery maker, approved by the Obama administration, boosted Beijing's military forces and satellites and threatened the security of the US electrical power and communications grids, according to National Security officials.[237]

And let us not forget the Uranium One sale to Russia.

In 2010, the Obama administration approved a business deal that gave Russia's Atomic Energy Agency control of a company with uranium mining interests in the United States, effectively granting Russia control over 20 percent of American uranium production. At the time of approval, the FBI was investigating Russia's corrupt business practices in the nuclear industry; it was unclear whether members of the committee that signed off on the deal, including Secretary of State Hillary Clinton, were aware of the inquiry, which presumably would have factored into their decision.[238]

In fairness, his book also revealed the profiteering made by the family of the wife of Senator McConnell (R-KY).

Wouldn't it be refreshing if the media would at least attempt a pretext of being unbiased?

Beginning in the fall of 2016, the media initiated its full-court press regarding both Russian involvement in the presidential election and the possibility that the Trump campaign collaborated with them. They repeatedly told us that we were only seeing "the tip of the ice-

---

[237] *Boston Globe—Chinese Owned Firm Completes A123 Purchase*—January 2013
[238] *Washington Post—Making Sense of Russia, Uranium One and Hillary Clinton*—October 2017

berg," only to discover that there was no *iceberg*. The partisan media showed no interest in reports that the Russians had been attempting to interfere during 2014 and 2016, during the Obama years; they expressed little interest in the suspicious activities of the Hillary Clinton campaign.

Gross media bias was further exhibited by the headlines following the release of a summary of the Mueller Report regarding potential collusion between our president, his campaign, and Russia. After two years of investigation, with highly motivated, predominantly anti-Trump biased investigators, Mueller found no criminal conspiracy.

Attorney General William Barr and Assistant Attorney General Rod Rosenstein reviewed the Mueller Report and announced in a press conference that Mueller had found that Russian interference was "deeper and broader than we had known." It concluded that the "Russian operation did not have any cooperation of the President, his campaign or, for that fact, any American citizen."

According to Barr and Rosenstein, the Mueller Report concluded that "the evidence did not establish obstruction of justice"; while there was no proof of "obstruction," the president could not be "exonerated."[239]

Shouldn't all Americans celebrate that there was no collusion, that our president is not a traitor? Shouldn't this be considered a national victory? On the day following the Mueller Report release, the news media did not rejoice in the overarching conclusion. Instead, the headlines now refocused on obstruction rather than collusion, announcing thus:

- *The New York Times*: "Mueller report lays out Russian contacts and Trump's frantic efforts to foil inquiry."
- *The Baltimore Sun*: "Trump attempted to disrupt probe."
- *The Boston Globe*: "No charge, no exoneration."
- *Chicago Sun Times*: "This is the end, Trump feared."

---

[239] The Mueller Report: *Report on the Investigation into Russian Interference in the 2016 Election*

- *The Washington Post*: "Mueller details Russian interference, Trump's attempt to disrupt probe."
- *Miami Herald*: "Mueller details efforts to thwart inquiry."
- *The Record*: "Trump attempted to thwart probe."
- *Los Angeles Times*: "Mueller defers to Congress' judgement."

And to think *The New York Times* and *Washington Pos*, each won a Pulitzer Prize for their "collusion" reporting. It is such a travesty.

In my view, these are no longer serious people; they have compromised their credibility. The mainstream media seems to operate in a moral vacuum.

So what are the unintended consequences?

We have seen for the most part that media is biased, either right or left. Media is driven by greed, maximizing "clicks and eyeballs" and their own political philosophy rather than a passion or commitment to honestly inform the public. Many seem to disregard a potential risk to national security in their quest for more readers, viewers, and retweets. What does this all mean?

Could we be at a place where it has become the "American people versus the media"? Are we at the point where news reflects partisans pushing an agenda rather than journalists reporting the news?

> If people in the media cannot decide whether they are in the business of reporting news or manufacturing propaganda, it is all the more important that the public understand that difference, and choose their news sources accordingly. (Thomas Sowell, senior fellow, Hoover Institution, Stanford University)

Social media is like a relentless sledgehammer constantly pounding our minds with the opinions of others, with "news" that may not be, and with such rapidity that we may be unable to question. Opinions are expressed with such certitude that they are often accepted as fact.

I think younger people are either too busy pursuing life, job, school, family, etc. that they seem indifferent to anything that doesn't have an impact on their personal orbit. Many older folks, however, seem uninformed because they choose to be; they are either lazy, disinterested, entrenched in their own tribal perspective, or comfortable in accepting others' views as their own. Few of us seem to have the time to understand the issues, to responsibly question the media. Each of us should challenge what is presented with an open mind and consider both sides of an argument and have the intellectual strength to formulate our own views, opinions, beliefs, and decisions.

It has been said that *military intelligence* is an oxymoron; perhaps *responsible journalism* is rapidly becoming one as well.

In 1982 and 1983, I was an adjunct professor at New York University School of Continuing Education, teaching a graduate course in magazine publishing management.

I taught that advertising rates were a function of circulation numbers, readership—in today's terms, *clicks, eyeballs, views, audience*. One measure of the quality of a publication is its "ad-edit ratio," that is, the percentage of editorial or written content versus advertising content. Which is more predominant, journalism or greed?

Today, the case could be made that the media business is driven by its audience, feeding "the beast" what they prefer to hear as opposed to providing responsible reporting. The media seems to understand and is willing to cater to its target market in its quest for higher circulation, therefore higher advertising revenue.

When Jeff Bezos purchased the venerable *Washington Post* in a dying newspaper industry, was it for profit or political presence?

Alas, we live in an increasingly imperfect world, where our standards, mores, morals, and customs continue to decline.

In 1897, Adolph Ochs, the owner of *The New York Times*, created its famous slogan, "All the News That's Fit to Print," which continues to appear on its masthead today. He wrote that slogan as a declaration of the newspaper's intention to report news impartially.[240]

---

[240] *Read Write Think*

In August 2019, Dean Baquet, executive editor of *The New York Times*, held an editorial department staff meeting, wherein he disclosed the new editorial direction of the newspaper. A *Times* staff member surreptitiously recorded the conversation, which was subsequently reported in *The Washington Examiner*. Baquet advised his staff, "The day Bob Mueller walked off that witness stand, two things happened, our readers who want Donald Trump to go away suddenly thought, 'Holy shit, Bob Mueller is not going to do it,' and Donald Trump got a little emboldened politically.

"I think…for obvious reasons…the story changed. A lot of the stuff we're talking about started to emerge like six or seven weeks ago. We're a little tiny bit flat-footed. I mean, that's what happens when a story looks a certain way for two years…the story changed but the fact is, the conspiracy-coordination allegation the *Times* had devoted itself to pursuing turned out to be false.

"Beyond that, Democrats on Capitol Hill struggled to press an obstruction case against the President. The Trump-Russia hole came up dry. I think that we've got to change.

"The *Times* must write more deeply about the country, race, and other divisions. Coverage for the next two years is…How do we write about race in a thoughtful way, something we haven't done in a large way in a long time? That, to me, is the vision for coverage."[241]

And for this, the *Times* received two Pulitzer prizes.

In September 2019, *The New York Times* published an article on the Opinion page headlined "Brett Kavanaugh Fit in with the Privileged Kids. She Did Not." The story accused Kavanaugh of additional sexual harassment charges while a student at Yale University.

It turned out that the *Times* News section had previously rejected the article because it could not be corroborated.

When printed on the Opinion page, the article failed to disclose that the injured party had no recollection of the incident and had declined to be interviewed for the piece. The *Times* editor reportedly *deleted* these salient details.

---

[241] *The Washington Examiner—New York Times chief outlines coverage shift—*August 2020

## UNINTENDED CONSEQUENCE

The paper's agenda was apparent. Once again, a *Times* article had to be retracted. The *Times* has become so unambiguously biased and it so liberally warps the news that they are committing journalism malpractice.

Perhaps they should revise the "All the News That's Fit to Print" slogan to "All the News That Supports Our Opinion," and their *New York Times* masthead to *Not Yet Truthful*.

When I was a young boy in New Jersey, I delivered newspapers for *The Bergen Evening Record*, with the cost of thirty-three cents a week. Having grown up with the paper, now *The Record*, managed by the Borg family, I appreciated its balanced, informative editorial style.

In 2016, the *Record* was purchased by the Gannett Company, and its editorial style became blatantly biased toward liberal opinion.

In his book *1984*, George Orwell warned us about the power of the media and the danger of twisting truth to serve political ends.

The Gannett Company now owns over 100 daily newspapers and nearly 1,000 weekly newspapers, with operations in forty-three US states and six countries, all delivering similar content.[242] Recently, the Gannett Company announced their merger with Gatehouse Media, publisher of 154 daily newspapers.[243],[244] This merger will further consolidate daily newspaper publishing. At what point does this extensive control over news publication become a perilous detriment to the notion of a "free press"?

> We've always known you can gain circulation or viewers by cheapening the product, and now you're finding the bad driving out the good. (Walter Cronkite)

Most recently, The McClatchy Company, publisher of the *Miami Herald, Fort-Worth Star Telegram,* and *The Sacramento Bee*

---

[242] Gannett Company
[243] *The Washington Post-Gannett Merger: GateHouse newspaper deal announced—August 2019*
[244] GateHouseMedia.com

in California, filed for bankruptcy. This is yet another sign of the broader decline of newspapers across the country. According to a 2019 Associated Press analysis, "More than 1,400 cities and towns in the U.S. lost a newspaper over the past sixteen years." McClatchy's financial troubles reflect the struggles of most print media, and does not bode well regarding the future of printed newspapers in the United States, where publishers are attempting the transition to a digital format.

I question whether facts and honesty will ever make a comeback in American journalism.

# Chapter VIII

# National Moral Compass

*A rusty nail placed near a faithful compass, will sway it from the truth, and wreck the argosy.*
—Walter Scott,
Scottish historical novelist

Who has the moral authority to set the ethical compass of our nation? Is it politicians, clergy, educators, or family? Or is it some combination of all these?

> When we speak the truth, we are correct. When we do not speak the truth because it would be politically unacceptable to admit to believing it, we are politically correct.[245]

To speak the truth, the unvarnished truth, the simple, unassailable truth, is the essence of principle.

I grew up in a time of families, neighborhoods, and communities, when authority was respected, and achievement rewarded. It was the last innocent time, a period before drugs, promiscuity, AIDS, blatant corruption, and violence. We have moved from a time when

---

[245] National Admissions Test for Law

we experienced the mystery of anatomy to one where there is no mystery at all.

We have seen marvelous accomplishments—civil rights advancements, man walking on the moon, *Explorer* surveying Mars, and the development of a space station.

We have experienced the explosion of computer technology, development of the internet, cell phones, iPods, Blackberries, texting, Twitter, and Facebook. We have seen advancements in technology that exceeded our ability to absorb and apply. We have seen an eruption of both wealth and poverty. We have seen women become CEOs, senators, congresswomen, secretaries of state, and presidential candidates. We have seen blacks achieve similar goals and, more, even become president of the United States. We have seen the improvement to, and the evolution of, many areas of our societal evils. There remains much more progress to be made, much more to be done. In my time, we have witnessed dreadful things as well—assassinations of John Kennedy, Bobby Kennedy, and Martin Luther King; race riots of the sixties; assassination attempts on Presidents Ford and Reagan; the Vietnam War and Middle East conflicts; the sexual revolution; the "911" attack; and the Columbine massacre. We have seen advancements in technology tainted, misused, and become weapons of hate. We have seen corruption of principle, the emergence of obscene greed, the lowering of the bar on acceptable behavior, and the compromising of the moral fabric of the nation. We left a time when pastors, teachers, doctors, and policemen were respected and deserved respect. We seem to have lost these values.

How did we become so angry and partisan? How did we become so fractured as a nation? Where did this toxic mix of conflict emanate from? In the past, we, as a people, concentrated on what united us, our common interests and common values, on our country and being American; we embraced our "sameness."

> Since this country was founded, each generation of Americans has been summoned to give testimony to its national loyalty. (President John F. Kennedy's inaugural address, January 1961)

We had survived the Great Depression and won World Wars as Americans, as a nation.

In Plato's *The Republic*, Socrates contends that the "greatest social good is the cohesion and unity that results from the common feelings of pleasure and pain which you get when all members of society are glad or sorry for the same successes and failures."

The moral fabric of the United States was torn, and civility began its aggressive descent at the 1968 Chicago Democratic Convention. At the height of the Vietnam War, and after a year of assassinations, riots, and a breakdown in law and order, it seemed as if the country were coming apart. Ten thousand demonstrators gathered in Chicago for the convention, where they were met by twenty-three thousand police and National Guardsmen. The rioting demonstrated a loss of faith in politicians, in the political system, in the country, and in its institutions. The violence that erupted at the convention throughout that week, captured live on television, confirmed both the Democrats' pessimism and the country's judgment of a political party torn by dissension and disunity.[246]

America is an idea. A spirit, not to be sacrificed or fettered for any political party or agenda. We have created a society divided between the elites and the realists. The elites believe they deserve, that they are owed, that they are entitled. The realists recognize what they want, what they desire, and they are committed to working to achieve them. The elites believe that they know what is best and that the realists are merely in their way.

Today, we obscss upon what divides us—political party, ethnicity, and religion. Our culture has become divided, supported by hundreds of cable stations offering fodder to whatever splinter group we identify with. We have become alone, together.

> It was the best of times, it was the worst of times, it was the age of wisdom, it was the age of foolishness, it was the epoch of belief, it was the epoch of incredulity, it was the season of Light, it was

---

[246] *The Smithsonian Magazine: The 1968 Democratic Convention*—August 2008

the season of Darkness, it was the spring of hope, it was the winter of despair, we had everything before us, we had nothing before us, we were all going direct to Heaven, we were all going direct the other way. (Charles Dickens, *A Tale of Two Cities*)

In our recent decades of sporadic legislation, increasing animus between political parties, of opportunities taken and opportunities missed, of our proclivity to seek solutions to problems *outside* our country as opposed to *within*, an argument could be made that Dickens was describing America in 2019.

The moral compass of America may be shifting. Some say that our national direction is morally reprehensible, that it is past time for a "mind shift."

Senator Ben Sasse (R-NB), in his book *Them*, lamented the loss of communities:

> Urban studies theorist Richard Florida divides Americans into the mobile, the rooted, and the stuck. Community is collapsing in America because the rooted are vanishing; the stuck have too many crises in their lives to think about much else; and the mobile are too schizophrenic to busy themselves with the care and feeding of their flesh-and-blood communities.[247]

What has happened to the fabric of our society? Why did our individual identity as Democrats, Republicans, liberals, conservatives, or independents become greater than our common identity as Americans?

In *Them*, Sasse suggests that "one reason for the ever growing chasm is that almost all of us are convinced that our position is 100 percent right, and that the other side is 100 percent wrong—no mat-

---

[247] *Them*—Senator Ben Sasse—Macmillan 2018

ter how silly it seems, when you think about it, to assume there are only two sides to big debates. We like being told that there are black hats and white hats. It's easier that way."

Further, he added, "A pair of researchers at Ohio State University gave 156 people the chance to read articles that affirmed or contradicted their political ideas. The participants spent far more time reading articles that confirmed what they already thought than articles that taught them anything new…people work hard to confirm their biases, not to challenge them."[248]

Why does our society so fear rational discussion and debate? Why do liberal mobs suppress free speech if it opposes their view? Why do liberal thugs vandalize property, pepper spray and attack groups with views that differ from theirs? Where are the moderate Democrat voices? Why are they as silent as the moderate Muslims? Have they lost their conviction, or has radical liberalism and socialism steamrollered them? What has happened to the Democratic Party?

Why the mind shift? Has it been usurped by Saul Alinsky?

We are now at a place where all the 2020 Democratic presidential contenders are tripping over one another to see who can promise the most "free stuff," who can move furthest left, who can endorse the most "big government," who can be, in the liberal jargon, the most "woke."

This is a dramatic departure from the philosophy of Democrat president William Clinton, who proclaimed, in 1996, "These are the seven challenges I set forth Tuesday night—to strengthen our families, to renew our schools and expand educational opportunity, to help every American who's willing to work for it achieve economic security, to take our streets back from crime, to protect our environment, to reinvent our government so that it serves better and costs less, and to keep America the leading force for peace and freedom throughout the world. We will meet these challenges, not through big government. The era of big government is over."[249]

---

[248] *Them*—Senator Ben Sasse—Macmillan 2018
[249] President William Clinton—Radio interview—January 27, 1996

Is it unreasonable to

- secure our borders and attempt to curtail illegal immigration and the flow of illicit drugs;
- notify Immigration Customs Enforcement if an illegal is apprehended in the commission of a crime;
- attempt to replace a health-care system that everyone recognizes is about to implode;
- recognize that $22 trillion in debt is a bad thing;
- agree that reducing bloated government could help reduce annual deficits;
- accept job growth and infrastructure repair is a "good thing"; and
- recognize that Islamic terror is a greater threat to the LGBT community than limited "bathroom choice"?

These seem to be elements of a political agenda that should unite us. Must we sacrifice the good in pursuit of the perfect? Is it impossible for us to replace polarization with common sense, to place country ahead of party?

Moderate Americans spoke loudly in November of 2016—cannot we heed their demand for more responsible government? Is anyone in Washington, DC, listening?

Some strategies to promote diversity are problematic and damaging. Over time, liberal policies are deconstructing America. They insist upon diversity, unless your views are diverse from theirs; preach diversity but practice division, exclusion, and identity politics. Placing too much emphasis on individual rights sacrifices those similar rights of the majority, resulting in unequal burden and disparity.

My point is that changing our laws or establishing new laws to support a splinter of our society should not be at the expense of the majority. (I cited transsexual access to bathrooms in public schools as a dramatic example.) It goes to the philosophical question of the "greater good."

We are becoming embroiled in a social civil war.

It is my sense that, in pursuit of diversity, we have weakened our national moral fiber. Organic diversity can be a strength, whereas forced diversity compelled through failed policies results in weakness.

*E Pluribus Unum* is defined as "out of many, one." Liberal policies seem to prefer from the one many. We seem to have traded conscience for convenience.

Our national history of, and experience with, the legislative process has been fraught with flaws, inconsistencies, and demonstrated limited vision. There are a lot of dark shadows lurking behind many legislative policies.

## Abortion

The 1973 *Roe v. Wade* Supreme Court ruling legalized abortion, diminished individual responsibility, and led to the sacrifice of over sixty million fetuses since the decision was handed down.[250]

Genocide is "the deliberate and systematic destruction of a racial, political, or cultural group." Are fetuses a "cultural group"? How could such a seemingly enlightened society allow this to happen?

Liberals contend to be committed to both women's health and to contraceptives and abortion. However, abortion is not meant to restore healthy functions of a diseased organ; it is intended to prevent the natural function of a healthy one.

We have easily accessible contraception—the pill, condoms, IUDs, even the morning-after pill—so then why are the millions of abortions necessary? Laziness? Carelessness? Has abortion casually become just another form of contraceptive? Has abortion allowed our society to devolve from one of responsibility to one of mindless, guiltless convenience? Where has parental guidance and the character development of children gone?

Abortions in the United States peaked in 1990 at 1,608,000 and has been steadily declining since then to 906,000 in 2015.[251]

---

[250] US Department of Justice—Roe v Wade—1973
[251] Abort73.com—*Abortion and Race*

The Guttmacher Institute is a leading research and policy organization committed to advancing sexual and reproductive health and rights in the United States and globally. According to Guttmacher, the statistical breakdown of abortions performed upon women aged fifteen to forty-four in 2008 was categorized: 40 percent black, 30 percent Hispanic, 27 percent "others, non-Hispanic," and 3 percent white.[252]

The US Census reported in 2015 that the US government assistance program participation by race breaks down as follows: 41 percent black, 36 percent Hispanics, 17 percent Asians or Pacific Islanders, and 13 percent non-Hispanic white.[253]

The government assistance statistics follow the Guttmacher abortion statistics very closely. Some, at the risk of being considered racist, might view these statistics in a utilitarian way as demonstrating that abortion is an effective method of reducing welfare costs. We might ask: Is this not a form of eugenics?

After almost fifty years of abortion on demand, does a fetus have any rights? Isn't an unborn child worthy of protection? Where are the advocates for the unborn children? How is it that we mourn a miscarriage but acclaim abortion? Why would abortion remain an important plank in the Democrat platform? Have we become so callous that we now distinguish between "wanted" babies and "unwanted" babies? We have recently descended to a point where we are debating whether aborting a *newly born* baby should be allowed. Really? Have we completely lost our minds? I ask my liberal friends, Isn't the protection of an unborn child a basic human rights issue?

Liberals lament separating children from mothers at the southern border yet advocate for abortion. Kellyanne Conway, senior adviser to President Trump, succinctly summarized, "Children should not be separated from their mothers, in the womb or outside of it."

While I recognize the need for the abortion procedure in certain circumstances, I view it as a decision to be made between the parents,

---

[252] Guttmacher Institute—*Reported Annual Abortions—1973 to 2015*
[253] US Census Bureau—*21.3 Percent of US Population participates in US... Assistance...*—May 2015

their God, and their doctor. It is a place for prayer and responsible contemplation, not a place for political policy. Government should not be involved.

Our governing laws seem to conflict with one another. Abortion, killing a fetus, is permitted by law and is not homicide, yet if a drunk driver kills a pregnant woman in a traffic accident, the driver would be charged with a *double homicide*. Euthanasia, where a responsible adult is making a choice to terminate life when experiencing extreme pain or hopelessness, is prohibited, yet ending the life of an unborn baby, who has no choice, is permitted. True conundrums. Do you see the disconnect?

I might cynically suggest that the decision of life and death has become a financial one; both *abortions* and *continuing life efforts* generate medical income.

As a point of historical significance, Norma McCorvey is "Jane Roe," the woman who initially brought the case to the Supreme Court, who later recanted her position and became a pro-life activist.[254] Abby Johnson was a director in the Texas Planned Parenthood organization; after seven years, her views were inalterably changed. Her book *un-Planned* tells of that transformation, the whys and whens, making compassionate reading. I recommend it. She also provides a graphic description of the actual abortion process, intellectually transforming the word *abortion* from a philosophical concept to a cruel reality.

In 2018 and 2019, several states have passed laws restricting the "right" to abortion, some precluding the procedure after six weeks, others precluding it after a heartbeat is detected. Clearly, some of these laws are too restrictive; denying an abortion in the instance of rape or when the mother's life might be at risk would be unreasonable. While these laws are being challenged in court, they appear to be part of a larger effort to eventually challenge *Roe v. Wade* at the Supreme Court.

I wonder, just wonder, if the justices deciding *Roe v. Wade* had foreseen the sheer numeric magnitude of abortions it allowed to be

---

[254] *Dallas News—Norma McCorvey (Jane Roe) Obituary*—February 2017

performed, the decades of ardent division it would create in our society, and the "industry" that it would allow to be created by Planned Parenthood, would their decision have been the same?

We can view abortion morally, politically, or practically, but from any perspective, it has an unintended consequence.

In 1979, China adopted a one-child policy to control its population growth. It limited the number of children a family could have and continue to receive financial support from its communist government. While it was not prohibited, families were economically *discouraged* from having additional children. Additional children would cause a *reduction* in the amount of their government dole. Consequently, determined to continue the family name and line, male fetuses were valued more highly than female fetuses. Female fetuses were routinely aborted, and China became the international leader in abortion rate.[255] The unintended consequence of this policy, thirty years later, was that China has a shortage of women to marry the abundance of men in their population.

India adopted a similar policy, with the same consequence. By 2018, men outnumbered women in China and India by seventy million.[256]

One consequence of *Roe v. Wade* in the United States after almost sixty years of permitted abortions, beyond the extermination of tens of millions of fetuses, is that it has contributed to the 2019 lowest US birthrate in thirty-two years.[257]

The continuing unintended legacy of *Roe v. Wade* is the loss of an unknown number of scientists, inventors, philosophers, doctors, educators, and other leaders of thought and deed that might have been aborted. Perhaps we aborted the fetus that would have given us a cure for cancer, and in the name of what?

Women should be entitled to control their bodies; however, once a woman is impregnated by *choice or carelessness*, the fetus

---

[255] *The Guardian—13 million abortions carried out every year in China—*2009
[256] *Encyclopedia Britannica—*(China's) *One Child Policy*
[257] *Boston Globe—US birthrate fall to lowest in 32 years—*May 2019

should have rights as well. Each of us is a *former* fetus! Shouldn't we let reason triumph?

I anticipate that the spirit of *Roe v. Wade* will prevail; it will not be repealed, it will be revised with safer "curbs," it will place restrictions on late term, and it will protect the rights of the unborn baby.

## Aspiration versus Accomplishment

> *If a man does not keep pace with his companions, perhaps it is because he hears a different drummer. Let him step to the music which he hears, however measured or far away.*
> 
> —Henry David Thoreau

I feel compelled to offer a caveat prefacing this subchapter; my purpose is not to be a Trump defender. I am more a supporter of pragmatism than a supporter of President Trump.

That said, ahhh, nostalgia—our mind filters less-pleasant memories and allows the enjoyable ones to dominate. Those of us old enough will remember Woodstock for the epic party and the music; we choose to ignore the traffic jams, mud, drugs, lack of inhibition, unsanitary conditions, and illness. We remember the music. Ahhh, nostalgia!

So it is, often, with politics.

Prior to his death, while President Kennedy's public approval rating remained above 50 percent, it had dropped from over 80 percent, and his reelection was not guaranteed.[258]

There was no enchanted notion of Camelot before his assassination, yet today, when we think of JFK, we imagine Camelot. It was Jacqueline Kennedy who initiated the concept. It has been reported that "just days after JFK's assassination, Jackie Kennedy crafted a glit-

---

[258] Research—History in Pieces: JFK's Presidential Approval Ratings

tering fairytale about his presidency that would captivate the nation for decades to come."[259] Ahhh, nostalgia—perhaps it continues today.

I have queried in other chapters, How should a person be properly measured, by his words or his deeds?

> We must never forget that the highest appreciation is not to utter words, but to live by them. (President John F. Kennedy)

> Deeds, not words, shall speak me. (John Fletcher, writer and playwright)

My sense is that your answer to the question will be biased. Either words or deeds would be given predominance, depending on which satisfies your personal prejudice.

That notion seems to be bolstered by Senator Ben Sasse (D-NE) in his book *Them*, where he noted, "A pair of researchers at Ohio State University gave 156 people the chance to read articles that affirmed or contradicted their political ideas. The participants spent far more time reading articles that confirmed what they already thought than articles that taught them anything new…people work hard to confirm their biases, not to challenge them."[260]

Let's look at President Obama, a contrast between aspiration and accomplishment. From his regal, inspirational beginning, the eloquent words in his nomination acceptance speech, where he "promised fundamentally transforming the United States of America," backed by majestic Greek columns.[261]

---

[259] *People Magazine—How Jackie Kennedy Invented Camelot*—November 2017
[260] *Them*—Senator Ben Sasse—Macmillan 2018
[261] Barack Obama's Presidential nomination acceptance speech—August 2008

UNINTENDED CONSEQUENCE

Barack Obama's acceptance speech, August 2008
(Suzieqq, WordPress), through President Barack Obama's
massively attended inaugural address of 2009.

Above is President Barack Obama's first inaugural address, January 2009 (Darkroom, *Baltimore Sun*), wherein he promised thus:

> Our nation is at war against a…network of violence and hatred.…To those who seek to advance their aims by inducing terror and slaughtering innocents…we will defeat you.
>
> Our economy is badly weakened…our health care is too costly…there is a sapping of confidence across our land. The state of the economy calls for action…create new jobs…lay a foundation for growth…build roads and bridges…raise health care's quality and lower its cost.…
>
> …Those of us who manage the public dollars will be held to account, to spend wisely…and do our business in the light of day.…
>
> …We…proclaim an end to the petty grievances, the recriminations and worn-out dogmas that…have strangled our politics.…
>
> …We remain faithful to the ideals of our forebearers and true to our founding documents.…We will not give them up for expedience sake.[262]

President Obama promised much in 2009 but delivered little in the subsequent eight years.

Underneath the pleasantness of his personality and the power of his oratory were the failures of his administrations, demonstrating their inability to overcome inherited crises.

The facts are irrefutable: the Iraq war was replaced with ISIS, debt spiraled from $7 trillion to near $20 trillion, health-care costs increased while services declined, roads and bridges continued to crumble, an additional twelve million left the labor force, yielding the lowest labor participation rate in thirty-six years.[263] Families on

---

[262] Barack Obama's Inaugural Address—January 2009
[263] *The Patriot Post—Nearly 12 Million Have Left the Workforce Under Obama*—December 2014

food stamps had doubled to over forty-eight million, racial tensions grew greater than they had been since the 1960s, partisan politics became a blood sport, scandals permeated, while the president circumvented Congress and the Constitution with his executive orders. Yet after Obama's two terms as president, many blindly insist the accomplishments of the Obama administration were constructive and to be applauded.

If so, then why?

- If the "reset" with Russia was good policy, why had Putin emerged as a primary adversary?
- If the abandonment of Egypt's Mubarak was good policy, why was there such unrest in Egypt?
- If the attack on Libya's Gaddafi was good policy, why is Libya in turmoil?
- If the assertion that Benghazi was "caused by a video" had been disproven, why had that premise not been recanted?
- If the policy of dealing with Israel was productive, why was there such tension between the two governments?
- If the China policy was effective, why did China mock us, stealing our technology and building a military base on a man-made island in the South China Sea?
- If the decision to withdraw from Iraq without leaving an American military presence to protect the gains made at the expense of blood and treasure was prudent, then why had ISIS emerged?
- If President Obama was "outraged" by the IRS scandal, why had he not insisted that Eric Holder pursue the matter?
- If President Obama was "troubled" by the *Associated Press* and James Rosen's free press scandal, why didn't he insist that Eric Holder explain the matter?
- If, as President Obama has asserted, the gunrunning program *Fast and Furious* was a "program begun under the previous administration, and when Eric Holder found out about it, he discontinued it" was disproven, why had that statement not

been recanted and why had he not insisted that Eric Holder cooperate with the congressional investigation into the matter?
- If the Affordable Care Act is such a positive legislation, why did the Obama administration resort to lies and deception to obtain its passage despite the overwhelming objection of the American people?
- If, as President Obama stated in 2016, "our businesses are hiring 200,000 Americans a month. The unemployment rate has come down from a high of 10% in 2009, to 6.1% today…this is the longest uninterrupted stretch of private sector job creation in our history," then why had there been no reduction in the food stamp rolls?

Before becoming president, Barack Obama had enjoyed measurable success as a community organizer and Illinois State senator, providing leadership, bringing relief to the underserved in minority communities, especially black. His promise of *"hope and change"* was directed at that constituency.

In her book *Becoming*, Michelle Obama expressed her memory of Barack Obama's address to the Democratic convention on July 27, 2004: "He spoke for seventeen minutes that night, explaining who he was and where he came from—his grandfather a GI who'd joined Patton's Army, his grandmother who'd worked on an assembly line during the war, his father who'd grown up herding goats in Kenya, his parents' improbable love, their faith in what a good education could do for a son who wasn't born rich or well connected. Earnestly and expertly, he cast himself not as an outsider but rather as a literal embodiment of the American story. He reminded the audience that a country couldn't be carved up simply into red and blue, that we were united by a common humanity, compelled to care for the whole of society. He called for hope over cynicism. He spoke with hope, projected hope, almost sang with it."[264]

She wrote of her childhood in the South Side of Chicago and of the deterioration of her community. She wrote of the racial divide and her encounters with perceived racism. Then why, as pres-

---
[264] *Becoming*—Michelle Obama—Page 215

ident and first lady, did they do so little for the South Side or black Americans in general?

After President Obama's election, he surrounded himself with academics, in his Cabinet and as his advisers, strong on theory but short on actual accomplishment outside academia. Consequently, the president brought the uber-liberal bias, ideas, and strategies that had altered our national education system into his administration, with predictable results. Instead of expanding the reach of his own personal experience, the academics supplanted his socially sensitive vision with their own extreme progressive theories on health care, education, and the environment, which were impractical, economically disastrous, and unsustainable.

The president, knowingly or not, had abandoned his quest to advance the plight of the downtrodden and economically disadvantaged. He ignored his purpose of improving the status quo of minorities, in exchange for utilizing his eight-year administration as some progressive petri dish. President Obama's audacity of hope was suffocated by theoretical progressive nonsense and spearheaded by those academics. He may have squandered his probable place in history.

Yet Democrats and the media tout President Barack Obama as one of the greatest presidents ever. I suspect, however, that history, when written, might disagree.

Perhaps another Camelot? Ahhh, nostalgia.

By contrast, in January 2017, President Donald Trump delivered his inaugural address to a media-reported smaller audience and promised thus:

President Donald Trump's inauguration,
January 20, 2017 (*Daily Star*, UK).

We must protect our borders from the ravages of other countries making our products, stealing our companies, and destroying our jobs.

Protection will lead to great prosperity and strength. We will reinforce old alliances and form new ones—and unite the civilized world against Radical Islamic Terrorism, which we will eradicate completely from the face of the Earth.

We will seek friendship and goodwill with the nations of the world—but we do so with the understanding that it is the right of all nations to put their own interests first.

We will follow two simple rules: Buy American and Hire American.

We will bring back our jobs. We will bring back our borders. We will bring back our wealth. And we will bring back our dreams. We will build new roads, and highways, and bridges, and airports, and tunnels, and railways across our wonderful nation.

We will get our people off welfare and back to work rebuilding our country with American hands and American labor.

At the bedrock of our politics will be a total allegiance to the United States…and through our loyalty to our country, we will rediscover our loyalty to each other.[265]

The media continues to refer to President Trump as a serial liar. Admittedly, he is prone to exaggeration and braggadocio. However, I can think of no president in modern history that has kept more campaign promises. Trump was not lying about those.

*The Federalist* is an American conservative online magazine and podcast that covers politics, policy, culture, and religion. In June 2018, it published an article summarizing the accomplishments of the Trump administration, titled "Trump Releases List of 60 Promises Kept; Media Ignores."

The American economy is stronger, American workers are experiencing more opportunities, confidence is soaring, and business is booming.

President Trump has re-asserted American leadership on the world stage, secured vital investments in our military, and stood up against threats to our national security.

Nearly 3 million jobs have been created since…[he]…took office. 304,000 manufacturing jobs have been created and manufacturing employment stands at its highest level since December 2008; 337,000 construction jobs have been created and construction employment stands at its highest level since June 2008.

---

[265] President Trump's Inaugural Address—January 20, 2017

The unemployment rate has dropped to 3.8, the lowest rate since April 2000, and job openings have reached 6.6 million, the highest level ever recorded.

Consumer confidence has been restored with confidence among both consumers and businesses reaching historic highs.

President Trump signed the historic Tax Cuts and Jobs Act into law, cutting taxes for American families and making American business more competitive. American families received $3.2 trillion in gross tax cuts and saw the child tax credit double. The top corporate tax rate was lowered from 35% to 21% so American businesses could be more competitive.

President Trump successfully eliminated the penalty for Obamacare's burdensome individual mandate.

President Trump has rolled back unnecessary job-killing regulations…far exceeded his promise to eliminate regulations at a two-to-one ratio, issuing 22 deregulatory actions for every new regulatory action. The Administration rolled back rules and regulations harming farmers and energy producers, such as the Waters of the United States Rule and the Clean Power Plan.

President Trump has advanced free, fair, and reciprocal trade deals that protect American workers, ending decades of destructive trade policies…[and]…is working to defend American intellectual property from China's unfair practices through a range of actions.

The President has secured historic increases in defense funding in order to rebuild our Nation's military with the resources they need, after years of harmful sequester. The United

States has worked with international allies to decimate ISIS.

Despite limited resources and obstruction from Congress, President Trump has worked to take control of our border and enforce our immigration laws. President Trump has called on Congress to provide the resources needed to secure our borders and close loopholes that prevent immigration laws from being fully enforced.

The Trump Administration continues to combat the threat of MS-13, protecting communities from the violence the gang has spread. In 2017, the Department of Justice worked with partners in Central America to file criminal charges against more than 4,000 members of MS-13.

President Trump has confirmed the most circuit court judges of any President in their first year, and secured Justices Gorsuch's and Kavanaugh's confirmation to the United States Supreme Court.[266]

Facts are facts. They may be spun, but they cannot be denied. Aspiration versus accomplishment, politician versus businessman, political philosophy versus practical policy.

Democrats and the mass media could not accept that the 2016 presidential election was a repudiation of the Obama administration policies. Instead, they embraced a strategy of Trump resistance. Representative Pelosi (D-CA) declared "Armageddon," Senator Schumer (D-NY) predicted the "end of America as we know it," and liberals howled at the moon, lamenting the historic loss of Hillary Clinton. No coronation.

---

[266] *The Federalist: Trump Releases List of 60 Promises Kept; Media Ignores*—June 2018

So, too, did Shakespeare have King Macbeth rant about life after the death of his wife and before his downfall: "It is a tale told by an idiot, full of sound and fury, signifying nothing."

In an endless effort to deflect attention from the Trump administration's accomplishments and to stall legislative progress, Democrats and the biased media engaged in a dishonest pursuit of a fictional Russian conspiracy.

Senator Schumer (D-NY), Senator Warren (D-MA), and Hillary Clinton initiated and openly encouraged their "resistance" campaign. Resistance to what? Are Democrats *against* lower unemployment, higher consumer confidence, higher wages, record stock market values, and stronger military? Are they against reduced illegal immigration, having NATO members pay their fair share, or efforts to peacefully denuclearize North Korea?

What is the unintended consequence?

We are weakening our society. There has been an assault on our traditional values. The future of our country is in the balance. Continued incivility is a cancer that can only lead to increased civil unrest and perhaps to political civil war. Our politics are broken, and we are mired in a period of ferocious steadfast partisanship. We are experiencing a crisis of confidence in our government offices. We have reached the limits of lunatic fringe in terms of civility. It is past time for action.

As a people, we must galvanize to repair a bruised, wounded Uncle Sam.

Why do zealot Republican politicians insist on extreme "right" positions, sacrificing incremental progress, forgoing the good in pursuit of the perfect? It is time for our politicians and citizens to abandon their pursuit of ideological purity. It is time for all Democrats to put aside their consumption with hatred toward the president. It is time for Libertarians to abandon their pursuit of a utopian society that could never exist in our complex world. It is time for the media to forsake its reflexive anti-Trump obsession and begin emphasizing the positive accomplishments that are improving our country, economy, and society.

Isn't it time for our politicians and media to convey the real dangers of flirting with socialism? Isn't it time to reject the false premise being championed by Senators Bernie Sanders (D-NH), Elizabeth Warren (D-MA), and Cory Booker (D-NJ) and Representatives Alexandria Ocasio Cortez, Ilhan Omar, and others?

> Do you want to know who you are? Don't ask. Act! Action will delineate and define you. (Thomas Jefferson)

How should a person be properly measured, by his words or his deeds? I believe that the answer lies in advice offered by the celebrated football coach at Notre Dame University Lou Holtz: "Don't criticize the performer, criticize the performance."

## Congressional Investigations

Most congressional investigations seem to be politically motivated, fruitless, divisive, and expensive. They often conclude with little accomplishment regarding their original intent and end up punishing unfortunates caught in their web with "process crimes." The policy of entrapment into process crimes to pressure witnesses into cooperating with the government investigation is devious and immoral. It appears to be the prevalent go-to strategy for these probes. One might question whether our legislators and the special counsels that are appointed are up to the task of finding justice, or do they simply pursue political advantage?

I offer, perhaps, a lesson in civics.

In 1951, anticommunist crusader Senator Joseph McCarthy (R-WI) convened the Army-McCarthy Hearings in Washington, DC, intended to investigate suspected members of the Communist Party being employed by the Department of the Army and the US State Department. McCarthy charged that the State Department and its secretary, Dean Acheson, harbored "traitorous" communists.

The Red Scare aggressively pursued and randomly accused Americans of being communist. McCarthy extended his targets to include additional government agencies, the broadcasting and defense industries, universities, and the United Nations.[267] J. Edgar Hoover allowed his agents to generate salacious material attacking targets of the hearings in pursuit of his own conservative social and political agenda.

Special counsel for the Army Joseph N. Welch, in a heated exchange with Senator McCarthy, questioned, "Have you no sense of decency, sir? At long last, have you left no sense of decency?"

The hearings were broadcast live, gavel to gavel, on ABC, CBS, and the Dumont television networks. Those broadcasts, as well as Edward R. Murrow's scathing editorial on his television show *See It Now*, greatly contributed to McCarthy's decline in popularity and his eventual censure by the Senate.[268],[269]

The investigation concluded without identifying any communists within the US government, achieved a circus quality with the political participants verbally sparring with one another, destroyed personal lives and careers, and provided one classic quote.

I was unable to confirm the cost to US taxpayers for the Army-McCarthy hearings. Little positive purpose, if any, was served.

The Watergate Scandal began with the arrest of five men caught breaking into the Washington, DC, Democratic National Committee headquarters in June 1972. A historical lesson would be learned here: while President Richard Nixon had no foreknowledge of the break-in, the Senate investigation proved he participated in the cover-up. The cover-up cost Nixon his presidency, demonstrating to America that the cover-up can be worse than the *crime*.

The Republicans proved in this instance of overzealousness that they, too, could be equally guilty of partisan dirty politics. The abuses included bugging the offices of political opponents and people of whom Nixon or his officials were suspicious. The president

---

[267] *Encyclopedia Britannica—McCarthyism*
[268] *Encyclopedia Britannica—McCarthyism*
[269] George Mason University—*History Matters*

and his close aides ordered investigations of activist groups and political figures, using the FBI, the CIA, and the IRS as political weapons.

*The Washington Post* broke the story, with reporting by Bob Woodward and Carl Bernstein, initially based upon leaks from a clandestine source identified only as Deep Throat. Decades later, in 2005, *Vanity Fair* magazine identified a former top FBI official named Mark Felt as Deep Throat, the secret source high in the US government who helped *Post* reporters Woodward and Bernstein unravel the Watergate conspiracy. Here again, an FBI agent showed political bias. Woodward, Bernstein, and *The Washington Post* editors confirmed the story.[270]

The FBI investigation discovered a connection between cash found on the burglars and a slush fund used by the Committee to Reelect the President, the official organization of Nixon's campaign. The Senate investigation revealed that Nixon had secretly tape-recorded conversations in his offices. The nation watched the proceedings on television and came to witness, firsthand, just how corrupt our government could be. The scandal led to the discovery of multiple abuses of power by members of the Nixon administration, led to the commencement of an impeachment process against the president and, ultimately, Richard Nixon's resignation. Several Nixon aides went to prison.[271]

I was unable to confirm the cost of the Watergate hearings to US taxpayers. In this instance, the congressional hearing did lead to justice.

The Iran-Contra Affair began in the middle of President Ronald Reagan's second term. During his campaign for reelection, Reagan had promised to assist anticommunist insurgencies around the globe, but the so-called Reagan Doctrine faced a political hurdle following devastating 1986 midterm election losses for the Republicans.[272]

Soon after taking control of Congress, the Democrats passed the Boland Amendment, which restricted the activities of the CIA and

---

[270] *Vanity Fair*: *"I'm The Guy They Called Deep Throat"*—July 2005
[271] *Encyclopedia Britannica—Watergate Scandal*
[272] U.S. Department of State—Archive: *Reagan Doctrine—1985*

Department of Defense in foreign conflicts. The politically motivated amendment by the anti-Reagan Democrats was specifically aimed at Nicaragua, where anticommunist Contras were battling the Sandinista communist government.

The 1987 Iran-Contra Affair was a secret Reagan administration arms deal that traded missiles and other arms in exchange for Americans held hostage by terrorists in Lebanon. Reagan, in defiance of the Democrats and in a determined effort to support the Contras and release the hostages, agreed that an arms deal with Iran could support both of those objectives and help the United States improve relations with Lebanon, providing the United Sates with an ally in a region where it desperately needed one.[273]

The funds derived from that deal were used to support the Contras in their armed conflict in Nicaragua. The controversial deal-making and the ensuing political scandal threatened to bring down the presidency of Ronald Reagan.

Attorney General Edwin Meese launched an investigation into the weapons deal and found that some $18 million of the $30 million Iran had paid for the weapons was unaccounted for. Lieutenant Colonel Oliver North, USMC, a member of President Reagan's National Security Council, came forward to acknowledge that he had diverted the missing funds to the Contras in Nicaragua, who used them to acquire weapons. North said he had done so with the full knowledge of national security adviser Admiral John Poindexter. Poindexter was initially indicted on seven felonies and tried on five. He was found guilty on four of the charges and sentenced to two years in prison, his convictions later vacated.[274]

A seemingly well-intended and successful foreign policy gambit by the Reagan administration, perhaps better kept a secret, was exposed by the Democrats only to embarrass a Republican administration. I understand that the Boland Amendment was violated, but which was the "greater good," releasing the hostages and funding the anticommunist Contras or abiding by a politically motivated law?

---

[273] *Encyclopedia Britannica—Iran Contra Affair*
[274] *Encyclopedia Britannica—Iran Contra Affair*

The Iran-Contra investigation cost taxpayers $47 million.

This was an example of politics given priority over country.

In 1994, Kenneth Starr was appointed special counsel to conduct the Whitewater Investigation. David Hale, a banker and the key witness against President William Clinton in the investigation, alleged that in November 1992, Clinton, while governor of Arkansas, pressured him to provide an illegal $300,000 loan to Susan McDougal, a partner with the Clintons in the Whitewater land deal.

Hale revealed that he had pleaded guilty to two felonies and secured a reduction in his sentence in exchange for his testimony against Clinton. President Clinton denied that he pressured Hale to approve the loan.[275]

Starr drafted an impeachment referral to the House of Representatives in the fall of 1997, alleging that there was "substantial and credible evidence" that President Clinton had committed perjury regarding Hale's allegations, and he disclosed new evidence of sexual misconduct.

The Clinton-Lewinsky scandal involved forty-nine-year-old president William Clinton and a twenty-two-year-old White House intern, Monica Lewinsky. The sexual relationship took place between 1995 and 1997 and came to light in 1998. Clinton ended a televised speech in late January 1998 with the statement that he "did not have sexual relations with that woman, Ms. Lewinsky."[276]

By April 1998, Starr's investigation in Arkansas was winding down, with his Little Rock grand jury about to expire. Hubbell, Jim Guy Tucker, and Susan McDougal had all refused to cooperate with Starr. Susan McDougal charged that Starr offered her "global immunity" from other charges if she would cooperate with the Whitewater investigation. McDougal refused to answer any questions under oath. When the Arkansas grand jury did conclude its work in May 1998, after thirty months in panel, it only came up a contempt indictment against Susan McDougal, leading to her being imprisoned for civil

---

[275] *Encyclopedia Britannica—Iran Contra Affair*
[276] *The Washington Post—William Clinton: "I did not have sexual relations with ...."*—January 1998

contempt of court for the maximum eighteen months, including eight months in isolation.

In September 1998, independent counsel Starr released his findings concerning offenses alleged to have been committed by President William Clinton as part of the Lewinsky scandal. The report mentioned Whitewater only in passing. The investigation led to charges of perjury and to the impeachment of President Clinton by the House of Representatives. He was subsequently acquitted on all impeachment charges of perjury and obstruction of justice in a twenty-one-day Senate trial, with a Republican majority.

Tucker and McDougal were later pardoned by President Clinton.

After four years of independent counsel investigation, no corroboration was found regarding the Whitewater matter, and two people were convicted on what are referred to as process crimes.[277]

The cost? Eighty million dollars of taxpayer money, young Americans being introduced to the notion of oral sex on nightly television, and the reputation of a young Whitehouse intern ruined. Was it worth it? You decide.

The Benghazi, Libya, and US diplomatic compound and CIA annex were attacked in early September 2012 by an estimated 150 Islamic militants affiliated with al-Qaeda. Four Americans, including US ambassador Christopher Stevens, were killed.

Susan Rice, US ambassador to the United Nations, went on the Sunday news television programs, representing the Obama administration, and she misled America, telling all that the attack was in reaction to an anti-Islam video that had been posted on YouTube. Later, the administration attributed the attack to the escalation of demonstrations that had occurred in front of the compound a day earlier; however, neither a link to the video nor evidence of those earlier demonstrations could be substantiated.

Did President Obama and his administration mislead the public when they initially claimed that the attack on the US consulate

---

[277] *Encyclopedia Britannica—Watergate Scandal*

UNINTENDED CONSEQUENCE

in Benghazi began "spontaneously" in response to an anti-Muslim video?

Eventually, other evidence emerged confirming that the attacks were premeditated by the al-Qaeda affiliate group Ansar al-Sharia.[278]

On the threshold of the 2012 presidential election, President Obama and his administration repeatedly refused to refer to the event as a terrorist attack, fearing it would influence the election. As a result, the question would not go away.

The Benghazi attack, the administration's spurious explanations, and the reported suggestion that the United States had military resources available that might have mitigated the attack, perhaps saving the American lives lost, created public controversy. Consequently, the House of Representatives and the US Senate each initiated a committee to investigate.

The House of Representatives select committee, created in May 2014, conducted hearings on Benghazi and released its report in June 2016. The committee chairman, Representative Trey Gowdy (R-SC), called the report the "final, definitive accounting."

A series of investigations ultimately placed responsibility for the attacks on insufficient bureaucratic measures that failed to prevent and respond properly to the assault.[279]

The report severely criticized the military, CIA, and Obama administration both for their response as the attacks unfolded and for their subsequent explanations to the American people. It cited incompetence at various governmental levels, including failure to deploy needed military assets, CIA intelligence reports that were rife with errors, and misguided planning.[280]

The House committee findings were challenged by every Democrat on the committee, although the Democrats did not call one witness on their own.

The US Senate Select Committee on Intelligence began hearings on Benghazi in October of 2012. The Senate report drew con-

---

[278] *Encyclopedia Britannica—2012 Benghazi attack*
[279] *Encyclopedia Britannica—2012 Benghazi attack*
[280] *USA Today—House Benghazi committee files final report—December 2016*

clusions like the House report and made specific recommendations regarding future conduct, procedures, and protections.[281]

The House investigation cost US taxpayers almost $8 million. I was unable to determine the cost of the Senate investigation or the cost incurred by the State Department needed to respond to information requests, although estimates have exceeded $40 million.

I could not uncover any evidence that the findings of either committee led to any significant policy revision.

The House committee investigation disclosed that Secretary of State Hillary Clinton had used a private email server, but the FBI initially declined to pursue the matter.

More party politics over policy and justice.

Exposing of the existence and use of Hillary Clinton's private email server while she was secretary of state created another scandal and led to another congressional investigation.

"Government employees are allowed to use private emails for government work; however, the practice is discouraged, and the agency must ensure that federal records sent or received on such systems are preserved in the appropriate agency record keeping system."

National Archives and Records Administration clarifies that personal email "can only be used in emergency situations and that emails from personal accounts should be captured and managed in accordance with agency record-keeping practices."[282] Using private emails to transmit classified information is always prohibited. In 2009, the Clinton email server was initiated. In 2012, congressional investigators asked Hillary Clinton if "she uses a personal email," but she ignored the question.

After the existence of Clinton's private server was exposed in 2014, the State Department formally requested that Clinton turn over the approximately thirty thousand emails. In December of that year, President Obama signed "an update to the Federal Records Act, that clarifies how private emails are allowed to be used."[283]

---

[281] US Senate Select Committee on intelligence—*Terrorist Attacks on Benghazi*—January 2014
[282] *CNN Politics—Timeline of Hillary Clinton's email scandal*—November 2016
[283] *CNN Politics—Timeline of Hillary Clinton's email scandal*—November 2016

In March of 2015, the State Department announced, "There is no indication that Secretary Clinton used her personal email account for anything but unclassified purposes." The next day, the House committee investigating Benghazi issued a subpoena for Libya-related emails.[284]

On March 10, 2015, *The New York Times* reported that Hillary Clinton had regularly deleted half of her emails as secretary of state. Clinton aides destroyed her phones with a hammer and had a data destruction company wipe her server clean with BleachBit, in defiance of a subpoena for those records. A total of 31,830 personal emails were deleted "sometime between March 25 [and] 31, 2015," according to the FBI. That was about three weeks *after* Clinton received a House subpoena for the records on March 4, 2015.[285]

Over the next fifteen months, the emails were provided in a series of tranches, and on July 26, 2015, Clinton stated that she did not send classified emails from here private server: "I am confident that I never sent nor received any information that was classified at the time it was sent or received."[286]

In January 2016, Intelligence Community inspector general I. Charles McCullough III wrote to the congressional intelligence committees that "emails on Clinton's private server have been flagged for classified information, some of which is considered the highest 'top secret' level of classification."

In May 2016, the State Department inspector general reported that "Clinton failed to follow the rules or inform key department staff regarding her use of a private email server." In the final analysis, of the 52,000 emails reviewed, 2,101 were considered classified, with 22 being classified "top secret."[287]

In response to the outcry from Congress and the American people, the Justice Department was compelled to open an investigation, and Attorney General Loretta Lynch assured, "The investigation…is

---

[284] *CNN Politics—Timeline of Hillary Clinton's email scandal*—November 2016
[285] FactCheck.org—*The FBI Files on Clinton's Emails*—September 2016
[286] *CNN Politics—Timeline of Hillary Clinton's email scandal*—November 2016
[287] *CNN Politics—Timeline of Hillary Clinton's email scandal*—November 2016

going to be handled like any other matter…they will follow the facts and follow the evidence wherever it leads and come to a conclusion."

Attorney General Lynch met with former president William Clinton in June 2016, while the FBI was investigating the private email server. Clinton boarded Lynch's plane while it was on the tarmac at Phoenix's Sky Harbor International Airport. After news broke about the airport meeting, the FBI's reaction was to scramble to identify the source who leaked the encounter to the media, intending to discipline them.[288]

Contrary to normal FBI investigative procedures, Hillary Clinton was interviewed by the FBI without being required to take an oath. Her testimony was not recorded. Five aides to Hillary were granted immunity for their testimony, generally only given in exchange for salient criminal information, and their personal computers were not retained as evidence.

After the FBI investigation was completed in July 2016, FBI director James Comey announced that he would not recommend charges against Hillary Clinton. While Clinton and her aides were "extremely careless" in handling classified information, she did not "intentionally and willfully" disclose that information.[289] How could Comey possibly know Clinton's intentions? Comey later testified before Congress that Attorney General Lynch asked him to refer to the probe as a "matter," a request that made him feel "queasy."

Classified Hillary Clinton emails were then found on the computer of disgraced former House representative Anthony Weiner (D-NY), husband of Clinton aide Huma Abedin.

Following the close of the FBI investigation, the House and Senate each initiated their own examinations, uncovering the biased nature of the FBI scrutiny. The conclusions of the Senate study were revealing:

---

[288] *Newsweek—After Clinton—Lynch Tarmac Meeting, FBI Scrambles—December* 2017
[289] FBI Press Office—*Investigation of Secretary Hillary Clinton's Use of a Personal E-mail*—July 2016

## UNINTENDED CONSEQUENCE

Text messages raise several questions about the FBI and its investigation of classified information on Secretary Clinton's private email server. Strzok and Page discussed serving to "protect the country from the menace" of Trump "enablers," and the possibility of an "insurance policy" against the "risk" of a Trump Presidency. The two discussed then-Attorney General Loretta Lynch knowing that Secretary Clinton would not face charges—before the FBI had interviewed Secretary Clinton and before her announcement that she would accept Director Comey's prosecution decision. They wrote about drafting talking points for then-Director Comey because President Obama "wants to know everything we're doing." Strzok and Page also exchanged views about the investigation on possible Russian collusion with the Trump campaign—calling it "unfinished business" and "an investigation leading to impeachment," drawing parallels to Watergate, and expressing Strzok's "gut sense and concern there's no big there there." The text messages raise several important questions that deserve further examination:

- Whether, and the extent to which, any personal animus and/or political bias influenced the FBI's investigation;
- Whether, and the extent to which, the Obama Department of Justice or White House influenced the FBI's investigation; and
- Whether, and the extent to which, any personal animus and/or political bias influenced the FBI's actions with respect to President Trump.

> We should all recognize the harm done to our rule of law when crimes go unpunished because government officials look the other way for the wealthy, famous, or powerful. Americans rightly expect a single and impartial system of justice for all, not one for the well-connected and a separate one for everyone else.[290]

The culture of political bias evidenced by the Federal Bureau of Investigation was initiated by J. Edgar Hoover during the Army-McCarthy hearings, continued through the Watergate era of Mark Felt, and endures today with the conduct of James Comey, Peter Strzok, and Lisa Page regarding the Clinton server scandal and the Trump-Russia investigation.[291] Interestingly, no one was ever charged with obstruction of justice, no one was indicted for a process crime, no one was cited for violating government policy and procedure, and grants of immunity were freely given without required testimony.

It has been estimated that the investigations cost the US taxpayers $20 million. Party politics over justice.

The Mueller Investigation seems to have been motivated by the Democrats' anger with the loss of the 2016 presidential election. Its primary objective should have been to determine the extent, if any, of Russian interference in America's election process. Instead, it became an attack on the integrity of our president, with some media outlets accusing President Trump of treason.

After Attorney General Jeff Sessions recused himself from the matter, Assistant Attorney General Rod Rosenstein appointed former FBI director Robert Mueller to serve as special counsel, charged with investigating possible Trump campaign involvement with the Russian interference in the 2016 presidential election.

The Mueller team, clearly biased, was comprised of "eighteen angry Democrats" and avid Hillary Clinton supporters. It is a case

---

[290] U.S. Senate—*The Clinton E-Mail Scandal and The FBI's Investigation of It*—February 2018

[291] *The Washington Post: The dark side of Hoover's FBI*—January 2016

where one political party tried to use this investigation to remove the president of the United States.

The Mueller Report concluded that the Russian operation did not have any cooperation of the president, his campaign, or for that fact, any American citizen.

He found no criminal conspiracy or collusion: "As soon as news broke out that Trump had been elected President, Russian government officials and prominent Russian businessmen began trying to make inroads into the new Administration. They appeared to not to have preexisting contacts and struggled to connect with senior officials around the President-Elect."[292] Mueller could not prove obstruction: "If we had confidence after a thorough investigation of the facts that the President did not commit obstruction, we would so state… the evidence we obtained about the President's actions and intent presents difficult issues that prevent us from conclusively determining that no criminal conduct occurred. Accordingly, while this report does not conclude that the President committed a crime, it does not exonerate him."[293]

The White House fully cooperated, did not claim executive privilege, and did not redact any material provided.

The Mueller Report concluded that "the evidence did not establish obstruction of justice"; while there was no proof of "obstruction," the president could not be "exonerated."

What does that even mean? Mueller could not prove that the president obstructed, but the investigation could not prove that he did *not* obstruct. This seems to be a colossally flawed legal reasoning.

At St. Peter's College, the Jesuits taught, in philosophy, the notion of a "negative proof fallacy," to wit: "The negative proof fallacy occurs when it is claimed or implied that because a premise cannot be proven false, then the premise must be true; or that if a premise cannot be proven true, then the premise must be false." One cannot prove a negative. Isn't innocence presumed if guilt cannot be proven? Has justice been sacrificed to appease political philosophy?

---

[292] *The Mueller Report—Page 144—Volume I*
[293] *The Mueller Report—Page 2—Volume II*

The final report of the special prosecutor ended up being a bit of a Rorschach test; its conclusions were subject to interpretation. It provided fodder for both sides. Unfortunately, Mueller was indecisive. The overarching finding was that Russia, via social media and misinformation, attempted to wreak havoc and influence our presidential election. Mueller, while failing to mention any aspect of the Clinton campaign involvement with the fabricated "Russian dossier," found that Russian interference was "deeper and broader than had been recognized."

The report detailed ten issues that President Trump discussed, which might have been interpreted as attempts at obstruction but were never carried out. The law cares about what is done, not what is discussed. Are we to be judged by our thoughts rather than our actions? Again, we are faced with the dilemma: Which has predominance, words or deeds?

It is ruinous that Mueller made no effort to examine the "dossier" that served as the bedrock underpinnings of the allegation, as well as the basis for a FISA warrant required to launch the initial investigation. Had he done so, the entire investigation might have been appropriately considered "fruit of a poisoned tree" and dismissed. Where did this false narrative begin? Will we ever know?

It appears that effort is underway to answer those questions.

Attorney General William Barr has initiated an investigation into these issues with the Department of Justice inspector general Michael Horowitz and Special Prosecutor John Durham to investigate the matter more broadly. Durham's inquiry has widened to become a criminal investigation.[294] The criminal investigation is targeting senior Obama administration officials: John Brennan, former CIA director; James Clapper, former director of National Intelligence; and Peter Strzok, former FBI special agent.[295]

The House Democrats then pursued "obstruction" and "cover-up," continuing to howl at the moon, focusing predominantly

---

[294] *The New York Times: Justice Dept. to Open Criminal Inquiry*—October 2019
[295] *Washington Examiner: John Durham Opens Criminal Inquiry*—October 2019

upon impeachment instead of legislation that is urgently needed by our nation.

It seems that in Congress, "truth" is in the eye of the beholder, but "truth" should not be a matter of perspective. Why are we so willing to tear our nation apart in pursuit of political ideology? Shouldn't all Americans celebrate that there was no collusion, that our president is not a traitor? Shouldn't this be a national victory?

It appears that the only authentic collusion, as regards to the Mueller investigation, was between the Democrats and the media. The Mueller Report may have exonerated the president on the legal side, but certainly not on the political side. Apparently, Trump derangement syndrome has no cure. House Democrats, like a pit bull with a bone, would not let go. So they abandon their claims of "collusion" and pursue an investigation into "obstruction"—obstruction of something the president said he did not do and the Mueller investigation determined he did not do. This must be the height of senselessness.

Now the Democrat-controlled Congress pursues "process crimes." Representative Jerry Nadler (D-NY) initiated a congressional investigation into the process crimes, to no apparent avail, and by October 2019, his committee became silent.

In July 2019, Robert Mueller appeared before two congressional investigation committees at the insistence of the Democrat chairmen, Representative Schiff (D-CA) and Representative Nadler (D-NY). Shockingly, Mueller demonstrated a dearth of knowledge of the contents of the investigative report bearing his name, seemingly confirming that his investigation ignored any aspect that might have reflected poorly upon Democrats.

The cost to taxpayers of the Mueller investigation has been estimated as $35 million, plus the untold cost to the private citizens that were dragged into it. The veracity of the FBI, Justice Department, and Obama administration has been called into question. Was it worth it?

Still, they would not let go of their quest for impeachment, and in September of 2019, the Democrats in the House of Representatives initiated hearings on an impeachment inquiry via *edict* by Speaker

Nancy Pelosi (D-CA). This was contrary to longstanding norms and precedent exercised in the impeachment hearings of Presidents Nixon and Clinton. The "impeachment inquiry" was initiated *without a vote* in the House, a deviation designed to protect Democrats in the House from publicly, and on the record, revealing their position on the inquiry and to deny the president due process.

Using this solemn and extreme impeachment process as political theater, the investigation committee chairman was Representative Adam Schiff (D-CA). Schiff made unproven allegations regarding improper conduct of President Trump during a telephone conversation Trump had with the president of Ukraine in July of 2019. President Trump declassified the transcript of the conversation in question and released it to the public. Schiff, whose veracity had been brought into question during the Mueller Investigation, made a contrived dishonest opening statement, then, with questionable authority, began calling for witnesses to appear and documents to be provided. All testimony was taken behind closed doors, shielded from the public. Schiff released only those portions of text messages, without context, that would support his allegations.

In early October, the Whitehouse announced that the executive branch would not respond to the House Investigation Committee until an actual impeachment inquiry vote was taken. In late October 2019, Speaker Pelosi relented in response to severe public and political criticism and ordered a vote in the House of Representatives, not to authorize the impeachment inquiry, but to codify the procedure undertaken. However, the procedures continued to restrict the Republicans in their opportunity to defend the president.

At the time of this writing, Speaker Pelosi has won her partisan impeachment in the House of Representative, in spite of bi-partisan objection, and after she delayed the transfer of the Articles of Impeachment to the Senate for trial, the senate's Constitutional obligation was completed and President Trump was acquitted, primarily along political party lines. All of this begs the question; How much of their moral compass are Democrats willing to sacrifice for political power? It is unlikely that similar theatrics will end before Election Day. Isn't it shameful that Nancy Pelosi's place in history might not be remembered as the first female Speaker of the House, but rather as the Speaker that presided over and created completely political and partisan articles of impeachment—forever establishing the impeachment procedure as a political strategy. Speaker Pelosi further maligned her own reputation when she petulantly ripped her copy of President Trump's 2020 *State of the Union Address* on national television. What possible purpose did that serve other than to make a partisan political statement? She demonstrated that her loyalty to party exceeds her concern for the nations well-being.

The 2018 Kavanaugh hearings held by the Senate Judiciary Committee on the nomination of conservative judge Brett Kavanaugh to the Supreme Court were nothing short of a national disgrace. The hearing was emotional, contentious, and dramatic. Christine Ford made allegations that Kavanaugh sexually assaulted her more than thirty years ago, while they were in high school. Another accused Kavanaugh of organizing a series of gang-rape parties. Kavanaugh denied the accusations.

Senator Flake (R-AZ) sided with the Democrats and held up the hearings to afford the FBI an opportunity to investigate the allegations. Neither of the allegations could be corroborated by the FBI based upon what I would suggest was a *motivated* FBI search.

During the hearings, partisan politics crushed common decency. It was a low point in American politics. Democrats used this public hearing to ravage the nominee, in hopes of blocking his nomination. The brutality and insipidness of the senators' questioning was nothing short of cruel, attesting to just how far fundamental civility has fallen. Democrat senators took Kavanaugh to task for his drinking in high school and college. Kavanaugh admitted to the behavior. Senator Whitehouse (D-RI) grilled Kavanaugh about his 1983 Georgetown Prep yearbook, which revealed his adolescent love of drinking beer, sports, and partying. At one point, the senator forced Kavanaugh to explain references to beer and flatulence. The Democrat senators' questioning was debasing and childish. Most crimes have a legal statute of limitations; what is the statute of limitations on adolescence?

Among the Republican lawmakers on the Judiciary Committee, Senator Lindsey Graham (R-SC) appeared the most outraged, assuring Kavanaugh that he was on his side and that Kavanaugh had "nothing to apologize" for. He sounded off on partisan efforts to "ruin this guy's life."

Graham, in an impassioned statement, called the hearing overly political, accusing Democrats of acting in bad faith concerning how they handled Ms. Ford. Graham said, "To my Republican colleagues, if you vote 'no,' you're legitimizing the most despicable thing I have seen in my time in politics."

Senator Graham expressed remorse for the way Kavanaugh and his family had been treated:

> If you [Democrats] wanted an FBI investigation, you could have come to us. What you [Democrats] want to do is destroy this guy's life, hold this seat open and hope you win in 2020. You said that, not me....[Judge Kavanaugh] you got nothing to apologize for. When you see Justice Sotomayor and Kagan, say hello because I voted for them. I'd never do to them what you've [Democrats] done to this guy. This is the most unethical sham since I've been in politics and if you really wanted to know the truth, you sure as hell wouldn't have done what you've done to this guy.
>
> I cannot imagine what you and your family have gone through. Boy, you [Democrats] want power, all want power. God, I hope you never get it. I hope the American people can see through this sham…that you knew about it and you held it. You had no intention of protecting Dr. Ford. She's as much of a victim as you are. God, I hate to say it because these have been my friends, but let me tell you, when it comes to this, if you're looking for a fair process, you came to the wrong town, at the wrong time.

>   This is hell. This is going to destroy the ability of good people to come forward because of this crap.
>
>   I hope you're on The Supreme Court. That's exactly where you should be. And I hope that the American people see through this charade. I wish you well, I intend to vote for you, and I hope everybody who's fair minded will.[296]

Kavanaugh was ultimately approved and appointed a justice on the Supreme Court.

I suspect that his wife and daughters continue to wear the emotional scars of this hearing.

Article 1, Section 1 of the US Constitution states, "All legislative Powers herein granted shall be vested in a Congress of the United States, which shall consist of a Senate and House of Representatives."

What is the purpose of a congressional investigation? Ideally, I would answer thus: to obtain information essential to the legislative process and oversight of the conduct of government. Nowhere is it suggested that the power of investigation should be used for purposes of advancing political philosophy, yet in the most recent seventy years, the congressional investigation mandate, responsibility, and privilege have been misused to achieve brazen, blatant political aims. Time, treasure, and personal reputations were sacrificed to the altar of what has become a political blood sport.

I think that the American people have had enough and want to see an end to these politically motivated, perpetual investigations.

How may we correct this miscarriage? Elect more responsible statesmen and stateswomen; encourage—no, demand—our politicians pursue the *people's business* rather than *reelection*; and speak out when abuse is evident.

An appropriate time for legislating term limits may very well be at hand.

---

[296] *The New York Times—Furious Lindsey Graham calls Kavanaugh Hearing...—* September 2018

## Our Bible, Our Flag, and Our History

"In God We Trust" is our national motto. It is fundamental to our country's underpinning and woven into our American identity.

Those principles are facing growing opposition from liberally biased political action groups, the Supreme Court, and our own government. Each seemingly targeting faith, our flag, and the symbols of our heritage. We continue to chip away at what are the cornerstones of Americana.

During a political speech in April 2008, presidential candidate Barack Obama demeaned a swath of the electorate with his comment regarding the attitude of some Americans toward the words of the Bible. He said, "It's not surprising, then, they get bitter, they cling to guns or religion," to which Hillary Clinton responded, "I was taken aback by the demeaning remarks Senator Obama made about people in small-town America, His remarks are elitist and out of touch."[297]

When did it become in our national best interest to discourage faith, even to ridicule it? How could it possibly be to our nation's advantage to dissuade patriotism and suppress the education of the rituals of our democracy during our children's primary education? By what measure has it become chic to destroy symbols of our history and heritage?

The liberal quest for "political correctness," which began to aggressively manifest itself in this century, has replaced the will of the majority in the pursuit of any minority celebre-cause-du-jour. Historical monuments are being desecrated and removed in the interest of what is considered defensible actions intended to protect the sensibilities of small groups of our citizenry.

Religious faith and patriotism have ceased being fashionable in our current culture. These actions undermine the "Norman Rockwell" portrait and aspiration of the American family, the "together" spirit of the United States, and, in turn, weaken our national moral compass.

---

[297] *The Guardian—Obama angers voters with guns and religion remark—April 2008*

# UNINTENDED CONSEQUENCE

We seem to be deciding these issues in the courts rather than in our hearts. Political activism and judicial "legislating from the bench" appear to have replaced reason.

Faith in our government is dwindling. American trust has declined, whether it involves faith in one another or confidence in the federal government and its institutions.

A 2019 Pew Research study found 73 percent of US adults under thirty believe that people "just look out for themselves most of the time," 71 percent say most people "would try to take advantage of you if they got a chance," and 60 percent say most people "can't be trusted." Pew Research also stated, "Across all three of these questions, adults under 30 are significantly more likely than their older counterparts to take a pessimistic view of their fellow Americans."[298]

Are we conceding Americana?

In 1962, the *Engel v. Vitale* Supreme Court decision banned prayer in public schools, led to a broader compulsory separation of church and state, and sowed the seeds of a more faithless society.[299]

Organized religions have drifted from the "fear of God" teaching of my youth to the "love of God" philosophy of today. My sense is that fear was a more powerful motivator. This notion, compounded with my belief that Americans have become too lazy—or it has become just too inconvenient—to participate in church, synagogue, or mosque, has created a great decline in attendance.[300]

---

[298] Pew Research Center—*Young Americans are less trusting*—August 2019
[299] *Encyclopedia Britannica—Engle v Vitale*
[300] Religious News Service—*The Great Decline—60 Years in One Graph*—January 2014

The Great Decline: 60 years of religion in America

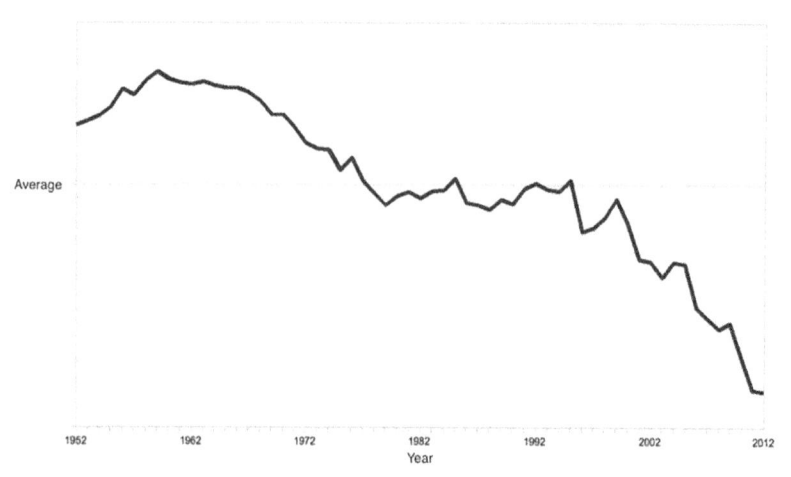

Graph by Corner of Church & State, a Religion News Service blog
Source: Aggregate Religiosity Index, J. Tobin Grant. *Sociological Forum.*

In 1980, the Supreme Court first addressed the constitutionality of public religious displays in *Stone v. Graham*. The court reviewed a Kentucky law requiring public schools to display the Ten Commandments in classrooms and determined that the Kentucky measure amounted to government sponsorship of religion, violated the First Amendment's Establishment Clause, and was therefore unconstitutional.[301]

In 1984, the court heard *Lynch v. Donnelly*, its first case specifically involving religious holiday displays. The court ruled that a Christmas nativity scene in the municipal square of Pawtucket, Rhode Island, "was constitutionally acceptable because the city's annual Christmas decorations were in a prominent park owned by a non-profit and included a display with a Santa Claus house, a sleigh and reindeer, carolers, a Christmas tree, and a 'season's greetings' banner. The display included a 'creche,' also called a nativity scene, which had been annually making appearances for over 40 years. The creche simply recognized the historical origins of the holiday, one

---

[301] JUSTIA—US Supreme Court—*Stone v. Graham—1980*

that has secular as well as religious significance." The justices then concluded, "In those circumstances, the nativity scene did not reflect an effort by the government to promote Christianity."[302]

In 1989, the Supreme Court heard *County of Allegheny v. ACLU* and ruled that a nativity scene on the staircase of a Pittsburgh, Pennsylvania, courthouse was unconstitutional. Unlike the situation in Pawtucket, where the crèche was shown together with more secular symbols, the Pittsburgh crèche was prominently displayed on its own and thus amounted to a government endorsement of religion.[303]

As a society, we seem to praise God one day a week, if at all, and we have become insistent that we remove any reference to religion from our schools and the public square.

The Philadelphia Flyers have banned the playing of Kate Smith's rendition of "God Bless America" because of the lyrics in a song that she recorded *ninety years ago.* Her statue standing in front of their arena since 1987 was initially covered with a tarp and ultimately taken down. The Flyers management explained that the decisions were made because the lyrics were "incompatible with the values of [their] organization and evoke painful and unacceptable themes."[304]

"In God We Trust" has nothing to do with political affiliation. Without religion and the moral code that most espouse, I believe we have, and will, become a less civil society.

Fortunately, there is evidence that reason might be creeping back into our national conscience. During the past few years, several states have passed laws requiring that the national motto be prominently displayed in their public schools.

In 2018, Florida passed a state law requiring school boards to conspicuously display "In God We Trust" in all schools and associated buildings. This legislation was agreed to in response to the tragic shooting earlier that year at Marjory Stoneman Douglas High School in Parkland, Florida. Kara Gross, legislative counsel for the Florida branch of the American Civil Liberties Union, is studying

---

[302] JUSTIA—US Supreme Court—*Lynch v. Donnelly*—*1984*
[303] Pew Research Center—*Religious Displays and the Courts*—June 2007
[304] *The Washington Post*—*Kate Smith Statue Removed by Flyers*—April 2019

the law and looking for ways to protect Floridians' rights, saying, "Public schools are for secular learning. The concern is that mandating a religious enforcement goes against the very crux of church and state." Kimberly Daniels, Democrat Florida State representative, responded, "He is not a Republican or a Democrat. He is not black or white," referring to the Christian God. "He is the light, and our schools need light in them like never before."[305]

A 2019 law in South Dakota requires all public schools to display the "In God We Trust" motto. Students returning to school that fall were greeted by the message, which supporters say is meant to "inspire patriotism." Governor Kristi Noem signed the law requiring that the message be obviously displayed in all 149 South Dakota school districts on the first day of classes that year.[306]

In 2019, schools across Kentucky were working to fulfill a new state law requiring that the national motto "In God We Trust" be displayed in a noticeable place before classes began. Some school districts put up plaques, while others used artwork in common areas. The law was sponsored by Representative Brandon Reed (R-KY), who said, "The motto is ever-present in society and is prominently displayed in the Kentucky legislature." The American Civil Liberties Union opposed the bill, saying the motto "has the appearance of endorsing religion."

In June 2019, the Supreme Court ruled "that a gigantic Latin cross on government land in Bladensburg, MD, does not have to be moved or altered in the name of church-state separation." The justices reasoned that the forty-foot cross was erected as a World War I memorial, not an endorsement of Christianity.[307]

This assault on our national sensibilities extended beyond religion and targeted our national flag, when the Supreme Court ruled on the issues of *flag burning* and mandatory *participation* in our Pledge of Allegiance.

---

[305] NPR—North Central Florida—*"In God We Trust" to be displayed in public schools*—May 2018

[306] CBS News—*South Dakota will require "In God We Trust" signs in all public schools*—July 2019

[307] *USA Today: Supreme Court Allows Cross on State Land*—June 2019

# UNINTENDED CONSEQUENCE

An initial Supreme Court ruling regarding the US flag came in 1907, where *Halter v. Nebraska* prohibited showing contempt for, or defacing, the flag in any manner. During the Vietnam War, this ruling was reinforced by the Federal Flag Desecration Law, passed in 1968. It banned any display of contempt directed at the flag. However, as liberal efforts escalated between 1968 and 1988, the courts ruled in a series of cases that desecrating a flag was protected under the Constitution as free speech.[308]

In 1989, the US Supreme Court upheld the right of protestors to burn the American flag in *Texas v. Johnson*, citing, "Johnson's actions were symbolic speech, political in nature, and could be expressed even at the expense of our national symbol and to the affront of those who disagreed with him."[309]

Later, the ACLU prevailed in allowing students to "opt out" of reciting the Pledge of Allegiance in public schools.

In 1965, three students in Des Moines, Iowa, wore black armbands to school, in protest of the Vietnam War. After they refused to remove the armbands during the Pledge of Allegiance, they were suspended.

In February 1969, the Supreme Court heard the case *Tinker v. Des Moines Independent Community School District* and ruled that the armbands were an expression of free speech and therefore allowed.[310] Following the Tinker ruling, the ACLU aggressively pursued similar cases in the appeals courts of several states, guaranteeing the rights of students. "The U.S. Supreme Court upheld the right of students to silently protest…remaining seated during the Pledge is a form of silent expression. A student may maintain 'respectful silence' whether seated or standing."[311] The Supreme Court may have signaled that it might be tempering in its position regarding the pledge in school.

In 2004, the Supreme Court heard *Elk Grove Unified School District v. Newdow*, in which the atheist unmarried father of a third-grade schoolgirl objected to his daughter participating in the pledge

---

[308] The Thought Co.—*The History of U.S. Laws Against Flag-Burning*—May 2019
[309] US Supreme Court—*Texas vs. Johnson*—June 1989
[310] *Encyclopedia Britannica—Tinker vs. Des Moines Board of Education*
[311] ACLU—*The Pledge of Allegiance in Washington Public Schools*—June 2012

because it included the phrase "Under God." The child's mother had no issue with her daughter reciting the pledge. The court dismissed the case, ruling that Mr. Newdow lacked standing to present the case, because the mother had legal custody of the child.

However, Justice Rehnquist offered a poignant opinion:

> To give the parent of such a child a sort of "heckler's veto" over a patriotic ceremony willingly participated in by other students, simply because the Pledge of Allegiance contains the descriptive phrase "under God," is an unwarranted extension of the establishment clause, an extension which would have the unfortunate effect of prohibiting a commendable patriotic observance.[312]

As we sit today, the Pledge of Allegiance continues to be recited daily in most public schools. While students have the defined right to opt out, I suspect most do not. I could find no statistic to either support or refute this notion. I conducted an informal, unscientific survey of several teachers, parents, and students from New York, New Jersey, and Florida and found *no occasion* in their experience where students had "opted out."

The anthem, another national ritual, has become the focus of disrespect in the guise of political protest.

During the 1968 Olympics, medal winners raised their black-gloved fist in a black-power salute during the playing of the US national anthem; in 1996, a basketball player for the Denver Nuggets refused to stand for the anthem at the NBA games; in 2016, a quarterback for the San Francisco 49ers refused to stand and took a knee during the playing of the anthem; in 2016, an American woman soccer player knelt during the national anthem before a game between the USA and Thailand; the same player, after winning the Women's World Cup in 2019, decided to kneel during the anthem; in August 2019, one Olympic gold medalist took a knee during the playing of

---
[312] Education Law—Elk Grove Unified School District v. Newdow

the anthem during the award ceremonies at the Pan American Games in Peru; while another raised a clenched-fist, black-power salute.

In October 2016, a youth football team in Beaumont, Texas, decided to take a knee; an eight-year-old St. Louis youth football team decided to kneel during the national anthem in September 2017; in September 2017, members of a private school girls' soccer team in Maine knelt during the anthem before their match; and in 2017, a high school band, after playing the national anthem before a Monday-night Oakland A's baseball game, took a knee.

Were these youthful actions spontaneous or the result of coaches and teachers using those children, in the words of Justice Rehnquist, as "heckler's vetoes"?

Professional athletes are taking a knee during the national anthem at sporting events, and schoolchildren are emulating them. The symbols of our nation have become punchlines on late-night television.

America remains the greatest country in the world in terms of freedom, strength, and opportunity, but it is admittedly flawed historically. Decisions made in the past supporting our economy, security, expansion, and the politics of the era are being viewed in retrospect as misguided. Generals, presidents, and others of historical significance who answered the call of their day, considered statesmen and heroes of their time, are being unceremoniously discarded, like so much trash in a seemingly flawed quest of political correctness.

Let's examine the definition of *politically correct*: "When we speak the truth, we are correct. When we do not speak the truth because it would be politically unacceptable to admit to believing it, we are politically correct."[313]

We cannot erase history: Hitler tried it, Stalin tried it, and Kim Jong-un is trying it. It cannot and should not be attempted.

Mascots, having been tradition for decades or longer, are now declared offensive to small segments of our society—the Washington Redskins, Atlanta Braves, Cleveland Indians. Much of this perceived distress is being rejected by most of the supposedly "offended" parties.

---

[313] National Admissions Test for Law

A *Washington Post* survey conducted in 2016 found that "90% of Native Americans who live outside traditional Indian reservations, and 53% of Indians on reservations, did not find the images discriminatory."[314]

At George Washington University, more than two hundred students signed a petition to rid the school of their mascot because they found "Colonials extremely offensive." The petition states that "the historically, negatively-charged figure of Colonials has too deep a connection to colonization and glorifies the act of systemic oppression."[315]

The Colonials mascot has been around since 1926 and was a tribute to the university's namesake, George Washington. Its original intent was to reference colonial America and the Continental Army. GWU has more than twenty-seven thousand students. Should a minority or two hundred be allowed to prevail? The bias against the university mascot demonstrates the student's mindless propensity to protest on college campuses. Poppycock.

Black students at the University of California-Los Angeles have demanded that they be segregated from white peers, calling for "safe spaces" for students of color on campus. To students that are demanding safe space on campus, I ask, "For whom? From what?"[316] Weren't the Civil Rights Act and Affirmative Action programs intended to eliminate segregation? Do we really want to turn the clock back in the one instance while crying racism in the next? This is foolishness.

Students seem more intrigued with their *right to protest* than they are with their *opportunity to learn*. Perhaps this is just the result of their education being biased by liberal and socialist concepts. Free speech is being suppressed in schools, on college campuses, and in other public forums. It seems that only predominantly liberal views are offered, permitted, or encouraged.

In July 2019, a San Francisco, California, board of education voted to remove an eighty-three-year-old mural adorning walls in a

---

[314] *Washington Post—Poll of Self-Identified Native Americans*—May 2016

[315] *The GW Hatchet—Students launch petition to abandon "offensive" Colonial mascot*—May 2013

[316] *The Washington Post—A group demanded a space for students of color*—March 2017

local high school that is dedicated to the life of George Washington. The 1600-square-foot mural shows white colonists stepping over a dead Native American and slaves laboring at Washington's Mount Vernon home. Their decision was, "It's demeaning. Destroy it."

More than five hundred educators, from California and elsewhere, urged the board members to revisit the decision.

A Stanford University art professor suggested that the mural could help build an understanding of the times if it were built into a lesson program. Rachel DeLue, a Princeton University professor of art history, warned, "If we cover it up and we whitewash it, not only are we doing a disservice to history, but we're also doing a disservice to those who suffered at the hands of European-descended Americans; Slaves and Native Americans who were traumatized and killed."[317]

On the Fourth of July 2019, Nike withdrew a sneaker from the market because the Betsy Ross thirteen-star flag depicted offended Colin Kaepernick. Kaepernick felt that the flag on the shoe represented a time of American slavery.[318] Preposterous! When did any athlete become the arbiter of American morality? Why would a shoe manufacturer override the conclusions of their market research and product development teams to acquiesce to the misguided opinion of a retired, mediocre quarterback?

Students of *nonbinary* sexual orientation are being allowed to choose which bathroom they will use in public schools. How is this not an awkward imposition on the rest of the student body? While these actions cater to small segments of our society, they discriminate against the larger population.

Sadly, America and family have become casualties of this societal reengineering. The family unit that forms an individual's character and personality has been sacrificed to liberal philosophy and the social media. We seem to have abdicated parental guidance in the areas of patriotism, religion, and character to our children's teachers and to our courts.

---

[317] *USA Today—Washington Mural: Historic or Offensive?*—July 2019
[318] *The Washington Post—After Colin Kaepernick complaint, Nike pulls shoe*—July 2019

While prayer may be prohibited in schools and abstaining from reciting the Pledge of Allegiance and the burning of our flag may not be illegal, those acts are considered extreme and are hurtful to most Americans.

An August 2006 Pew Research survey showed that 69 percent of Americans "favor looser, not tighter," limits on religion in public schools. In the same poll, more than two-thirds of Americans agreed that "liberals have gone too far in trying to keep religion out of the schools and the government. And 58% favor teaching biblical creationism along with evolution in public schools."[319]

In 2005, the Pew Research Center conducted a survey in which 83 percent of Americans felt that displays of Christmas symbols should be allowed on government property. In another poll, 74 percent said they believe it is proper to display the Ten Commandments in government buildings.[320]

In a 2008 Pew Research Center poll, about two-thirds of Americans polled said that they fly the American flag, close to 75 percent said flag burning should be illegal, and 50 percent said it should be unconstitutional.[321]

A 2016 Marist poll found that 52 percent of respondents thought failing to stand during the national anthem, regardless of why, is "disrespectful to the freedoms the Anthem represents" and that leagues should require their athletes to stand; 53 percent felt such a display should not be mandated.[322]

Our national history is our national history. It cannot be rewritten to assuage the contemporary sensibilities of the "politically correct," nor can we erase our national disgraces, such as slavery and the oppression of the Native Americans. We must learn from those mistakes, not bury them. Everything in the milieu of political correctness seems intolerant, ironic, and hypocritical. It is time for the

---

[319] Pew Research Center—*Religion in the Public Schools*—May 2007
[320] Pew Research Center—*Religious Displays and the Courts*—June 2007
[321] Pew Research Center—*No Clamor for Amendment from Flag Waving Public*—June 2008
[322] Marist Poll—*Protesting the National Anthem: Disrespectful or Expression of Freedom*—Sept 2016

American people to refocus priorities upon what makes us the same rather than what makes us different. Why do we allow progressives to dictate, to "run the asylum"?

If our Constitution prohibits public prayer, if our Constitution allows the desecration of our flag, if our Constitution encourages disrespect of our anthem, if our Constitution mandates the destruction of historical monuments, then, perhaps, it is time to *amend* our Constitution.

Two visionary, literary figures, one a poet of the United Kingdom and the other a recipient of the Presidential Medal of Freedom, have offered keen insight into the human condition.

Alfred, Lord Tennyson, published his famous *Ulysses* in 1842 and used the aging Ulysses's monologue as a metaphor for the aging British Empire. The final lines reflect what I believe to be the coming trials of our great nation:

> We are now that strength which in old days
> Moved earth and heaven, that which we are, we are:
> One equal temper of heroic hearts,
> Made weak by time and fate, but strong in will
> To strive, to seek, to find, and not to yield.

American literary icon Maya Angelou read her inspirational poem "On the Pulse of Morning" at Bill Clinton's inauguration in 1993 and so eloquently encouraged us to persevere:

> History, despite its wrenching pain,
> Cannot be unlived, and if faced
> With courage, need not be lived again.

Our future is in our own hands; the past need not be prologue.

## Slavery: America's "Original Sin"

In consideration of the magnitude of this topic, I will be devoting an entire chapter to slavery, racism, and reparations. I feel that this subject is also vital to any discussion of our national moral compass and ask that you consider my thoughts from that chapter in this context as well.

## Supreme Court

The Supreme Court of the United States, established by Article III of the US Constitution, first met on February 2, 1790, and heard its first case in 1792. It would take 189 years before the all-male court would more accurately reflect the composition of the nation it presided over, with the advent of the court's first female associate justice.

Sandra Day O'Connor received her undergraduate and law degrees, in 1950 and 1952 respectively, from Stanford University. Upon graduation, as a woman, she was unable to find law firm employment. She was only offered secretarial positions, and O'Connor eventually pursued private practice in Arizona. She had an impressive law and political career, culminating in her appointment to the Arizona Court of Appeals.

Sandra Day O'Connor was the first woman to be nominated to the Supreme Court. Nominated by Republican president Ronald Reagan in 1981, the conservative justice O'Conner was approved unanimously and would become a swing-vote justice.[323] Reagan would go on to appoint three additional justices to the court: William Rehnquist, Antonin Scalia, and Anthony Kennedy.

In its over-two-hundred-year history, only three other women justices have served: Ruth Bader Ginsburg (1993–present); Sonia

---

[323] *Encyclopedia Britannica—Sandra Day O'Connor—United States Jurist*

Sotomayor, the first Hispanic to serve (2009–present); and Elena Kagan (2010–present), each appointed by a Democrat president.[324]

Over time, with the evolution of the court's composition based upon presidential nominations, its bias wafted between liberal and conservative, with each political party fighting aggressively to retain the advantage.

The long history of political infighting goes back as far as the President George Washington administration. But the incivility seems to have begun in 1939, when President Franklin Roosevelt appointed Felix Frankfurter to the court. Frankfurter, a founder of the American Civil Liberties Union, received substantial bipartisan opposition because he was Jewish, extremely liberal, and not American born. He would not be the first Jewish justice. That was Louis Brandeis, appointed by President Woodrow Wilson in 1916. However, Frankfurter was the first nominee to be required to appear before the Senate Judiciary Committee, changing the selection process thereafter.[325]

In 1968, both Republicans and Southern Democrats filibustered and blocked President Lyndon Johnson's recommendation that Justice Abe Fortas be elevated to chief justice.[326]

The partisan-fueled bias began to emerge with the nomination of Robert Bork by President Ronald Reagan, which, if appointed, would have shifted the court to a more conservative majority. Until this point, objections to a nominee were bipartisan, primarily focusing on the *qualifications* of the candidates. However, in 1987, Senator Ted Kennedy (D-MA) would redirect the concern from *qualification* of an individual to *managing the composition* of the court. The Democrats were concerned that too many conservative justices being appointed would hinder liberal legislation, as it had with FDR's New Deal.

Liberal Democrats, led by Senator Ted Kennedy, fearing the shift in the court, initiated an aggressive campaign to block the nom-

---

[324] *Encyclopedia Britannica—Brandeis, Frankfurter, Ginsburg; Sotomayor; Kagan*
[325] *Encyclopedia Britannica—Brandeis, Frankfurter, Ginsburg; Sotomayor; Kagan*
[326] CBS News—*The long history of political fights over Supreme Court Seats*—April 2017

ination. Kennedy took to the Senate floor and challenged, "Robert Bork's America is a land in which women would be forced into back-alley abortions, Blacks would sit at segregated lunch counters, rogue police could break down citizens' doors in midnight raids, [and] schoolchildren could not be taught about evolution." Kennedy's scare tactics, while demonstrably fallacious, successfully convinced a Democrat-controlled Senate to reject Bork's nomination by a 58–42 vote.

In the course of this philosophical assassination, "a new verb was born, 'Borking' judicial nominees, vigorously questioning their legal philosophy and political views to derail their nomination."[327]

In 1990, President George W. Bush nominated Clarence Thomas to be an associate justice on the Supreme Court. Initially, the hearings lasted three days and concentrated on the nominee's legal philosophy and judicial experience.

During the Thomas hearings leading into 1991, the "Borking" strategy was expanded to encompass sexual accusations. Senator Ted Kennedy (D-MA) was advised of rumors relating to Thomas sexually harassing women that had worked for him, and he insisted that the committee chairman, Senator Joe Biden (D-MD), investigate further. The alleged victim, Anita Hill, chose not to testify. Biden was reluctant and warned his colleagues, "I believe there are certain things that are not at issue at all…and that is his character.…This is about what he believes. I know my colleagues, and I urge everyone else to refrain from personalizing this battle."

After *NPR* broke the Anita Hill story on October 6, Hill agreed to testify. The Thomas hearings took on ugly sexual, racist overtones with Hill and Thomas, two Yale Law School graduates from poor rural backgrounds, sparring about sexual intimidation that was alleged to have occurred when Hill worked with Thomas. Democrats violated their promises to Hill "that only the committee would investigate the allegation and that the charges would be kept confidential." Instead, Democrats engaged the FBI to investigate the matter

---

[327] History.com—*How Robert Bork's Failed Nomination Led to a Changed… Court*—October 2018

and forced the televised hearings in which there was sexually explicit testimony, while the world was watching. Biden opened the hearings.

> Professor Hill made two requests to this committee. First, that the committee investigate the charges and, second, that the charges remain confidential. I believe we have honored both her requests, but the landscape has changed, and we are thus here today, free from the restrictions, which had previously limited our work.[328]

(As a point of interest, the Democrats would use a similar strategy twenty-seven years later, violating the trust of Dr. Christine Blasey Ford in the Kavanaugh hearings.)

The Republicans on the committee responded "with a vengeance," resorting to attempts at Hill's character assassination. In the end, Anita Hill was humiliated. Clarence Thomas called the exercise "a national disgrace…a high-tech lynching for uppity blacks who in any way design to think for themselves." Clarence Thomas was confirmed 52–48, the narrowest margin in more than a century.[329]

The animus between the political parties escalated thereafter, disappointing many that might have believed the Thomas-Hill debacle to be definitive low point in decorum.

In 2016, President Barack Obama nominated Merrick Garland to the Supreme Court, but the Republican-controlled Senate refused to schedule a hearing, citing a long-held practice of not allowing a "lame-duck" president to fill the court.

In 2017, President Donald Trump nominated Neil Gorsuch to the court. Democrats filibustered the nomination, until the Senate majority leader broke the filibuster by changing the Senate rule from a sixty-vote requirement to end the filibuster to a simple majority.

---

[328] NPR—*A Timeline of Clarence Thomas—Anita Hill Controversy*—September 2018
[329] NPR—*A Timeline of Clarence Thomas—Anita Hill Controversy*—September 2018

Gorsuch was confirmed with a 54–45 vote. Three Democrats voted for him.[330]

In 2018, President Trump nominated conservative judge Brett Kavanaugh to the Supreme Court; the confirmation hearing was emotional, contentious, and dramatic. The vitriol reached unimaginable proportions during the hearing to appoint him.

Christine Ford made allegations that Kavanaugh sexually assaulted her more than thirty years earlier, while they were students in high school. Ford had been promised by Democrats that her testimony would remain confidential. Senator Dianne Feinstein (D-CA) violated that confidence. Someone else accused Kavanaugh of organizing a series of gang-rape parties. Kavanaugh denied the accusations.

Senator Jeff Flake (R-AZ) sided with the Democrats and held up the hearings to afford the FBI an opportunity to investigate the allegations. Neither of the allegations could be corroborated by the FBI based upon what I would suggest was a *highly motivated* FBI search.

During the hearings, partisan politics crushed common decency, a low point in American politics. Democrats used this public hearing to ravage the nominee, in hopes of blocking his nomination. The brutality and insipidness of the senators' questioning was nothing short of cruel, attesting to just how far fundamental civility had fallen. The theatrics of the Democrats violated Dr. Ford's trust and demonstrated on live television how inept and uncompassionate our politicians could be. The Kavanaugh hearings were not an attempt to investigate the character and qualifications of the nominee; they were nothing less than an effort at character assassination. Kavanaugh was confirmed by a vote of 50–48.

Time and cultural standards change, but we seemed to have lost our humanity, our civility in this process. All because of the mandate of political party.

---

[330] CBS News—*The long history of political fights over Supreme Court Seats*—April 2017

# UNINTENDED CONSEQUENCE

In August 2019, Senator Sheldon Whitehouse (D-RI) sent a brief to the Supreme Court warning that the court should not hear a case involving a New York City gun control law. Senator Whitehouse suggested that the court's Republican-appointed majority was too tainted to deliver a valid ruling. Whitehouse argued that the court had become too partisan and has produced too many ideologically divided rulings, damaging the public's trust in the federal judiciary. He warned of looming changes the political branches could force on the court should it fail to show restraint:

> The Supreme Court is not well. And the people know it, perhaps the court can heal itself before the public demands it be "restructured" in order to reduce the influence of politics, a nation desperately needs it to heal.[331]

I wonder where the senator's expression of concern was when a myriad of rulings was passed from the predominantly liberally biased court over the past decade. This was a blatant attack on judicial independence. Politics over justice. Subsequently, Judicial Watch submitted a complaint to the Bar Association charging Whitehouse with "threatening the Supreme Court."[332]

There have been times in our history when the composition of the court, specifically the appropriate number of justices, had been questioned. Most notable by President Franklin Delano Roosevelt in 1936.

During the Great Depression, President Roosevelt was pushing through the New Deal legislation, and beginning in May 1935, the Supreme Court began to strike down a number of those laws, overturning more pieces of legislation than at any other time in US history. To combat these setbacks, FDR planned to add five additional justices to the court. His plan was met with instant opposition

---

[331] *The Washington Post—Republican Senators tell Supreme Court not to be "cowed" by Democrat Senators*—August 2019

[332] *The National Sentinel—Sen. Sheldon Whitehouse Hit with Bar Complaint*—August 2019

and was recognized as the blatant power grab that it was. President Roosevelt had badly miscalculated national reverence for the court and its independence and eventually abandoned the idea.[333]

A 1937 political cartoon with the caption "Do we want a ventriloquist act in the Supreme Court?"

Several 2020 Democratic presidential hopefuls have already suggested that they would propose expanding the Supreme Court to as many as fifteen justices if they are to win the White House. Their intent would be to fill those seats with liberal members to counter the current conservative 5–4 majority on the court. Would this not be another "blatant power grab"?

This contemporary idea of packing the court was rejected by Justice Ruth Bader Ginsburg, its most senior liberal member. "Nine seems to be a good number, and it's been that way for a long time," Justice Ginsburg said in an interview with NPR.[334]

Most cases submitted to the Supreme Court are inspired by or initiated with the American Civil Liberties Union. The ACLU

---

[333] History—*This is How FDR Tried to Pack the Supreme Court*—October 2018
[334] *The Washington Times*—Democrats warn Supreme Court it's too unhealthy…— August 2019

was founded in 1920. Its stated mission is "to defend and preserve the individual rights and liberties guaranteed to every person in this country by the Constitution and laws of the United States." It is "officially non-partisan."[335]

Anyone following the activities of the ACLU would agree that it has become militantly liberally biased, pursuing the most extreme interpretations of the Constitution, seemingly mocking it rather than revering it. It has served as the catalyst of legal aggression against most of the American population and in favor of splinter minority groups.

The America I grew up in appears to have been forfeit in the name of "liberal progress." In an antiutilitarian sense, we have placed the need of the few over the good of the majority.

The moral and social fabric of America has been worn thin, perhaps torn; decadence in our society has emerged, and our individual and often collective vices, self-absorption, ignorance, and arrogance sometimes draw us toward ignoble behavior.

Court decisions should be neither liberal nor conservative; they should be reasonable, moderate, and they should consider the longer-term impact on all Americans. Decisions made by the court have far-reaching and long-lasting consequence. One can count the number of seeds in an apple, but it is impossible to count the number of apples in a seed. So it is with court decisions, each seemingly noble at first, but many are ultimately destructive to society due to unintended consequences.

Democrats have expanded the strategy of impeachment beyond President Trump to reshape the court. Liberals have moved to solicit support to impeach conservative justices Kavanaugh and Thomas.[336], [337]

Our government is structured with three equal but separate branches: the executive, the legislative, and the judicial. This system was designed by our forefather visionaries to provide balance of power

---

[335] American Civil Liberties Union
[336] *Newsweek: Impeach Brett Kavanaugh*—October 2018
[337] *Newsweek: The Case to Impeach Supreme Court Justice*—February 2018

within our government and to cross-check between the branches. No single branch would be superior. We cannot allow political party or philosophy to disrupt that balance. We must preserve that construct and circumstance. Blatant attacks on judicial independence must not be tolerated.

## Technology and Incivility

> *We are losing sight of civility in government and politics. Debate and dialogue are taking a back seat to the politics of destruction and anger and control. Dogma has replaced thoughtful discussion between people of differing views.*
>
> —James McGreevey, New Jersey governor

> *More than one-half of Americans (54%) expect the general tone and level of civility in the country to decline even further during the next few years. Among this group, 57% believe that the Internet and/or social media are to blame—a factor that tops a list of nineteen possible choices measured this year. The impact of incivility on our politics is significant. A majority believes that incivility leads to political gridlock (73%), less political involvement (71%) and fewer people running for public office (61%).*
>
> —KRC Research[338]

Technology has presented a double-edged sword to society. It provides powerful tools and capabilities that can be used for good or evil: instant communication, fingertip availability of information and knowledge, and platforms to broadcast personal views and opinions to potentially limitless audiences. Unfortunately, computer

---

[338] Weber Shandwick-Powell Tate—KRC Research: *Civility in America 2019*

games and social networking have also created the opportunity to undermine our core values, our mores, and our civility. It enables anyone to become an antagonistic, nameless, faceless bully.

Facebook was in vogue, a social imperative, when launched in 2004. Now when combined with Twitter, Instagram, and Snapchat, they have power and influence that have become destructive. They have spawned the "social media mob" phenomenon, where participation is unaccountable, leaving contributors without any personal responsibility.

The combination of website technology with contemporary music and film allows, endorses, and even encourages vulgarity and viciousness. They have all fed a youthful culture that celebrates violence and has become desensitized to their own mortality. They have conditioned our youth to believe that death can be undone simply by hitting the Restart button. It would be intellectually dishonest to deny that these influences have contributed to the rash of suicides and mass shootings over the past two decades. While there may be an absence of specific data to support such a claim, empirical observation would.

Technology has enabled and prompted a society of self-absorbed narcissists. A recent column in my local newspaper summed it up succinctly:

> But enough about me, let's talk about me. While we are at it, let's post about me, text about me, Snapchat about me. The "selfie" generation may not be more self-absorbed than any other, but they sure have more platforms on which to love themselves.[339]

In her book *The Power of Off*, Nancy Colier observes, "We are spending far too much of our time doing things that don't really matter to us, disconnected from what really matters, from what makes us feel nourished and grounded as human beings. It's connections to other human beings—real-life connections, not digital ones—that

---

[339] *The Record—Selfie Museum pops up in Paramus—*August 2019

nourish us and make us feel like we count. Our presence, our full attention is the most important thing we can give each other. Digital communications don't result in deeper connections, in feeling loved and supported."[340]

We have become addicted to these devices. In a restaurant, at a ball game, on the street, or in a supermarket, and you will observe people obsessing over their electronic apparatus, oblivious to all around them. Children at school, at the dinner table, or on the playground seem chained to them. They text, not talk, and make eye contact with a device, not a person, denying themselves the opportunity to develop essential interpersonal skills. Today's technology has adversely influenced our attention span and ability to focus, making us lazy and distracted. Smartphones and iPads are replacing books and newspapers, where circulation per capita has declined from 35 percent in the mid-1940s to under 15 percent today.[341]

Kindle and Nook are replacing hardcover and paperback books, with sales of adult fiction dropping 16 percent since 2013, almost a billion-dollar decline.[342] We are casting the joy of the weight of a hardcover book in our hand, the sensation of turning the page, the inconvenience of newspaper ink smudging our fingertips onto the junk heap of obsolescence created by technology.

The introduction of smartphones seems to be converting our society into collective robots. This detachment encouraged by technology over the decades has persuaded us to become a much less civil society. Behavior that would have been considered unacceptable thirty years ago is now the new normal.

Parents teach their children these new standards by example; film and music reinforce racism, violence, and misogyny, while government and educators emphasize nonbinary relationships.

President Trump lowered the bar dramatically during the 2016 presidential campaign and after with his barrage of name-calling and unproven accusations. He has stirred incivility with his incessant use

---

[340] *The Seattle Times—How smartphone addiction is affecting our physical…health—*January 2017
[341] Wikipedia—Network and media audience
[342] *The New York Times—The Last Great American Novelist—*August 2019

of Twitter, mocking, belittling, and criticizing. The combination of President Trump's conduct and the social network has been devastating to our notion of respect. His proclivity to tweet his opinion on issues unrelated to the presidency creates distraction and exacerbates the condition. In this regard, he has harmed the Office of the Presidency and the social attitude of the nation.

Democrat senators established a new low in personal and social decorum during the Kavanaugh hearings for his Supreme Court nomination. The degree of rancor and venom displayed in that forum was unprecedented.

Pause and imagine the potential misinterpretation thirty years hence of some of your own social media posts, or yearbook remarks, written primarily to impress peers and feed our own personal narcissism. Comments made, often as adolescents, may be considered "cringe worthy" in an "adult" tomorrow.

Technology has expanded our audience to incite. Our absence of decorum seems to have no boundary.

- In June 2018, Representative Maxine Waters (D-CA) told a crowd "If you see a member of Trump Cabinet, push back....Let's make sure we show up wherever we have to show up. And if you see anybody from that Cabinet in a restaurant, in a department store, at a gasoline station, you get out and you create a crowd. And you push back on them. And you tell them they're not welcome anymore, anywhere."[343]
- In June 2018, a diner called other activists, alerting them that Kirstjen Nielsen, secretary of homeland security, was having dinner in the restaurant. The activists used social media to organize a crowd, a "social media mob," who rushed to the scene, chanting, "If kids don't eat in peace, you don't eat in peace!" Nielsen was essentially shamed out of the restaurant.[344]

---

[343] *Time Magazine—"They're not Welcome Anymore"*—June 2018
[344] *The New York Times—Kirstjen Nielsen Confronted by Protesters*—June 2018

- The proprietor of a northern Virginia restaurant asked White House Press Secretary Sarah Huckabee Sanders to leave in June 2018.[345]
- Antifa protestors surrounded Charlie Kirk, Turning Point USA's founder and president, and Candace Owens, who works as the organization's communications director, as they left a restaurant. One protester poured water over the heads of Kirk and Owens in August 2018.[346]
- In October 2018, Senate Majority Leader Mitch McConnel and his wife, labor secretary Elaine Chao, were confronted in a restaurant. Someone came off the street, grabbed their dinner, went out the front door, and threw it on the ground. He came back in and got into a back-and-forth with Secretary Chao. The unidentified man was shouted down by customers before leaving the restaurant.[347]
- In June 2019, an unidentified waitress spit at President Trump's son Eric in a Chicago cocktail bar.[348]

Has there been no journalistic curiosity to identify the perpetrators of these acts of incivility because the victims were conservative or Republican? It is just another demonstration of media bias. How did this behavior become acceptable?

- A riot was narrowly averted in Portland, Oregon, in late August 2019 when the entire one-thousand-member Portland Police Department was activated to thwart an inevitable conflict between the "flag-waving" far-right group Proud Boys and Antifa. Associated Press reported, "As of early afternoon, most of the right-wing groups had left the area via a downtown bridge. Police used officers on bikes and in riot gear to keep black-clad, helmet- and

---

[345] *USA Today—Sarah Huckabee Sanders booted from Red Hen*—June 2018
[346] *Village Voice—ANTIFA Protestors Confront Conservatives Charlie Kirk*—August 2018
[347] *The Washington Post—Mitch McConnel confronted in Louisville restaurant*—July 2018
[348] *The Washington Post: June 26, 2019*

mask-wearing anti-fascist protesters—known as Antifa—from following them."

One can only conclude, in this instance, that Antifa was the aggressor in attempting to incite conflict. However, that was not the way most media reported it.[349]

- In July 2019, *Newsweek* magazine ran an opinion piece, suggesting that Antifa "was less frightening than a golden retriever." What an absurd premise! Show me a retriever that harasses private citizens, conservatives, and journalists. The writer attempted to minimize the uncivil conduct and rationalize Antifa's behavior. This stretch of reasoning is intellectually dishonest and demonstrates the extent to which media will go to justify violence that is not directed at liberals.[350]
- In the summer of 2019, a spate of incidents occurred in New York City, where NYPD policemen were attacked, doused with water, or targeted with projectiles. Each incident was captured on videotape and went viral on social media.[351]

Is there no end to manufactured social outrage? Has our society reverted to being Neanderthal? Have we become unable to suppress an impulse? What lesson does this conduct teach our children?

Technology has expanded our audience to accuse. We are now witnessing the ever-present charges of racism, an extremely serious accusation, rapidly becoming a hackneyed Democrat trope.

There is only one intellectually honest debate tactic: pointing out errors or omissions in your opponent's facts or your opponent's logic. Sadly, it seems that when Democrats lack an intellectually sound rejoinder, they default to "racism."

---

[349] *Associated Press—Arrests and shields, metal poles, were seized at Portland protest—*August 2019
[350] Newsweek—*Ban Antifa? I've Met Golden Retrievers Who Scared Me More*—July 2019
[351] *The Daily News—Groups of jeering men douse NYPD cops*—July 2019

At the risk of being accused a Trump apologist, although I believe that I have demonstrated that I am not, I feel it necessary to distinguish between *reason* and *racism*. The allegation of President Trump being a racist is anchored more in opinion than fact. Trump is a street fighter, counterpuncher. He is often insensitive and chooses imprudent words, allowing him to be viewed at times as a tactless social moron. Let us coolly examine the actual record with less bias.

- Between 2011 and 2015, Donald Trump joined 20 percent of Americans in questioning if President Barack Obama was an American citizen. Trump was accused of racism against the first black president, and while Trump's claim was foolhardy, it was not seeded in racism. There was, and continues to be, an uncommon dearth of information available on President Obama's youth, education, or personal life prior to his becoming a political activist and community organizer. No tell-all from a college lover, no memoir from a childhood friend, either of which could easily have become a national best seller, generating millions of dollars for its author. This scarcity of Obama's personal history feeds the conspiracy theory. Trump's preoccupation was more curious than racist.[352]
- In 2016, Candidate Trump suggested that Judge Gonzalo Curiel might not be impartial in ruling on a case involving Trump University because of Curiel's Mexican heritage and Trump's opposition to weak immigration policies and his commitment to "building a wall." Trump was accused of racism. Counterpuncher, yes. Racism? I think not.[353]
- In 2016, Candidate Trump opined on Colin Kaepernick's refusal to stand for our national anthem prior to a National Football League game: "I have followed it and I think it's personally not a good thing, I think it's a terrible thing, and you know, maybe he should find a country that works

---

[352] *The New York Times—Donald Trump Clung to 'Birther Lie'—*September 2016
[353] *The Atlantic—Trump Attacks a 'Mexican' U.S. Federal Judge—May* 2016

better for him." Trump was called a racist, yet his comment had nothing to do with the color of Kaepernick's skin. It was in response to Kaepernick disrespecting our flag and national anthem. Perhaps a patriotic opinion, but not racist.[354]

- In 2017, President Trump proposed a travel ban on migrants from six predominantly Muslim countries. Democrats immediately cried "racism" and "anti-Muslim xenophobia" when, in fact, his intent was in the interest of national security. Trump was targeting immigrants from countries that were hotbeds of terrorism, not because they were Muslim, but because there was a serious security concern. Trump's proposal was in defense of our country, not racist. Had his proposal precluded *anyone* from *any* Muslim-majority country, that would have been racism, but it did not.[355]
- After the civil unrest in Charlottesville, Virginia, during August of 2017, President Trump commented, "We condemn in the strongest possible terms this egregious display of hatred, bigotry and violence, on many sides." The media, Democrats, and some Republicans ranted "white nationalism" and "racism," slicing, dicing, and parsing the words "on many sides."[356]

While it might not support the biased narrative of the media, a more reasonable response to Trump's comments might have been to acknowledge that there were *two groups*: protesters and counterprotesters. The protesters were the right-wing groups that organized the rally, and the counterprotesters were the far-left groups like Antifa and racial justice activists that opposed the rally, with each contributing to the disorder, death, and destruction. I believe an honest interpretation of the president's intended meaning of "On many sides"

---

[354] *Sports Illustrated*—Donald Trump: Colin Kaepernick should find another country—August 2016

[355] *The New York Times—Trump's New Travel Ban Blocks Migrants*—June 2017

[356] CNN News—*Donald Trump's incredibly unpresidential statement on Charlottesville*—August 2017

would be that all sides were wrong. This was media-manufactured racism.[357]

Incidentally, Virginia's Democrat governor Terry McAuliffe said of the demonstrators, "Let's be honest, they need to leave America, because they are not Americans." Where was the media outrage regarding McAuliffe's comment?[358]

- In July 2019, President Trump lashed out at Representative Cummings (D-MD) in a tweet: "Rep. Elijah Cummings has been a brutal bully, shouting and screaming at the great men and women of Border Patrol about conditions at the Southern Border, when actually his Baltimore district is FAR WORSE and more dangerous. His district is considered the Worst in the USA." Trump was called a racist.

Trump was defending the men and women of the Border Patrol after the way Representative Cummings, grandstanding for television and political purpose, savagely treated those officials during his congressional hearing. Trump criticized Cummings's *conduct*, not his *color*. The charge of racism was reckless.[359]

- In July 2019, President Trump criticized four congressional representatives, "women of color," that had made public statements viewed by many as anti-American and anti-Semitic; he suggested that they leave the country, and he was widely criticized as a racist. Admittedly, Trump could have used more elegant words. I believe the concept of "love it or leave it," made popular during the Vietnam War, was the essence of his meaning.

His poor choice of words gave the liberals a cudgel to beat him with accusations of racism. A more impartial assessment could con-

---

[357] *The New York Times—Who Were the Counter protesters in Charlottesville?*
[358] *CNN News—Virginia governor on white nationalists: They should leave America—*August 2017
[359] *USA Today—Trump attacks Elijah Cummings Baltimore district—*July 2019

clude that he was reacting to their unpatriotic comments and conduct, not the color of their skin or gender.[360]

I believe that the president was making this point: if you are so unhappy with the United States, you are welcome to leave.

President Kennedy inferred a similar message:

> I do not believe that any of us would exchange places with any other people or any other generation. The energy, the faith, the devotion which we bring to this endeavor will light our country and all who serve it. (President John F. Kennedy's inaugural address, January 1961)

Conversely, if we fail to bring "*faith* [and] *devotion…to this endeavor*," we will surely continue the slide into the oblivion of disdain and rancor.

How valid are the endless charges of racism? Again, we revisit the question, Should we measure someone's intent more by their *words* or *deeds*?

The Trump administration accomplishments directed toward minorities, which have doubled his support in the black community to 29 percent, include these six: black and Hispanic unemployment are at record lows, there has been a significant increase in black business ownership, youth unemployment is at a fifty-two-year low, he enacted opioid restriction laws, he signed the Criminal Reform Act, and he signed an executive order creating a national historic park for Martin Luther King Jr.[361]

In the words of Fox television personality Greg Gutfeld, "If Trump is a racist, he sucks at it."

One might think that President Trump would anticipate the media and the political left parsing his words and become more introspective and anticipatory.

---

[360] *The Atlantic—Trumps White-Nationalist Attack on Four Congresswomen*—July 2019
[361] *Washington Examiner—Medias Blackout: Trump's 60-point accomplishment list*—June 2018

> Civility means a great deal more than just being nice to one another. It is complex and encompasses learning how to connect successfully and live well with others, developing thoughtfulness, and fostering effective self-expression and communication. Civility includes courtesy, politeness, mutual respect, fairness, and good manners. Taking an active interest in the well-being of our community and concern for the health of our society is also involved in civility. (P. M. Forni, educator and author)

What factors or conditions have allowed our technological advancements to lead to the unintended consequence of aggressive incivility?

Parents, or the single parent, seem to have relinquished their child-nurturing responsibilities to schoolteachers, video games, and childhood peers. Political vitriol seems to be the consequence of antagonistic commitment to party over country. Legislators appear to be concentrating on what divides us rather than what unites us. Common sense has seemingly been abdicated for mob rule.

What must be done to encourage more civility in our society? Where are the parents? *Parents* must reassume their role in child-rearing. *Politicians* and *citizens* must reclaim "America first" and abandon the "party-first" philosophy. *Legislators* must allow more consideration toward the impact of legislation's implication upon the majority population.

We cannot be playing a game measured by political party wins or losses; rather, it is the consequence upon our nation that is in balance. It is no game.

We no longer live in a world of simple solutions. Should we legislate "curbs" on social networking companies? Would social rancor be less pervasive without Twitter? Has the absence of stricter censorship over film and music led to the erosion of the ethical fabric of our youth and of our society? Or are these just the unavoidable costs of free speech? These are the questions our politicians and legislators should be addressing, rather than their pointless pursuit of impeachment.

We must return to a time when we speak *to* each other, not *at* each other. We must put down our electronic devices and engage in real conversation, must show some consideration for those with opinions differing from our own, and must try to understand their perspectives. Do unto others. We must be better than this. Be courteous to others. Attack ideas, not people.

There is hope, but it requires reason, compassion, and understanding.

> It has become appallingly obvious that our technology has exceeded our humanity. (Albert Einstein)

## The Sexual Revolution

As we begin this subchapter, I will concede that I am writing this from the perspective of a man, a husband, and a father of two children, one son and one daughter.

In a similar context, it is also important to acknowledge that I view the sexual revolution as distinct and separate from the feminist movement. The sexual revolution challenged traditional codes of behavior related to sexuality and interpersonal relationships, whereas the feminist movement was intended to advance the political, economic, and social equality of the sexes; some might reasonably view the latter as being of greater importance.

Please remember we are focusing on the sexual revolution here, not feminism.

The liberal activism of the 1960s has encouraged the ongoing erosion of social conduct, seen vividly in today's attitude, dress, and comportment. This has been especially harmful to our young ladies. Today, many parents seem indifferent as to how their daughters provocatively dress. Parents seem to be competing to demonstrate who is most "liberated," through their children.

Yesterday's role models for young women, usually depicted in film, were discreet, sensible, demure, considerate, well-mannered, and poised: Elizabeth Taylor in *National Velvet*, Doris Day in *Pillow Talk*, Debbie Reynolds in the *Tammy* series, Sandra Dee in *Gidget*, and Audrey Hepburn in *Breakfast at Tiffany's*.

Today's role models for young women are derived more from music, music videos, and television rather than film. They are provocative, unrealistic, bold, inconsiderate, impolite, and insecure: Madonna, Miley Cyrus, Ariana Grande, and the Kardashians.

The media overwhelms us with sexual messages in music, movies, TV shows, and advertising.

In Ward, Day, and Epstein's 2006 book *Uncommonly Good*, they suggest that adolescent initiation with sexuality is related to exposure:

> The messages conveyed about sexuality (in the media) are not always ideal…and they are often limited, unrealistic, and stereotypical. Dominating is a recreational orientation to sexuality in which courtship is treated as a competition, a battle of the sexes, characterized by dishonesty, game playing, and manipulation.…Also prominent are stereotypical sexual roles featuring women as sexual objects, whose value is based solely on their physical appearance, and men as sex-driven players looking to 'score' at all cost.[362]

Most people agree that today's young lasses are more sexualized than ever. Does this serve societal progress or enlightenment? Have these revisions to societal norms created unwarranted social pressure upon them, encouraging, even demanding, sexual activity at much earlier ages? What was once considered perverse has become acceptable. What magic, mystery, and innocence have our children sacrificed to achieve this liberal agenda?

---

[362] *Uncommonly Good*—Ward, Day and Epstein—2006

A 1999 survey of students indicated that 40 percent of ninth graders across the United States report having had sexual intercourse.[363] I was unable to find a comparative statistic for 1959; however, I am confident that it would be pointedly lower.

While the content of Sharlene Azam's 2009 book *Oral Sex Is the New Good Night Kiss* has been challenged by Dr. Tina Read, who holds a PhD in human sexuality from the unaccredited San Francisco, California, Institute for Advanced Study of Human Sexuality, the mere existence of such a writing should be confounding.[364]

This social movement challenged the traditional norms related to sexuality. Since its advent, we have seen increased acceptance of, and even encouragement for, premarital sex, homosexuality, and alternative forms of sexuality.

Were our children emotionally better off and better protected yesterday or today? Where has this revolution taken us?

During the 1960s and 1970s, the sexual revolution cultivated promiscuity, stifled accountability and responsibility, and contributed to countless single-parent families. On July 27, 2013, CNN anchor Don Lemon reported that 72 percent of African American births are out of wedlock. This was confirmed in a *National Review* article.[365] The sexual revolution lowered the bar of acceptable standards, mores, and norms. An argument could be made that this repositioning contributed to the predatory conduct that seems so prevalent today. If someone leaves money lying in open public places, isn't the act of theft being encouraged? What response does provocative dress engender?

Is there a cause-and-effect relationship between yesterday's sexual revolution and today's attitude toward promiscuity? Are we intentionally attempting to bring our society to the level of depravity depicted in the biblical story of Sodom and Gomorrah?

---

[363] *Child and Adolescent Development for Educators*—Judith Meece—2008
[364] SMS Nonfiction Book Reviews—*Oral Sex is the New Good Night Kiss*—April 2010
[365] SMS Nonfiction Book Reviews—*Oral Sex is the New Good Night Kiss*—April 2010

Since that revision to our mores, America has experienced a series of widely publicized sexual assault allegations, each ultimately proven to be a hoax:

- In 1987, Tawana Brawley, a fifteen-year-old African American woman from New York, falsely accused four white men of raping her. The charges received widespread attention because of her age and the persons accused, including police officers and a prosecuting attorney. Brawley's adviser, racial agitator Al Sharpton, gave the case national prominence. Ms. Brawley alleged that she was raped and left in a trash bag with racial slurs written on her body and covered in feces. A grand jury, hearing the evidence, concluded that Brawley had not been the victim of a forcible sexual assault and that she herself might have created the appearance of such an attack.[366]
- In March 2006, Crystal Mangum, a black student at North Carolina Central University who worked as a stripper, escort, and dancer, accused three white Duke University lacrosse team players of raping her at a party hosted by the school's lacrosse team. Her attorney suggested that the alleged rape was a hate crime. Al Sharpton injected himself into this case as well.

    In *anticipation* of the investigation, Duke University suspended the lacrosse team for two games, forced the lacrosse coach to resign, and then canceled the remainder of the 2006 season.

    The following year, the North Carolina attorney general dropped all charges, declaring the three lacrosse players "innocent" and victims of a "tragic rush to accuse."[367]
- In 2013, Morgan Triplett, twenty, visited the University of California–Santa Cruz for a lesbian, gay, bisexual, and transgender conference. While there, she claimed that she

---

[366] *New York Times -Tawana Brawley Hoax*—October 1988
[367] *The Federalist—Fantastic Lies*—March 2016

had been raped in broad daylight on the Santa Cruz campus. Triplett's story was a hoax. The bizarre truth is that she used Craigslist to locate a stranger who agreed to "punch, kick, and bruise her" in exchange for sex. In another advertisement, she sought somebody to "shoot her in the shoulder."[368]

- In 2017, Sabrina Erdely, a writer for the *Rolling Stone* magazine, asserted that five members of the Phi Kappa Psi fraternity gang-raped a freshman named Jackie at a frat house party, then left her in a bloodstained dress. *The Washington Post* reported both that Jackie fabricated much of her rape tale and that Erdely failed to properly investigate it.[369]

These fraudulent accusations only inspire a degree of suspicion toward future claims of abuse, harassment, and rape. The power and impact of actual crimes are diminished and often met with disbelief.

Has the sexual revolution, its erosion of style and of acceptable social behavior, encouraged the contemporary torrent of harassment activity? Clearly, there are boundaries that are being breeched. The mantra of "They should be believed" pronounced when accusers come forward is weakened by those fraudulent sex and racist allegations. When these scandals are reported, liberal politicians seemed to be in lockstep, proclaiming that "women should be believed." I recognize that all sexual abuse allegations should be heard; most have merit and prove true. Accusers should be heard, but evidence should be believed. Imagine the *falsely accused* being your son, father, or husband.

Newton's third law of physics, as I remember, suggested that "for every action there is an equal and opposite reaction." The Me Too movement may well be the *equal* and *opposite* reaction to the sexual revolution, and perhaps its unintended consequence.

---

[368] *City on A Hill Press -Rape Hoax Reaches Conclusion*—February 2013
[369] *Washington Post—The Full Demise of Rolling Stone's Rape Story*—December 2014

Activist Tarana Burke started the Me Too movement in 2006, encouraging women to show solidarity with one another, specifically when it came to sexual harassment.

The Me Too movement went viral in 2017 when actress Alyssa Milano used it in support of Rose McGowan's allegations of sexual harassment against Harvey Weinstein. Since that time, numerous celebrities, business executives, and politicians have been exposed as predators.[370]

In 2018, Democrats exploited the power of the Me Too movement in their attempt to undermine the Brett Kavanaugh nomination to the Supreme Court. The hearing became a tortured application of the movement's purpose, providing another example of a noble objective poisoned for purely political advantage.

The height of liberal hypocrisy was demonstrated when Senator Ted Kennedy (D-MA), of Chappaquiddick fame, died. The city of Washington, DC, shut down for his funeral. Where were the liberals' or, for that matter, our nation's moral outrage? Had the death of Mary Jo Kopechne been dismissed or forgotten? Was this not a convenient double standard expressed by the media and liberals because Kennedy was a Democrat?

The culmination of our societal indifference, complicity, and moral corruption was evidenced with the 2019 revelation of the poster child of perversion, Jeffery Epstein.

He objectified young girls, stole their innocence, and cheated them of their childhood for the pleasure of a reportedly wide catalog of public personalities, including politicians, celebrities, business executives, and royalty. Yet with Epstein's suicide, pursuit of his alleged co-conspirators has been forgotten. Had the alleged co-conspirators been conservatives or Republicans, I can assure you that the investigation and revelation would have continued.[371]

It has been reported that the US House of Representatives disbursed between $12 and $17 million to settle harassment charges against their members. Representative Jackie Speier (D-CA) told

---

[370] CBS News Report—*Rose McGowan on Alyssa Milano*—January 2018
[371] *Vanity Fair*—"*The Girls Were Just So Young*"—*The Horrors of Jeffery Epstein*—July 2019

# UNINTENDED CONSEQUENCE

MSNBC that the millions have been doled out to alleged victims of harassment from congressional members over the past decade. "There is about $15 million that has been paid out by the House on behalf of harassers in the last ten to fifteen years." The identities of lawmakers or their aides who reach misconduct settlements aren't disclosed.[372] Don't you find it strange that the perpetrators have never been identified and that there has been no evidence of journalistic curiosity regarding them? Another example of political party over justice.

So what has been gained? Was rampant promiscuity the goal of the sexual revolution or the unintended consequence? Either way, we have reengineered gender relationships from the ground up, and our society appears to have suffered. Were the burning of bras, the protests, and the sacrificing of a standard of acceptable social behavior worth what has been achieved in terms of feminine sexual equality? Was the price of youthful innocence worthy of the outcome?

It would seem to me that American women have had their "sexual revolution," and they have lost. I, for one, still believe in chivalry and miss the wistfulness of putting women on a pedestal. Call me a romantic.

In the most recent 2018 rendition of *A Star Is Born*, Lady Gaga and Bradley Cooper posed the lyrical question that I humbly posit today:

> Tell me somethin', girl,
> Are you happy in this modern world?
> Or do you need more?
> Is there somethin' else you're searchin' for?

Just askin'.

The sexual revolution is a perfect example of a perhaps noble concept distorted by extremes. The eventual consequence of which was unforeseen and, I pray, unintended.

---

[372] Politico—*Congress' sexual harassment system, decoded*—November 2017

## Voting Rights

The Declaration of Independence states, "We hold these truths to be self-evident, that all men are created equal, that they are endowed by their creator with certain inalienable rights, that among these are life, liberty, and the pursuit of happiness."

With those rights, however, come certain responsibilities. One of the most important is the duty to vote, to exercise your franchise.

US election laws date back to 1787, when Article 1 of the Constitution gave states the responsibility of overseeing federal elections. However, it did not establish any specific rule regarding who could vote. That would be determined in the states. The states had laws to limit the "franchise" to only white male landowners.

In 1848, a group of women activists gathered in Seneca Falls, New York, to discuss the problem of women's rights. They were invited there by the reformers Elizabeth Cady Stanton and Lucretia Mott. Most of the delegates agreed American women were autonomous individuals who deserved their own political identities.[373]

In 1868, politics eclipsed purpose. After the Civil War, the Fourteenth Amendment to the Constitution was ratified, extending the constitutional voting protection to all *male citizens*, protecting the right to sue, to make contracts, to buy and sell property, specifically excluding women.[374]

The Fifteenth Amendment, ratified in 1870, gave African American *men* the right to vote but continued to exclude women. Many black Americans couldn't exercise this right because some states imposed literacy tests, poll taxes, and other barriers to make it harder to vote. The poll tax was law in Southern states: Florida, Alabama, Tennessee, Arkansas, Louisiana, Mississippi, Georgia, North and South Carolina, Virginia, and Texas.[375] Poll taxes were also in place in some Northern and Western states: California, Connecticut, Maine,

---

[373] History.com—*Women's Suffrage*
[374] *Encyclopedia Britannica—14th Amendment to the Constitution*
[375] *American History USA: Poll Tax in the USA*

# UNINTENDED CONSEQUENCE

Massachusetts, Minnesota, New Hampshire, Ohio, Pennsylvania, Vermont, and Wisconsin.[376, 377]

In 1869, Elizabeth Stanton and Susan B. Anthony formed a group called the National Woman Suffrage Association and began to fight for a women's voting rights amendment to the US Constitution. Later, the organization's name would change to the National American Woman Suffrage Association.[378]

Woman suffrage advocates Stanton and Anthony saw the ratification of the Fifteenth Amendment as their chance to push lawmakers for truly universal suffrage. They refused to support the Fifteenth Amendment and even allied with racist Southerners who argued that white women's votes could be used to neutralize those cast by African American men.[379]

The motives of women varied by group, some less seemly than others. Temperance advocates wanted women to have the vote because they thought it would mobilize an enormous voting bloc on behalf of their cause. Many middle-class white people were swayed by the argument that the enfranchisement of white women would "ensure immediate and durable white supremacy, honestly attained."[380]

The Nineteenth Amendment to the Constitution, ratified in 1920, gave American women the right to vote.[381] In November of that year, more than eight million women across the United States voted in elections for the first time.[382]

Republican president Dwight Eisenhower signed the 1957 Civil Rights Act, ensuring that all Americans could exercise their right to vote. In the House of Representatives, 107 Democrats voted against the bill; 18 senators voted against it as well. Senator John Kennedy (D-MA) voted against the bill for political reasons. JFK wanted to

---

[376] USA.GOV—*Voting and Election Laws*
[377] *Encyclopedia Britannica—15th Amendment to the Constitution*
[378] History.com—*Women's Suffrage*
[379] History.com—*Women's Suffrage*
[380] History.com—*Women's Suffrage*
[381] USA.GOV—*Voting and Election Laws*
[382] History.com—*Women's Suffrage*

deny the Republicans of a symbolic step ahead in the civil rights movement.[383] Another example of politics over country.

At that time, only 20 percent of blacks were registered to vote, despite being the majority in numerous congressional districts in the South. Blacks had been effectively disenfranchised in Southern states by discriminatory voter registration rules and laws in those states that had been instituted by Southern Democrats. Civil rights organizations began to collect evidence of these discriminatory practices, such as the enforcement of literacy and comprehension tests and poll taxes, to support their argument against these voter-suppression techniques.[384]

The Twenty-Fourth Amendment to the Constitution was ratified in 1964, making all these suppression methods illegal, and it lowered the voting age for all elections to eighteen.[385]

After the court struck down these methods of suppressing the black vote, Southern Democrats resorted to gerrymandering to navigate around the Twenty-Fourth Amendment and continued to dilute the influence of the minority vote.

Gerrymandering is the practice of drawing the boundaries of electoral districts in a way that gives one political party or voting group an unfair advantage over its rivals, diluting the voting power of members of political, ethnic, or linguistic minority groups. The term is derived from Democrat governor Elbridge Gerry of Massachusetts. His administration enacted a law in 1812 defining new state senatorial districts that gave disproportionate representation to Democratic Republicans. The practice has been employed by both Democrat and Republican governors to wrest political advantage over the other and continues to this day.

Until the 1980s, disputes regarding political gerrymandering were generally considered "not to be decided by federal courts on the presumption that they presented political questions" that are properly decided by the legislative or the executive branch.[386]

---

[383] *Encyclopedia Britannica—Civil Rights Act 1957*
[384] *Encyclopedia Britannica—Civil Rights Act 1957*
[385] USA.GOV—*Voting and Election Laws*
[386] *Encyclopedia Britannica—Gerrymandering*

# UNINTENDED CONSEQUENCE

In 1986, the Supreme Court held, in *Davis v. Bandemer*, that political gerrymanders could be found unconstitutional (under the equal protection clause) if the result of gerrymandering "is arranged in a manner that will consistently degrade a voter's or a group of voters' influence in the political process as a whole." However, the justices felt that those conditions did not exist in that specific case.[387]

In 2017, the court ruled, in *Cooper v. Harris*, that the district gerrymandering done in North Carolina was unconstitutional.[388] It wasn't until 2018 that the Supreme Court once again took up the issue of the jurisdiction of political gerrymandering claims in *Rucho v. Common Cause*. There the court declared (5–4) that "partisan gerrymandering claims present political questions beyond the reach of the federal courts." The court found that nonpartisan gerrymandering would be permissible.[389]

Seeing a political advantage after the 2020 census, former president Barack Obama and former attorney general Eric Holder have taken up gerrymandering as the focus of his postpresidential political life, to gain a political advantage for the Democrats. Obama and former attorney general Eric Holder plan to focus on state-by-state campaigns to promote wider use of nonpartisan methods of drawing districts. The issue of gerrymandering may significantly change in the next Congress, with court challenges as a strategy to discount voter results. It seems that any avenue available will be used to "reshape" election results if necessary.[390]

The accuracy of the American election process is vital to our democracy. The potential of voter fraud creates a stain upon it. While fraud has been repeatedly asserted by conservatives and Republicans, it has been vehemently rejected by liberals and Democrats. Once again, politics over purpose. It is reasonable to strive to ensure that only American citizens participate in the election process. All parties should embrace that principle, yet liberals use canards to impede its guarantee.

---

[387] *Encyclopedia Britannica—Gerrymandering*
[388] *Encyclopedia Britannica—Gerrymandering*
[389] *Encyclopedia Britannica—Gerrymandering*
[390] *Red State—Gerrymandering is fine, except when Republicans do it—May 2017*

While it is necessary to have a license to drive an automobile, a photo identification to board an airplane or purchase tobacco or alcohol, valid identification is not required to perform your most solemn duty as a citizen—to exercise your franchise and vote. Liberals claim that requiring a state-provided voter ID is a form of suppressing the votes of minorities. That is pure twaddle.

In a July 2012 speech at the NAACP convention in Houston, Attorney General Eric Holder stated that "recent studies indicate that nationally, only 8% of white voting-age citizens but 25% of African-American voting-age citizens lack government-issued photo IDs."[391]

What effort would be required to have the states issue photo identification to these Americans? Would the effort not be justified by the ability to guarantee that all individuals that cast a vote are American citizens?

Is voter fraud a fact or a myth? The size of the voter fraud, as a percentage of votes cast, might be insignificant, but the advent of fraud should be terribly concerning and perhaps the first small leak in what might become a possible torrent.

Here are some adjudicated examples of recent voter fraud cases:

- In Knox County, Kentucky, Donnie Newsome, Democrat county chief executive, and co-conspirator Willard Smith were convicted of several charges for "organizing a conspiracy to pay several impoverished, handicapped, illiterate, or otherwise impaired persons to vote for Newsome and others by absentee ballot in the 1998 Democratic primary election." Newsome was sentenced to twenty-six months in prison. Smith received a twenty-four-month sentence.[392]
- In East Chicago, Indiana, in 2003, there was "extensive voter fraud" in the Democrat mayoral primary election. The fraud was so pervasive that the Indiana Supreme Court overturned the election and ordered a new special

---

[391] *PolitiFact—Holder says recent Studies show 25% of African American lack photo ID*—July 2012

[392] *The Daily Signal—Heritage Foundation—300 Cases of Voter Fraud in America*—August 2015

election. A local judge found "direct, competent, and convincing evidence" that supporters of the election's apparent victor, incumbent mayor Robert Pastrick, "orchestrated an elaborate scheme of absentee ballot fraud." A voter fraud task force secured forty-six convictions.[393]

- Dead people voting in Colorado. A CBS affiliate's evidence of voter fraud in Colorado in 2016 sparked an immediate investigation by Secretary of State Wayne Williams. His report exposed multiple incidents in recent years where dead Coloradans were still voting. A dead World War II veteran named John Grosso voted in a 2006 primary election, and a woman named Sara Sosa, who died in 2009, cast ballots in 2010, 2011, 2012, and 2013. Mrs. Sosa's husband, Miguel, died in 2008, but a vote was cast in his name one year later.[394]
- Illegals found voting in Virginia. A study by the watchdog Public Interest Legal Foundation found, in just eight Virginia counties, 1,046 alien noncitizens successfully registered to vote. These aliens were only accidentally caught when they renewed their driver's license and told authorities they were noncitizens. This study didn't include the metropolises of Fairfax County and Arlington. Moreover, the FBI opened an investigation in the state after twenty dead people turned in applications to vote.[395]
- Some Pennsylvania citizens voting twice. In 2015, Pennsylvania's secretary of state admitted data proving more than seven hundred Pennsylvania voters might have cast two ballots in recent elections yet said she's powerless to investigate or prosecute double voters. Nearly forty-three thousand voters in Pennsylvania had potentially duplicate

---

[393] *The Daily Signal—Heritage Foundation—300 Cases of Voter Fraud in America—*August 2015
[394] *The Washington Times—No, Voter Fraud isn't a Myth—*October 2016
[395] *The Washington Times—No, Voter Fraud isn't a Myth—*October 2016

registrations in either Pennsylvania or other states, data researcher Voter Registration Data Crosscheck found.[396]

- Illegal voters uncovered in Philadelphia. At least eighty-six noncitizens have been registered voters in Philadelphia since 2013, and almost half of them have cast a ballot in a recent election, watchdog Public Interest Legal Foundation noted this month. The number was only turned up after officials received specific requests from the voters themselves to remove their names from the rolls. "This is just the tip of the iceberg," Joseph Vanderhulst, the watchdog's attorney, told LifeZette on October 5. "Who knows how many are on and don't ask to be taken off?"[397]

- Voter rigging in Texas. In 2016, allegations of voter fraud in Tarrant County, Texas, prompted a state investigation. The suit targeted mail-in ballots, which allows for people to vote from their homes without any ID or verification of identity. There's concern of so-called vote harvesting, where political operatives fill out and return other people's ballots without their consent.[398]

- Indiana voter fraud investigation grows to fifty-six counties. According to a 2016 local NBC story, Indiana State Police were amid a statewide investigation into possible voter registration fraud. "Police believe there could be hundreds of fraudulent voter registration records with different combinations of made up names and addresses with people's real information."[399]

- Three under investigation in Oklahoma for voting twice in the presidential primary. An investigation was conducted into three Comanche County, Oklahoma, residents who voted twice in the 2016 Presidential Preference Primary Election, according to the local ABC 7 News station, KSWO. "All three submitted absentee ballots before show-

---

[396] *The Washington Times—No, Voter Fraud isn't a Myth*—October 2016
[397] *The Washington Times—No, Voter Fraud isn't a Myth*—October 2016
[398] *The Washington Times—No, Voter Fraud isn't a Myth*—October 2016
[399] *The Washington Times—No, Voter Fraud isn't a Myth*—October 2016

ing up to their polling place on March 1 and voted again in person."[400]
- Election fraud in Kentucky. A Franklin County grand jury indicted a Pike County man in 2016 on multiple felony counts of election fraud in connection with its statewide primary. Keith Justice was charged with four counts of intimidating an election officer and one count of interfering with an election officer in Pike County.[401]
- Underage voters found voting in Wisconsin's presidential primary. In 2016, Brown County election officials found six cases where underage voters cast a ballot in the state's presidential primary. County clerk Sandy Juno told a local reporter that six seventeen-year-old students registered and voted. Despite five of the students presenting a valid ID, poll workers never looked at the date of birth on them or on the registration forms they filled out. In one case, the student used a report card as identification.[402]
- Voter registration cards sent to illegals in Pennsylvania. In 2016, the secretary of state's office in Pennsylvania mailed about 2.5 million voter registration postcards to people who were not registered voters but were licensed drivers. Secretary of State Pedro Cortes admitted to the House of Representatives that seven people had reported that they received voter registration cards in error.

State Representative Daryl Metchalfe, a Butler County Republican who chairs the State Government Committee, said in a September testimony that there's several problems with the state's voter registration system. "There's certainly the potential for hundreds, if not thousands, of foreigners here legally and illegally to be on our voter rolls, and a certain percentage who are casting ballots,"

---

[400] *The Washington Times—No, Voter Fraud isn't a Myth*—October 2016
[401] *The Washington Times—No, Voter Fraud isn't a Myth*—October 2016
[402] *The Washington Times—No, Voter Fraud isn't a Myth*—October 2016

Mr. Metchalfe told LifeZette. "We've got a lot of integrity issues that need to be addressed."[403]

Candidate Donald Trump warned supporters that they were fighting against a "rigged system, rife with voter fraud and those eager to protect the status quo." Liberals and Democrats challenged that this type of talk was "dangerous" to the integrity of our electoral system and asked for proof of his voter fraud allegations.

According to an October 2016 article in *The Washington Times*, "the argument isn't whether voter fraud is real, but how widespread it is," offering examples documenting that "voter fraud isn't a myth and how Mr. Trump's claims aren't just speculation."[404]

Clearly, fraud, while not yet rampant, is not a myth.

Since 1950, the census asked some question relating to citizenship. In that decade, the question asked if the recipient was "foreign born, is he naturalized." In 1960, the question was revised to "place of birth," and in 1970, 1980, 1990, and 2000, the question asked, "Is this person a citizen of the United States?" In 2010 the citizenship question was removed by the Obama administration.[405]

In 2018, the Trump administration proposed reinstating the question on the 2020 census survey requiring responders to declare "if they were citizens of the United States." Democrats vehemently objected.

While this might have assisted in curtailing voter fraud, the primary concern of the Democrat objection was that the exclusion of noncitizens could affect the calculation determining the number of seats a state would have in the House of Representatives and the allocation of federal funds to states.

Shouldn't we know how many American citizens there are? Isn't this important information?

Almost 188 million Americans, 61 percent, voted in the 2016 presidential election, according to the US Census Bureau, below the almost 64 percent the Bureau says voted in 2008.

---

[403] *The Washington Times—No, Voter Fraud isn't a Myth*—October 2016
[404] *The Washington Times—No, Voter Fraud isn't a Myth*—October 2016
[405] NPR—*Has Citizenship Been a Standard Census Question?*—March 2018

Several long-standing trends in presidential elections include either white turnout increased and the nonwhite share of the US electorate remained flat since the 2012 election.[406]

Democrats disillusioned with the unthinkable Donald Trump victory in the 2016 presidential election, which had long been anticipated as a Hillary Clinton coronation, have offered several revisions to voting laws. They are proposing policy revisions that would increase the influence of the largest population states, which are historically liberal. They propose to lower the voting age to sixteen, give the vote to incarcerated felons, and eliminate the Electoral College. If allowed, that would lead to the coastal liberal elites choosing our president.

With all the intense effort expended by our forebears to establish voting rights for *all* Americans, isn't it a tragedy that only 51 percent of our voting age population exercise their franchise, while 49 percent willingly choose not to participate in the democratic process?[407]

Isn't it a bit ironic that many Americans find time to criticize and moan about their political representatives and the policies that they legislate, or not, yet the same individuals cannot find the time to vote and help choose them? Shameful. I believe that those who fail to vote deny themselves the right to criticize government conduct. Perhaps we might explore changing the franchise from a "right" to a "requirement," from a privilege to a duty.

Progress cannot be made if people are only willing to talk to others with the same opinion. Has ignorance dimmed our vision?

A productive, successful democracy requires well-informed voters. Americans should vote issues, not party; vote conscience, not hatred. Try to understand the issues and their consequence, disregard party, and focus on policy. Harsh division can only yield futile results.

Your vote is your power, your solemn obligation, your responsibility. Do not waste it or forfeit it. If you desire positive change, then you cannot stay home on Election Day. Prepare yourself as you would for an important test or interview. Study for it, understand the

---

[406] Pew Research Center—*Black voter turnout fell in 2016*—May 2017
[407] United States Election Project—*2016 November General Election Turnout Rates*

issues, choose wisely. Policy over party, process over passion, information over impulse.

Find your own voice. Then express your own views.

Our right to vote has been paid for in blood and treasure; we ought not squander it.

# Chapter IX

# Slavery, Racism, and Reparations

As I reflect upon my life, I realize that I have had acquaintances, college mates, business associates, and golf partners that were African American. However, I cannot state with complete candor that I ever had a true *friend* that is black.

This was not the result of racism, simply happenstance.

I write this chapter acknowledging that I have never been the victim of racism. I have never been scarred by the devastation of hate, nor have I walked in a "black man's shoes." Consequently, I fear that my musings might be viewed as naive or contrite. While I dismiss the notion of "white privilege" as simply another arrow in the quiver of racism, I accept the reality of past racial subjugation.

> Those who deny freedom to others, deserve it not for themselves. (Abraham Lincoln, sixteenth US president)

Candace Owens is a conservative commentator, political activist, and cofounder of Turning Point USA. She is known for her pro-Trump stance as well as her criticism of Black Lives Matter and the Democratic Party.

In her opening statement to a congressional committee studying "hate crimes and the rise of white nationalism" in April 2019, she expressed her practical, personal view:

> My grandfather grew up on a sharecropping farm in the segregated South. He grew up in an America where words like racism and white nationalism held real meaning under the Democratic Party's Jim Crow laws.
>
> My grandfather's first job was given to him at the age of five years old and his job was to lay tobacco out to dry in an attic in the South. My grandfather has picked cotton and he has also had experiences with the Democrat terrorist organization of that time, the Ku Klux Klan. They would regularly visit his home and they would shoot bullets into it. They had an issue with his father, my great-grandfather.
>
> There isn't an adult today that in good conscience would make the argument that America is a more racist, whiter nationalist society than it was when my grandfather was growing up.
>
> Here are some things we never hear. 75% of the black boys in California don't meet state reading standards. In inner cities like Baltimore within five high schools and one middle school, not a single student was found to be proficient in math or reading in 2016. Single motherhood rate in the black community, which was at 23% in the 1960's, is a staggering 74% today.
>
> There are more black babies aborted than born alive in cities like New York, and you have Democrat Governor Andrew Cuomo celebrating late-term abortions.
>
> My point is that White Nationalists, White Nationalism, does not do any of those things that

I just brought up. Democrat policies did. White supremacy, racism, White Nationalism, words that once had real meaning have now become nothing more than election strategies every four years. The black communities are offered handouts in fear, reparations and White Nationalism.

I believe the legacy of the ancestry of black Americans is being insulted every single day. I will not pretend to be a victim in this country. I know that makes many on the left uncomfortable

The biggest scandal in American politics is that Democrats have been conning minorities into the belief that we are perpetual victims, all but ensuring our failure. Racial division and class warfare are central to the Democrat party platform. They need blacks to hate whites, the rich to hate the poor. Soon enough it will be the tall hating the short.

Over the last fifty years, US political policy and legislation have devoted trillions of dollars to correcting inequities in the minority communities.

The network of social and economic support programs provided a two-edged sword, a "hand up" or a "handout." The recipient made the choice, walk through the opened door of economic opportunity or become dependent upon the government largess; move on or adorn new "chains," the economic shackles tied to the government dole.

It would seem trite to quote the old adage "You can lead a horse to water, but you can't make it drink"; instead, I will quote Zora Neale Hurston, who was an influential author of African American literature, anthropologist, and filmmaker. In her writing, she portrayed racial struggles in the early twentieth-century American South. In her book *Their Eyes Were Watching God*, a character, Jody Starks, poignantly explained the plight of the postemancipation black

American: "Us talks about de white man keepin' us down! Shucks! He don't hav tuh. Us keeps our own selves down."

As a country, we have endeavored to right the ship of slavery and racial prejudice, albeit belatedly, but we could not compel our fellow Americans to "drink."

Racism is the basest form of social conduct and has become the default position of most liberal disagreements or confrontations. When the merits cannot be argued, racism is alleged.

The 2020 presidential election may very well descend into a rhetorical battle of "racism" versus "socialism." It should not be; it should be an election about ideas and direction.

Racial unrest appears to be more problematic today than at any time since the 1960s. To understand racism in the United States, we need to view it in the context of our history.

Racism has unfortunately been a thread in the tapestry of American history. Prior to gaining our independence, the colonial Americans subjugated the Native and the slave populations. Clearly, these were our nation's most egregious and shameful acts. Our behavior is rife with acts of racism toward each new wave of immigrant throughout our history, some feared, some hated.

Ben Franklin warned of the "swarthy, stupid Germans" in the 1750s, followed by the fear of Catholics in the 1850s, certain that they were colluding with the pope. In the 1880s, it was the Chinese that were feared to be "taking American jobs"; we even passed legislation to prohibit their immigration into the United States. Then came the Irish "Micks," then the Italian "Dago Wops," then the Jewish "Kikes," and the Polish "Polacks."

During World War II, our government sanctioned the interment of all Japanese Americans, in "the interest of national security."

Each group was feared because they were different in language, culture, and/or appearance. Most recently, after the 9/11 terrorist attacks on the United States, the target has become the Muslims. But no national act of racism was more reprehensible than slavery, and I will focus on that disgrace.

Prejudice is taught, as it is not part of one's DNA at birth. *Shame on our parents and friends.* After untold investment in Affirmative

# UNINTENDED CONSEQUENCE

Action and similar initiatives, our colleges are reverting to segregation, with "safe spaces" and antiwhite curriculum. *Shame on our educators.* Racism is used as a weapon in deceptive political strategies. *Shame on our politicians.* The progress that had been made between the Civil Rights Act of 1964 and 2008 has been forfeit. *Shame on former attorney general Eric Holder and Al Sharpton.*

From the early colonies and until the 1860s, slavery was viewed as an economic necessity for the cotton and tobacco farms of the South but was never justified morally or ethically. During this period that slavery spread, it is estimated that 388,000 Africans were kidnapped, brought to America, and forced into slavery. The slave population had grown to four million prior to the Civil War. The buying and selling of human chattel were commonplace, slave trade was extremely lucrative, and it was an integral part of the Southern economy.[408]

The plight of the American slaves was effectively depicted within Alex Haley's epic 1976 novel *Roots*, which was later offered as a television miniseries winning nine Emmys, a Peabody, and a Golden Globe award. It provided an effective portrayal of the slave saga from 1750 through the post-Civil War period. In my opinion, *Roots* should be required viewing in every American grammar school.

Following the Revolutionary War, abolitionist laws were passed in most Northern states, and a movement developed to abolish slavery.

America's original sin will always be a blight on American history. The efforts of abolitionists offered a glimmer of hope, and abolitionism was the movement before and during the American Civil War to end slavery in the United States.

As the Constitution was in the process of being drafted, black people were not considered citizens, and even then, slavery was a significantly divisive issue. While the Southern "slave states" viewed slaves as chattel, those states recognized the advantage of including slaves in their state population numbers, which would determine the number of representative each state could send to Congress.

---

[408] PBS—*The African Americans*—Henry Lewis Gates, Jr.

In 1787, Charles Pinckney of South Carolina proposed a compromise: "Three-fifths of the number of slaves in any particular state would be added to the total number of free white persons...to determine the number of Congressmen each state would send to the House of Representatives."[409]

Originally, states were allowed one representative in Congress for each thirty thousand persons in their state. The three-fifths clause was part of a series of compromises enacted by the Constitutional Convention. Other clauses prohibited slavery in the Northwest territories and forbade US participation in the international slave trade after 1807.[410]

The intellectual, spiritual, and philosophical objection to slavery, as a principle, emerged almost immediately after the Constitution was ratified.

As the country expanded westward, it was determined that new territories and states in the West should be free states. Residents of newly created territories would decide the issue of slavery by vote, a process known as popular sovereignty. Northern states depended on free labor and all had abolished slavery by 1805.

The question of whether slavery would be allowed in the new Western states continued. In 1820, the Missouri Compromise attempted to resolve this question. It had admitted Missouri to the Union as a slave state and Maine as a free state, preserving the fragile balance in Congress. It stipulated that in the future, slavery would be prohibited north of the southern boundary of Missouri and in the rest of the Louisiana Purchase. The compromise did not apply to new territories that were not part of the Louisiana Purchase, and so the issue of slavery continued to fester as the nation expanded.[411] When Thomas Jefferson heard of the Missouri Compromise, he recognized its significance to the growing divide of national opinion

---

[409] *The Heritage Guide to the Constitution*—David Brennen, Professor—Case Western Reserve University

[410] *The Heritage Guide to the Constitution*—David Brennen, Professor—Case Western Reserve University

[411] History.com—*Westward Expansion*

regarding slavery, foresaw the Civil War, and reportedly opined that this would be "the knell of the Union."[412]

In 1857, the Supreme Court decided on *Dred Scott v. Sandford*. The case addressed a dispute regarding slave ownership between slave states and free states. Dred Scott was a *slave* whose owner had spent time as a resident in free states and territories. Scott sued over whether it was lawful for slave owners to hold a slave in a free state or free territory. The Supreme Court was stacked in favor of the slave states, as five of the nine justices were from the South. Chief Justice Roger B. Taney wrote the majority decision, which was issued in March 1857. The court held that Scott was not free based on his residence in the free state or free territory because he was *not considered a person* under the US Constitution; Scott was the *property* of his owner, and property could not be taken from a person without due process of law.[413]

In the 1860 presidential election, Republicans supported banning slavery in all the US territories. The Southern states viewed this as a violation of their constitutional rights and as the first step in a grander Republican plan to eventually abolish slavery.

Abraham Lincoln was the first Republican Party candidate to win the presidency. Prior to his inauguration, with slavery being the central concern, seven states with cotton- and tobacco-based economies declared secession and formed the Confederacy. The first six to declare secession had populations that were 49 percent slaves.[414]

Civil War hostilities began shortly after Lincoln's inauguration, in April 1861, when Confederate forces fired on Fort Sumter. It ended in April 1865, when Confederate general Robert E. Lee surrendered at Appomattox.

In September 1862, acting upon our social conscience, President Abraham Lincoln issued a preliminary warning that he would order the emancipation of all slaves in any state that did not end its rebellion against the Union by January 1, 1863. The Emancipation

---

[412] Abbeville Institute—*Thomas Jefferson, Southern Man of Letters*—November 2015

[413] *Encyclopedia Britannica—Dred Scott Decision*

[414] civilwarcauses.org—*Selected Statistics on Slavery in the United States*

Proclamation, signed in January 1863, outraged white Southerners, angered some Northern Democrats, and energized antislavery forces. The proclamation lifted the spirits of African Americans, both free and slave. It encouraged many slaves to escape from their masters and get to Union lines to obtain their freedom and to join the Union Army.[415]

Southern Democrats went to war, sacrificing their sons, to preserve slavery; Northern Republicans went to war to abolish it. The war cost between 620,000 and 750,000 lives and brought an end to the antebellum culture.[416]

After the war ended, during the Reconstruction Period of 1865–1877, federal laws provided civil rights protections in the Southern states for the recently freed slaves. The Freedman's Bureau was established to help solve everyday problems of the newly freed slaves, such as obtaining clothing, food, water, health care, communication with family members, and jobs.[417] "Forty acres and a mule" was a promise made by the United States government to aid formally enslaved black farmers. Approved by President Abraham Lincoln, it specifically allotted each family a plot of land no larger than forty acres.

General Tecumseh Sherman later ordered the army to lend mules for the agrarian reform effort. Many freed people believed and were told by various political figures that they had a right to own the land they had long worked for as slaves. They widely expected to legally claim forty acres of land and a mule after the end of the war.

Some land redistribution occurred under military jurisdiction during the war and for a brief period thereafter. However, federal and state policy during the Reconstruction Era emphasized *wage labor* for blacks, not *land ownership*. Almost all land allocated during the war was restored to its prewar white owners.[418]

Proclamations such as Special Field Order No. 15 and the Freedmen's Bureau Act were explicitly reversed by Lincoln's successor, Democrat president Andrew Johnson.

---

[415] *Encyclopedia Britannica—Emancipation Proclamation*
[416] American Battlefield Trust—*Civil War Facts*
[417] *Encyclopedia Britannica—Freedmen's Bureau*
[418] *Encyclopedia Britannica—Freedmen's Bureau*

## UNINTENDED CONSEQUENCE

By 1868, Democrats gradually regained power in the Southern legislatures, using paramilitary groups to disrupt Republican organizing, run Republican officeholders out of town, and intimidate blacks to suppress their voting. Extensive voter fraud was evident. While public schools had been established by Reconstruction legislatures for the first time in most Southern states, those for black children were consistently underfunded.

By 1877, the last of the federal troops were withdrawn from the South and white Democrats had regained political power in every Southern state. They enacted laws officially segregating black people from the white population. They passed laws, which came to be known as Jim Crow, to make voter registration and electoral rules more restrictive, decreasing political participation by most blacks and many poor whites.

The Jim Crow laws were statutes enacted by Southern states that legalized segregation between African Americans and whites. They restricted their right to use public facilities, schools, to vote, or to find decent employment. They prohibited black and white children from attending the same schools; required separate official records of black births, marriages, and deaths from records of white people; and prohibited a person of "pure white blood" from marrying or engaging in "illicit carnal intercourse" with anyone with African blood. They required separate coaches or sections for black passengers on public transportation; required separate waiting rooms and ticket windows; required segregation in libraries, inns, hotels, restaurants, bars, hospitals, theaters, circuses, parks, beaches, restrooms, cemeteries, and wherever whites and blacks might commingle. Whites and blacks were restricted from playing pool, baseball, basketball, football, cards, dominoes, checkers, or golf together. Factories and workplaces were required to maintain separate bathrooms.[419]

The Ku Klux Klan became the enforcement arm of the Southern Democrat Party. Founded between 1865 and 1866 by six former officers of the Confederate Army as a fraternal social club and insurgent movement promoting resistance and white supremacy during

---
[419] *Encyclopedia Britannica—Jim Crow Laws*

the Reconstruction era, the Klan targeted black freedmen and their white Republican allies with threats and violence, including murder, and seriously weakened the black political establishment.

Between 1890 and 1910, ten of the eleven former Confederate states passed new constitutions or amendments that effectively disenfranchised most blacks and tens of thousands of poor whites through a combination of poll taxes, literacy and comprehension tests, and residency and record-keeping requirements. Those who could not vote were not eligible to serve on juries and could not run for local offices. They were effectively erased from political life, as they could not influence the state legislatures, and their interests were overlooked.

In 1870 and 1871, the federal government passed the Enforcement Acts, which were intended to prosecute and suppress Klan crimes.[420]

In 1913, Woodrow Wilson, a Democrat from New Jersey born and raised in the South, became the first Southern-born president of the post-Civil War period. He appointed Southerners to his Cabinet. The Wilson administration introduced segregation in federal offices. Segregation and racial bias continued in the South for over one hundred years, and acts of racism continued to stain our history.

Prior to the *Brown v. Board of Education* Supreme Court decision in 1954, race relations in much of the United States were dominated by segregation; *Brown* asserted that segregation did not provide an equal education opportunity for blacks. The court's 9–0 decision in *Brown* declared that the "separate but equal" notion was unconstitutional for American public schools and educational facilities and paved the way for integration.[421]

Even during our World Wars, blacks serving in the US Armed Forces were segregated, until President Harry Truman initiated the integration process in 1948.

President Eisenhower signed the 1957 Civil Rights Act, ensuring that all Americans could exercise their right to vote. At that time, only a small percentage of blacks were registered to vote, despite

---

[420] American-Historama—*Enforcement Acts*
[421] U.S.Courts.gov—*History—Brown v Board of Education*

being the majority in numerous congressional districts in the South. Blacks had been effectively disenfranchised by discriminatory voter registration rules, poll taxes, and laws in those states instituted and propagated by Southern Democrats.

An interesting and revealing insight into the 1960s segregated South in Mississippi can be gleaned from a 2009 novel written by Kathryn Stockett, *The Help*, which was made into a movie in 2011, receiving several Academy Award nominations.

The civil rights movement for blacks did not begin in earnest until the 1950s. Martin Luther King Jr., an American Baptist minister and activist, became the most prominent, visible spokesman and leader in the civil rights movement from 1955 until he was assassinated in 1968. He attended segregated public schools in Georgia, graduating from high school when he was fifteen, and received a BA degree from Morehouse College in 1948. After three years of theological study at Crozer Theological Seminary in Pennsylvania, he was awarded the BD in 1951. He enrolled in graduate studies at Boston University, completing his residence and receiving his degree in 1955.

In December 1955, Rosa Parks, a civil rights activist, refused to surrender her seat on a Montgomery, Alabama, bus, in defiance of the city's segregation laws, and was arrested. Many consider Rosa Parks to be the first black nonviolent activist in the United States. The Reverend King, a new minister in a Montgomery church, became leader of the city's civil rights activists. In response to the Rosa Parks arrest, King staged a boycott of the city transit system.

In his first public speech, he said, "We have no alternative but to protest. For many years we have shown an amazing patience. We have sometimes given our white brothers the feeling that we liked the way we were being treated. But we come here tonight to be saved from that patience that makes us patient with anything less than freedom and justice."

Although King's home was dynamited and his family's safety threatened, he continued to lead the boycott until, shortly after a year, the city's buses were desegregated. Martin Luther King Jr. practiced a campaign of nonviolent civil disobedience with sit-ins and protest marches.

King joined other civil rights leaders in organizing the historic March on Washington in August 1963, where an assembly of more than two hundred thousand blacks and whites gathered peaceably to demand equal justice for all citizens under the law. Crowds were inspired by the emotional strength and prophetic quality of King's famous "I Have a Dream" speech, in which he emphasized his faith that all men, someday, would be brothers. He urged Americans to judge people by the content of their character as opposed to the color of their skin.[422]

> I have a dream that my four little children will one day live in a nation where they will not be judged by the color of their skin, but by the content of their character. (Martin Luther King Jr.)

King had hoped the rising tide of civil rights agitation would produce a rising anger of national opinion, and it did. The result was the passage of the Civil Rights Act of 1964.

At the age of thirty-five, King was the youngest man to have received the Nobel Peace Prize. He donated the $54,123 prize money to the furtherance of the civil rights movement.[423]

King prophetically told a crowd at a church in Memphis the night before he died, "I've seen the promised land. I may not get there with you. But I want you to know tonight that we, as a people, will get to the promised land." On the following evening of April 4, 1968, while standing on a balcony in his hotel room in Memphis, Tennessee, where he was to lead a march in support of striking garbage workers, he was assassinated.

However, there was another faction opposing integration and advocating for extreme segregation. Black nationalism, headed by Elijah Muhammad and Malcolm X, articulated the Nation of Islam's

---

[422] *Encyclopedia Britannica—Martin Luther King, Jr.*
[423] TheNobelPrize.com

racial doctrines on "the inherent evil of whites and the natural superiority of blacks."[424]

Malcolm X helped lead the movement during the period of its greatest growth and influence. He met Elijah Muhammad in Chicago in 1952 and then began organizing temples for the Nation in New York, Philadelphia, and Boston and in cities in the South. He founded the Nation's newspaper, *Muhammad Speaks*, which he printed in the basement of his home. Malcolm also criticized the mainstream civil rights movement and challenged Reverend King's central notions of integration and nonviolence. Malcolm argued that more was at stake than the "civil right to sit in a restaurant or even to vote." He saw the most important issues were black identity, integrity, and independence. In contrast to King's strategy of nonviolence, civil disobedience, and redemptive suffering, Malcolm urged his followers to defend themselves "by any means necessary."[425] Malcolm X helped change the terms used to refer to African Americans from *Negro* and *colored* to *black* and *Afro-American*, emphasizing our differences rather than our commonalities.

An internal dispute within the Nation of Islam led to the assassination of Malcolm X in 1968. Following the death of Elijah Muhammad in 1975, a new, even more militant, more controversial voice for the Nation of Islam emerged, Louis Farrakhan.

In 1966, the Black Panther Party was founded by Huey Newton and Bobby Seale to challenge police brutality against the African American community. Dressed in black berets and black leather jackets, Panthers monitored police activities and organized armed citizen patrols in the black communities of Oakland, California, and other US cities. Newton and Seale drew on Marxist ideology for the party platform and outlined the organization's philosophical views and political objectives in a "ten-point program"; it called for an immediate end to police brutality, employment for African Americans, and land, housing, and justice for all.

---

[424] *Encyclopedia Britannica—Malcolm X and The Nation of Islam*
[425] *Encyclopedia Britannica—Malcolm X and The Nation of Islam*

The Black Panthers were part of the larger black power movement, which emphasized black pride, community control, and unification for civil rights. In 1969, the J. Edgar Hoover FBI declared the Black Panthers a communist organization and an enemy of the United States government, labeling the Panthers as "one of the greatest threats to the nation's internal security."[426]

The black power movement incited social unrest and delayed the evolution process that would be necessary to achieve actual equality for blacks. By the summer of 1968, the common cause of blacks and whites marching together had been shattered as riots swept the Watts section of Los Angeles and, over the next two years, in cities across the country.[427]

These opposing views, representing conflicting goals between assimilation and separation, not only divided America but divided the black community within America as well.

The United States experienced the most widespread series of race riots in its history. Riots occurred in Alabama, New York, California, Illinois, Florida, Ohio, Georgia, New Jersey, and Michigan. Riots erupted in more than 110 cities the night Martin Luther King Jr. was assassinated.

The race riots of the 1960s led President Lyndon Johnson to establish a National Advisory Commission on Civil Disorders in 1967. The commission identified white racism as the main cause of the riots. Specifically mentioned were pervasive discrimination and segregation, black migration to the cities as whites left them, harsh ghetto conditions, frustration of hopes, and a feeling of powerlessness on the part of many blacks. There is little evidence that serious efforts were made to correct the problems raised by the commission. The Johnson administration, and those that followed, viewed the riots as law enforcement problems rather than a sign of social imbalance.[428]

Sadly, with all the intense effort expended, in blood and sacrifice, to establish voting rights for *all* Americans, isn't it a tragedy

---

[426] History.com—*Black Panthers*
[427] *The Smithsonian Magazine: The 1968 Democratic Convention*—August 2008
[428] *Encyclopedia Britannica—Race Riots of the 1960's*

that only 67 percent of our voting-age population exercised their franchise in 2012?

The turnout in 2008 and 2012 certainly was influenced by the first black candidate for president. However, in 2016, that participation dropped by 7 percentage points, to 59 percent, leaving 41 percent that chose not to participate in the democratic process.[429] Shameful. Those who fail to vote deny themselves the right to criticize government action.

In September 1960, as a seventeen-year-old US Navy sailor who had grown up in the integrated North, I boarded a train in Newark, New Jersey, heading for Miami, en route to Key West, Florida.

This trip, my first ever to Southern states, was revealing in many ways. When the train stopped in Charleston, South Carolina, for two hours, I embarked to see what I could see. I was stunned to see bathrooms and drinking fountains marked "Whites Only." I had been taught about segregation in high school but had never witnessed it. It offended me, making me feel uncomfortable. This was at a time when the civil rights movement was just beginning to emerge. I couldn't grasp the Southern mind-set, but I knew that this prejudice was just wrong.

Affirmative Action intended to promote opportunities for defined minority groups within our society, to give them equal access to that of the majority population, was first instituted in the United States by an executive order signed by President John Kennedy in 1961, "to ensure that applicants are employed, and employees are treated during employment, without regard to their race, creed, color, or national origin." It was intended to achieve nondiscrimination.[430]

The stated justification for affirmative action by its proponents is that it helps to compensate for past discrimination, persecution, or exploitation by the "ruling class" and to address existing discrimination.

In 1965, President Lyndon Johnson issued another executive order that required government employers to take "affirmative

---

[429] Pew Research Center—*Black voter turnout fell in 2016*—May 2017
[430] *Business Insider—JFK Wrote a Memo in 1961*—December 2015

action" to "hire without regard to race, religion and national origin." This was intended to prevent his administration from discriminating against members of disadvantaged groups.[431]

Weren't these a legislative form of reparations?

Unfortunately, executive orders do not have the permanence of legislation or law and could be reversed by the next president.

In considering the positive effects of Affirmative Action, we can see that it has helped break some stereotypes. For centuries, black people were considered less capable than whites, and the implementation of this policy gave them the chance to show they are every bit as capable. Stereotypes have started to change and will continue to change.

However, there have been negative effects as well.

Affirmative Action has created a "reverse discrimination," putting race as the dominant factor in employee recruitment and school admission policies rather than selecting the best people, regardless of color and race.

Affirmative Action presupposed that all people having the same color skin were from the lower class, needing help, and, in fact, reinforced existing stereotypes.

In my view, on balance, Affirmative Action policies have been positive, encouraging all Americans to be ambitious and excel, while opening doors to segments of our society that had previously been closed. We have seen black Americans rise to the summit of business, politics, and social positions.

Is it a bit ironic that this policy appears in conflict with other social safety-net projects that seem to encourage the opposite, staying home and receiving a government dole rather than striving for self-sufficiency and personal upward mobility?

The Civil Rights Act of 1964, signed by President Lyndon Johnson, made discrimination based on race, religion, sex, national origin, and other characteristics illegal. In the House of Representatives, ninety-six Democrats voted against the bill; in the

---

[431] American Association for Access, Equity and Diversity—*About Affirmative Action*

# UNINTENDED CONSEQUENCE

Senate, twenty-one Democrats and six Republicans voted against it.[432]

President Johnson's 1964 National War on Poverty was intended "not only to relieve the symptoms of poverty, but to cure it and, above all, to prevent it." The action was directed toward economically depressed communities, both black and white. The program, costing over $50 trillion since its inception, has created generations dependent upon the government dole, while having no measurable impact on our national poverty level.[433]

School busing was an attempt to compel the integration of public schools. In 1971, the Supreme Court decided on the practice of using mandatory busing and allowed it to continue in multiple cities across the United States.[434]

*The New York Times* explained the court ruling:

> It is not enough for school officials to draw school attendance lines that appear to be racially neutral. Officials must foster integration by such affirmative measures as gerrymandering school boundaries to include both races, pairing "white" and "Negro" schools, and drawing school zones that combine noncontiguous areas in racially diverse neighborhoods.[435]

Most Americans, both black and white, were opposed to busing. While busing might have succeeded in some areas, it also served to increase the racial divide and contributed to "white flight."

The Community Reinvestment Act, signed into law by President Jimmy Carter in 1977, was designed to assure that "banks serve the convenience and need of the communities that they serve." It was intended to target "redlining" practices and allow "affordable housing" to minorities and low-income families.

---

[432] United States Senate—*Roll Call Vote on Civil Rights Act*—June 1964
[433] *Encyclopedia Britannica—War on Poverty*
[434] *Encyclopedia Britannica—Busing*
[435] *The New York Times—Supreme Court Rules on Busing—April 20, 1971*

Improvements in education, employment, housing, and laws prohibiting discrimination were in the spirit of America. They elevated those of the black community that possessed ambition and a personal commitment to improve their lot in life.

By 2008, racial tensions in the United States had achieved substantial progress regarding antiblack prejudice. Mixed racial dating, biracial marriages and families were commonplace; social unrest seemed to have abated.

Biracial families were frequently represented in TV and print advertising. There was a clear black presence in the arts and industry. Blacks had risen to prominence in industry with Kenneth Frazier, CEO, Merck & Co; the military with General Colin Powell; and in politics with Condoleezza Rice, US secretary of state. To a great degree, social mores and customs had evolved. Agitators and race-baiters like Al Sharpton with his National Action Network and Jessie Jackson with his Rainbow Coalition had become substantially irrelevant.

Sharpton demonstrated his agitation motivation in 1993 when he incited a riot in the Crown Heights Jewish neighborhood of New York City with these words: "Talk about how Oppenheimer in South Africa sends diamonds straight to Tel Aviv and deals with the diamond merchants right here in Crown Heights. The issue is not anti-Semitism; the issue is apartheid. All we want to say is what Jesus said: If you offend one of these little ones, you got to pay for it. No compromise, no meetings, no coffee klatsch, no skinnin' and grinnin'."[436]

In 2008, the United States elected its first black president; his election symbolized the country's uplifting racial progress. Unfortunately, President Barack Obama's promise to resolve the remaining racial bias was unkept.

His appointment of Eric Holder as attorney general proved disastrous to race relations. I view Holder as the most racially divisive attorney general in the last century. He succeeded in relapsing our country back to the 1960s-era racial animus. Between 2009 and

---

[436] *The Daily News—Al Sharpton's true role in Crown Heights*—August 2011

2016, racial tensions in the United States had reversed course. One of Holder's first decisions as attorney general was to dismiss the legal case against several members of the New Black Panthers group, who had been charged with intimidating voters in Philadelphia during the 2008 presidential election. This was met by an outcry from Republicans.[437]

In July 2009, black Harvard professor and noted African American scholar Henry Gates Jr. was arrested near his home in Cambridge, Massachusetts, in response to a 911 call reporting a potential burglary. President Obama jumped into the race debate with both feet and offered his opinion: "I don't know, not having been there and not seeing all the facts, what role race played in that, But I think it's fair to say, number one, any of us would be pretty angry; number two, that the Cambridge police acted stupidly in arresting somebody when there was already proof that they were in their own home, and, number three, what I think we know separate and apart from this incident is that there's a long history in this country of African Americans and Latinos being stopped by law enforcement disproportionately."

Any pretense that Obama's election had transformed America into a postracial society was dispelled. Popular opinion divided along racial lines; blacks agreed with him, and whites thought he played the race card. These stumbling first steps were a harbinger of what was to come, creating a bitter national debate about racial profiling, six months into his first administration.

What positive purpose could be served by inviting Al Sharpton to the White House almost thirty times? What message did that send to those seeking racial harmony? President Obama's image as a racial healer never recovered.

Events such as the 2014 shooting of a black man in Ferguson, Missouri, which the media reported to be an "unprovoked police shooting," provided fodder for the agitators like Al Sharpton and AG Eric Holder. Each visited Ferguson and condemned the police. Their racial crusading, fueled by the media, led to the creation of

---

[437] *The Washington Times—Problems, Panthers surface at Pa. polls*—November 2012

new black activist groups like Black Lives Matter and a resurgence of racism, sparking antipolice legislation, rioting, and antipolice protest marches. The myth of "Hands up, don't shoot" was born. The pretext of police brutality was eventually disproven. Video surfaced that demonstrated that the man killed was a bully and a thug.

The revival of racial tension reignited by Obama administration missteps continues to this day.

In the 2020 presidential election primaries, Senator Cory Booker (D-NJ) and activist Al Sharpton are demanding that reparations be paid to black Americans in response to America's history of slavery.

What are *reparations*? The *Webster's Dictionary* definition is "the making of amends for a wrong one has done, by paying money to or otherwise helping those who have been wronged."

Wasn't the Civil Rights Act and Affirmative Action Plan intended to redress the long-lasting effect of slavery?

What would reparations be but the extraction of money from people who never owned slaves to give to people who never were slaves? Where is the demand for reparations pertaining to our scourge of the Native Americans? It is estimated that since arriving in America, through the Indian Wars, between five hundred thousand and one million Native Americans had been slaughtered. "From the time Europeans arrived on American shores...the U.S. government...authorize[d] over 1,500 wars, attacks and raids on Indians, the most of any country in the world against its indigenous people. By the close of the Indian Wars in the late 19th century, fewer than 238,000 indigenous people remained, a sharp decline from the estimated 5 million to 15 million living in North America when Columbus arrived in 1492."[438]

Is it too cynical to suggest that the appetite for reparations is a function of the size of the potential voting bloc?

At this point, I claim the right of author's privilege. I feel obliged to share a personal story regarding race-baiting.

---

[438] History.com—*When Native Americans Were Slaughtered in the Name of 'Civilization'*

# UNINTENDED CONSEQUENCE

Senator Corey Booker (D-NJ) grew up in my children's hometown of Harrington Park, New Jersey. His parents were executives with IBM.

To my knowledge, the Bookers were the first black family to live in Harrington Park. He attended the same schools at the same time as my children. I am unaware of any prejudice being experienced.

In June 2018, Booker made a speech in Virginia wherein he proclaimed that his parents "broke the color barrier in Harrington Park." Nonsense! My family had lived in Harrington Park since 1974; there was never a color barrier—perhaps an economic barrier, but never a color barrier, no "redline." This was simply another race-baiting comment by Booker, another grandstanding "Spartacus moment." His assertion offended me. I believe that he owes the people of Harrington Park an apology.

Racism is taught by parents and friends; it has been perpetuated by politicians and legislation, fueled by ignorance and hatred. Today the notion of racism is incited, aggravated, and perpetuated by the rhetoric of Dr. Cornel West, Van Jones, and Al Sharpton preaching victimhood and white privilege.

In 2019, Jemele Hill, a former ESPN anchor, now a columnist for *The Atlantic* magazine, published an article titled "It's Time for Black Athletes to Leave White Colleges." Her piece suggests that the athletes were being exploited by the "white" universities for profit. She believes that black athletes should self-segregate to benefit the "all-black" schools. Does Jemele Hill really want to turn the clock back to segregation?

Is this not a racist suggestion? Have the integration efforts by all schools and sports teams not been to the benefit of all athletes and fans? Did Jackie Robinson endure incivility and racism without purpose?

Black athletes have received scholarship opportunities and college educations as a direct result of desegregation; they have greater opportunity and diversity with their choice of university expanded.[439]

---

[439] *The Atlantic—It's Time for Black Athletes to Leave White Colleges*—October 2019

## WILLIAM L. KANE, SR.

In the 1958 theater production of *South Pacific*, Rogers and Hammerstein broke a social taboo by introducing aspects of prejudice, racism, and a multicultural relationship into its script. Included in the production was a song, "You've Got to Be Carefully Taught." The lyrics encapsulate the problem of tutoring racism:

> You've got to be carefully taught to hate and fear,
> You've got to be taught from year to year,
> It's got to be drummed in your dear little ear,
> You've got to be carefully taught.
> You've got to be taught to be afraid,
> Of people whose eyes are oddly made,
> And people whose skin is diff'rent shade,
> You've got to be carefully taught.
> You've got to be taught before it's too late,
> Before you are six or seven or eight,
> To hate all the people your relatives, hate,
> You've got to be carefully taught!

Alas, we are destined to have racism as a part of our human fabric. It provides weak-minded, unenlightened citizens with a target to address their personal feelings of incompetence and failure.

The following poem, written by Countee Cullen in the 1920s, conveys the lasting impression of the scars that are borne through racist acts:

### Incident
by Countee Cullen

> Once riding in old Baltimore,
> Heart-filled, head-filled with glee,
> I saw a Baltimorean
> Keep looking straight at me.

# UNINTENDED CONSEQUENCE

Now I was eight and very small,
And he was no whit bigger,
And so I smiled, but he poked out
His tongue, and called me, 'Nigger.'

I saw the whole of Baltimore
From May until December;
Of all the things that happened there
That's all that I remember.

Reparations will not end racism; only social and political civility will. If racism is taught, then we must endeavor to "unteach" it.
We can *do* better than this; we can *be* better than this.
We *must* be better than this.

# Chapter X

# Wars and Conflicts

*You may not be interested in war, but war is interested in you.*

—Leon Trotsky,
communist theorist and Soviet politician

Today is June 6, 2019, the seventy-fifth anniversary of the Allied invasion of Normandy, France, during World War II. The military action that would lead to the end of war in the European Theater and the end of Hitler's Third Reich.

I watched the tribute to those who served and especially to those who were lost during the invasion that changed the course of history. I listened to President Trump's eloquent, impassioned speech, as well France's President Macron, praising the men and women that served during that war. Trump, in part, said, "To more than 170 veterans of the Second World War who join us today—you are among the very greatest Americans who will ever live. You are the pride of our nation. You are the glory of our republic, and we thank you from the bottom of our hearts."

Tom Brokaw spoke of these heroic men in his book *The Greatest Generation*. Sadly, there are many young Americans that have never been taught about the war. Many don't even know who won or understand the sacrifices required to achieve that victory. *The*

*Greatest Generation* should be required reading in every high school in our country.

My father was a member of that generation, serving in the Navy in the Pacific Theater under Admiral "Bull" Halsey. Dad's diary of his experience cited places like Okinawa, Iwo Jima, and Leyte Gulf, names most Americans might never have known had it not been for the war. His diary provides an unemotional account of day-to-day life aboard a US warship up to and including the dropping of the two atomic bombs on Japan.

On April 19, 1951, General Douglas MacArthur made his farewell address to congress, in which he warned, "Once war is forced upon us, there is no other alternative than to apply every available means to bring it to a swift end. War's very object is victory." While it is commonly accepted that the United States has the most powerful armed forces in the world, I wonder if today's Americans have the same mettle as that "greatest generation."

General George Patton was fond of saying that "wars may be fought with weapons, but they are won by soldiers."

> The supreme art of war is to subdue the enemy without fighting. (Sun Tzu, *The Art of War*)

In 1775, the Revolutionary War was inspired by common people who felt overtaxed, overregulated, and denied personal freedom. The war lasted eight years.

In January of 1776, Thomas Paine published *Common Sense*, which argued for American independence. Most colonists considered themselves Britons, but Paine made the case for a new American. "Europe, and not England, is the parent country of America. This new world hath been the asylum for the persecuted lovers of civil and religious liberty from every part of Europe," he wrote.[440]

The Revolutionary War, fought to obtain freedom from the British crown, was successful and established our independence as the United States of America. Figures regarding casualties from the

---
[440] *Encyclopedia Britannica—Common Sense—Pamphlet by Paine*

Revolutionary War are estimates based upon a variety of sources. Statistics provided by the Department of Defense are 4,435 killed and 6,188 wounded, which are surprisingly low, considering the fierceness and closeness of the battles.[441]

In 1787, during the process of drafting the Constitution, slavery was a significantly divisive issue. While the Southern "slave states" viewed their slaves as chattel, necessary to their economy, Northern states viewed slavery as an abomination. The three-fifths clause was a compromise allowing "three-fifths of the number of slaves in any particular state [to be] added to the total number of free white persons [to determine the] number of Congressmen each state would send to the House of Representatives."

Other laws prohibited slavery in the Northwest territories and ended US participation in the international slave trade in 1807. This issue would foment public discord, ultimately leading to the Civil War.[442]

The War of 1812 was fought in reaction to British restrictions on US trade, their support of the Native Americans who were resisting our westward expansion, and the impressing of American merchantmen into the British Navy. In June, Democrat president James Madison, responding to heavy pressure from Congress, signed the American declaration of war. The United States took on the greatest naval power in the world, Great Britain.

Declaring war for the first time in our nation's history, we intended to stop British impressment, reopen the trade lanes with France, remove British support from Native American tribes, and secure our territorial honor and integrity in the face of our old rulers.[443]

The war lasted from June 1812 until February 1815, a span of two years and eight months. US casualties, as assessed by Wikipedia, were 3,860 dead and almost 9,000 injured. The primary result of

---

[441] 2006 Edition of Liberty Tree Newsletter—*Casualties during the American Revolution*

[442] *The Heritage Guide to the Constitution*—David Brennen, Professor—Case Western Reserve University

[443] American Battlefield Trust

the war was two centuries of peace between the United States and Britain.

After over one hundred years of Indian Wars and confrontations between American pioneers and settlers, Democrat president Andrew Jackson signed the Indian Removal Act in 1830. The law authorized the president to negotiate with Native American tribes for their transfer to federal territory in the West in exchange for the white settlements on their ancestral lands. The act has been referred to as an act of systematic genocide. It completely discriminated against an ethnic group to the point of certain death of vast numbers of its population. The act signed by Jackson was strongly enforced under his administration and that of Democrat president Van Buren until 1841.[444]

I could find no reliable estimate of how many Native Americans died during the Indian Wars; many tribes had been decimated by disease introduced by the Europeans.

The wars ended with the creation of the reservation system, establishing tracts of land for Native Americans to live on while white settlers took over their land. The main goals of Indian reservations were to bring Native Americans under US government control, minimize conflict between Indians and settlers, and encourage Native Americans to take on the ways of the white man.

The Civil War was initiated by Southern Democrats. Lincoln campaigned on an abolitionist platform promising to contain slavery to the states where it was practiced. New states in the west would come into the Union as free states. The Southern states had dominance in the Congress and realized that they would have diminishing influence as new free states entered the Union.

Retaining slavery was crucial to the agricultural South. South Carolina issued its Proclamation of Secession in December 1860. The importance of slavery to its way of life was the very reason for secession. In their attempt to secede from the Union and retain the "right" to own slaves, one month after Lincoln's inauguration,

---

[444] *Encyclopedia Britannica—Indian Wars and Indian Removal Act*

Southern forces fired on Fort Sumter in April 1861, the South fighting to retain slavery, and the North fighting to abolish it.

Lincoln issued the Emancipation Proclamation in January 1863.

The war lasted four years and ended in 1865, at a cost between 620,000 and 750,000 lives. The Northern troops prevailed, and the Confederate forces surrendered at Appomattox, Virginia. Confederate general Robert E. Lee surrendered to Northern general Ulysses S. Grant.[445]

The war resulted in the abolition of slavery, the freedom of black Americans, and the end of the antebellum South. However, it did not end the subjugation of the blacks in the Jim Crow South.

The Mexican American War was fomented in 1845 when President Polk made a proposition both to purchase California and New Mexico from Mexico and to agree upon the Rio Grande River as the southern border of United States. When that offer was rejected, Democrat president Polk asked Congress to declare war on Mexico and ordered US troops into the disputed areas. According to ThoughtCo, the war lasted a little over three months, with 13,000 US casualties, but fewer than 1,800 were killed in action and the rest from disease.

The Mexican American War ended with the signing of the Treaty of Guadalupe Hidalgo, giving vast expanses of the Southwestern territory to the United States. In return, the United States gave Mexico $15 million and an additional $3.25 million to repay debts owed to Mexican citizens.[446]

In February 1898, the battleship USS *Maine*, moored in Havana's harbor, sank after being rocked by two explosions, igniting the Spanish American War. Over 250 men on board were killed. "Hawks" in the media and within the government immediately blamed Spain, and Democrat president McKinley signed a decla-

---

[445] *Encyclopedia Britannica—The Civil War*
[446] *Encyclopedia Britannica—The Mexican American War*

ration of war against Spain. The war ended in four months.[447] The US incurred 3,549 killed in action, including those lost on the USS *Maine*, and 2,957 from disease.[448]

The 1898 Treaty of Paris negotiated the purchase of the Philippines from Spain for $20 million, Cuba was granted independence, and Guam and Puerto Rico became US territories.

Disagreement in Europe over territory and boundaries came to a head with the assassination of Archduke Ferdinand of Austria in 1914, and one month later, European war broke out.

In 1917, Germany began unrestricted warfare in war-zone waters, causing the United States to break diplomatic relations. Shortly thereafter, the American liner *Housatonic* was sunk by a German U-boat. In late March, Germany sank four more US merchant ships.

In April, Democrat president Woodrow Wilson appeared before Congress and called for a declaration of war against Germany. World War I would come to be referred to as the Great War.

In June 1917, the first US infantry troops landed in France, and the war ended on November 11, 1918. More than two million American soldiers had served on the battlefields of Western Europe, and some fifty thousand of them lost their lives.

The terms of the armistice were harsh: all occupied lands in Belgium, Luxembourg, and France, plus Alsace-Lorraine, held since 1870 by Germany, were to be evacuated within fourteen days; the Allies were to occupy land in Germany to the west of the River Rhine; German forces had to be withdrawn from Austria-Hungary, Romania, and Turkey; Germany was to surrender to neutral or Allied ports ten battleships, six battle cruisers, eight cruisers, and 160 submarines; Germany was also to be stripped off heavy armaments, including five thousand artillery pieces, twenty-five thousand machine guns, and two thousand airplanes; the naval blockade would continue; five thousand locomotives, 150,000 railway cars, and five thousand trucks would be confiscated from Germany; and Germany

---

[447] *Encyclopedia Britannica—The Spanish American War*
[448] The Spanish American War Centennial Website

would be blamed for the war and reparations would be paid for all damage caused.[449]

The Austro-Hungarian Empire, one of the oldest monarchies in Europe, was no more.

After the resolution of the Great War, leaders of the victorious countries joined in seeking a strategy that might prevent a recurrence of military conflicts. The solution was thought to be the creation of the League of Nations. Democrat president Woodrow Wilson was a driving force behind the league's formation and strongly influenced the form it took, but the US Senate voted not to join in November 1919.

The concept of a peaceful community of nations was first proposed in 1795 by philosopher Immanuel Kant in *Perpetual Peace: A Philosophical Sketch*. Kant argued for the establishment of a peaceful world community, not in a sense of a global government, but in the hope that each state would declare itself a free state that respects its citizens and welcomes foreign visitors as fellow rational beings, thus promoting peaceful society worldwide.

While the League of Nations enjoyed some success resolving local disputes around the world, the onset of the Second World War demonstrated that the league had failed in its primary purpose, the prevention of another world war. One of the reasons for this failure was that its power was limited by the United States' refusal to join.[450]

After Japan's attack at Pearl Harbor, Hawaii, on December 7, 1941, Democrat president Franklin Delano Roosevelt asked Congress to declare war on Japan. FDR then immediately followed with a declaration of war against the Axis Powers of Adolf Hitler in Europe. World War II involved more than thirty countries.

Sparked by the 1939 Nazi invasion of Poland, the world war dragged on for six years, until the Allies defeated Nazi Germany and Japan in 1945.

---

[449] *Encyclopedia Britannica—World War I*
[450] *Encyclopedia Britannica—League of Nations—Political History*

## UNINTENDED CONSEQUENCE

It was the deadliest conflict in human history, marked by fifty to eighty-five million fatalities, most of whom were civilians in the Soviet Union and China. It included massacres, the genocide of the Holocaust, strategic bombing, premeditated death from starvation and disease, and the initial use of nuclear weapons in war. The United States suffered 407,600 killed in action and 671,801 wounded, in both theaters.[451] When the war ended, Germany's Hitler and Japan's Tojo were defeated and Europe and Asia were destroyed. The United States embarked upon a series of aid programs that would finance reconstruction.

With time and experience, the Allies met after the war to form an organization that would replace the League of Nations. Spearheaded by Democrat president Delano Roosevelt, the United Nations was formed. Unfortunately, over time, the effectiveness of this body was compromised by corruption and vetoes inspired by regional political philosophies.[452]

The Korean Conflict is often referred to as the Forgotten War. It began in June 1950, when seventy-five soldiers and artillery from the North Korean People's Army crossed the 38$^{th}$ parallel, which was the boundary between the Soviet-backed Democratic People's Republic of Korea to the north and the pro-Western Republic of Korea to the south.[453]

Democrat president Truman believed if aggression went unchecked, a chain reaction would be initiated that would marginalize the United Nations and encourage communist aggression elsewhere.[454] The UN Security Council and United States Congress approved the use of force to help the South Koreans. While President Truman did not declare war against North Korea, it was considered a "police action."

The US immediately began using its air and naval forces. The decision to commit ground troops became viable when the Soviet Union confirmed it would not move against US forces in Korea. By

---

[451] *Encyclopedia Britannica—World War II*
[452] *Encyclopedia Britannica—League of Nations—Political History*
[453] USARMY.MIL
[454] National Archives—US Enters the Korean Conflict

July, American troops had entered the war on South Korea's behalf; it was a war against the forces of international communism. In July 1953, the Korean Conflict came to an end after some five million soldiers and civilians lost their lives.[455]

The Pentagon put US battle deaths at 33,652 and "other deaths," meaning deaths in the war zone from illness, accidents, and other nonbattle causes, at 3,262, yielding a total of 36,914.[456]

The Korean peninsula remains divided today.

Republican president Dwight Eisenhower promised South Vietnam prime minister Diem that the United States would provide whatever support necessary to ensure a noncommunist Vietnam. Following through on that commitment, he began United States aid to South Vietnam in January 1955, and American "advisers" began arriving in February to train the South Vietnamese army.

In 1961, Democrat president Kennedy approved sending four hundred Special Forces troops and one hundred other US military advisers to South Vietnam. Kennedy approved the start of clandestine warfare against North Vietnam to be conducted by South Vietnamese agents under the direction and training of the CIA and US Special Forces troops. Kennedy's orders also called for South Vietnamese forces to infiltrate Laos to locate and disrupt communist bases and supply lines there. Troop levels gradually grew from just under a thousand in 1959 to sixteen thousand in 1963.[457]

Democrat president Lyndon Johnson expanded the undeclared war and pursued an aggressive program of increasing US troops committed to Vietnam between 1964 and 1968, reaching a peak of 536,000.[458]

A significant milestone in the war was the Tet Offensive in February 1968. Attacks were staged by eighty-five thousand North Vietnamese troops, carried out against five major South Vietnamese

---

[455] National Archives—US Enters the Korean Conflict
[456] *Service and Casualties in Major Wars and Conflicts—1994*
[457] *Encyclopedia Britannica—The Viet Nam War*
[458] *Encyclopedia Britannica—The Viet Nam War*

## UNINTENDED CONSEQUENCE

cities, dozens of military installations, and scores of towns and villages throughout South Vietnam.

The US military forces were successful in quelling the attacks and became more optimistic. They saw that the successful rebuke of their enemies resulted in an undeniable weakening of communist forces and strength.[459]

However, Walter Cronkite, embedded in Vietnam, observed and reported a different picture:

> To say that we are closer to victory today is to believe in the face of evidence, the optimists who have been wrong in the past. To say that we are mired in a stalemate seems the only realistic, yet unsatisfactory, conclusion. It is increasingly clear to this reporter that the only rational way out then will be to negotiate, not as victors, but as an honorable people who lived up to their pledge to defend democracy and did the best they could. It seems now more certain than ever that the bloody experience of Viet Nam is to end in a stalemate.

While generally believed but unable to be confirmed, President Lyndon Johnson reportedly declared, "If I've lost Cronkite, I've lost middle America."[460] Whether he said that or not, I am certain that the president recognized the significance of Cronkite's broadcast.

This was the first US conflict where news reports were televised daily, submitted with graphic video by journalists following our troops into action. American antiwar anger accelerated when the reports of atrocities committed by US forces in the Vietnam village of My Lai became public in 1969.[461]

Opposition to the war bitterly divided Americans even after President Nixon ordered the withdrawal of US forces in 1973. This

---
[459] *Encyclopedia Britannica—Tet Offensive*
[460] *Getting it Wrong: Ten of the Greatest Misrepresented Stories…*—W. Joseph Campbell
[461] *Encyclopedia Britannica—The Viet Nam War*

was the first war involving the United States where unprecedented public opposition was evident in demonstrations, marches, and college campus disturbances.

Shortly after his inauguration, and in response to the growing US civilian outcry, Republican president Nixon began the gradual withdrawal of US troops in 1969, leading to the complete withdrawal in August 1973.

The Vietnam War was a long, costly, and divisive conflict that pitted the communist government of North Vietnam against South Vietnam and its principal ally, the United States. More than three million people, including over fifty-eight thousand Americans, were killed in the war.

After the withdrawal of US troops, communist forces ended the war by seizing control of South Vietnam in 1975, and the country was unified as the Socialist Republic of Vietnam the following year.[462]

In retrospect, we can speculate as to what the expenditure of American blood and treasure in Vietnam accomplished, if anything. The virulent antiwar sentiment in America at that time was aptly depicted in the 1990 Tom Cruise movie *Born on the Fourth of July*. The film was based upon the autobiography of Ron Kovic, who had been paralyzed in the Vietnam War. Feeling betrayed by the country he fought for, Kovic became an antiwar and pro-human rights activist.[463]

In January of 1991, the Iraq War was authorized by the United Nations Security Council, with a "coalition of the willing," and approved by Republican president George H. W. Bush after Iraq's president Saddam Hussein invaded Kuwait. The conflict, which lasted less than a month, was a conventionally fought war. A combined force of troops from the United States and Great Britain (with smaller contingents from several other countries) invaded Iraq and rapidly defeated the Iraqi military and paramilitary forces. The Iraqi army was destroyed, and Hussein was forced to withdraw from Kuwait. President Bush chose not to pursue Hussein and remove

---

[462] *Encyclopedia Britannica—The Viet Nam War*
[463] *Biography—Ron Kovic*—July 2019

## UNINTENDED CONSEQUENCE

him from office. Many speculate that had Bush pressed for Hussein's removal, the Second Iraq War might have been avoided.[464]

America's War on Terror (Afghanistan and Iraq) was announced by Republican president George W. Bush in the aftermath of the September 11, 2001, terror attacks in the United States. With US military forces, his administration was able to redirect the "ground zero" of that conflict to the Middle East rather than the soil of the United States. He was successful in doing so for the remainder of his presidency.[465]

After the inauguration of President Obama, the focus of our national foreign policy regarding terrorism shifted. Retargeted to protect the millions of innocent Muslims that were not part of the radical movement, the term *Islamic terrorist* was banned from Washington lexicon.

Americans were feeling a mix of anger, fear, and dismay regarding personal and national security. They were seeking reassurance and leadership. President Obama offered platitudes rather than a plan of action.

Imagine how the course of history might have been changed if he had, after his inauguration, addressed the nation and proposed thus:

> The United States has been attacked by radical Islamic terrorists. The attackers were radicalized in a perverted interpretation of the Islamic faith. This cancer has formed within the Islamic community and must be eradicated from within. Peace-loving Muslims must stand up against this blasphemy of their faith. You must be the catalyst to defeat it. The United States will join you. I am asking every Muslim, every mosque, and every Muslim-majority country allied with the United States to join me in defeating this scourge

---

[464] *Encyclopedia Britannica—Iraq War*
[465] *History—Americas War on Terror—Timeline*

and pulling ISIS out by its roots. To the individuals of the Muslim faith in America, if you see something, say something. To every imam in every mosque in America, if you sense a member might be undergoing a possible radicalization, say something.

To each Muslim country allied with the United States, I ask that you stand an army of twenty thousand men. Whether Sunni, Shia, or Kurd, place your philosophical differences aside for the moment to create this combined force to eradicate those who have hijacked your Islamic faith. The United States will assist you with all the weight of its military and diplomatic power.

Imagine how the course of our fight against terrorism might have been enhanced if we had been able to create a predominantly Muslim antiterrorist army.

In May 2011, President Obama authorized a US Navy SEAL raid on a compound in Pakistan and killed the al-Qaeda leader Osama bin Laden. *The Washington Post* headline read, "US Forces Kill Osama Bin Laden: Obama: 'Justice Has Been Done.'" The death of Bin Laden was a crushing blow to al-Qaeda.

Mitt Romney, the likely Republican nominee to run against Obama in 2012, said, "Congratulations to our intelligence community, our military and the President." Many congressional Republicans issued statements explicitly commending Obama, including House Speaker John Boehner and New York Republican Peter King. Rudy Giuliani, former New York City mayor, offered praise "for President Obama for making the decision." Even Rush Limbaugh had praise for President Obama.[466]

Shortly after taking office, President Trump revised the military rules of engagement and directed the US military to aggressively

---

[466] *Time Magazine: How Republicans Reacted to Bin Laden Killing*—May 2011

pursue the ISIS terrorists with remarkable success. The Heritage Foundation summarized their victory:

> One year into the Trump administration, the facts on the ground—in Syria and Iraq—have changed dramatically. ISIS lost control of Mosul, the second-largest city in Iraq, in July 2017. Three months later, ISIS' capital—the Syrian city of Raqqa—fell. Many fighters retreated to Deir ez-Zor in the country's east. In November 2017, that too fell. The "Caliphate" that Abu Bakr al-Baghdadi announced with such fanfare in the summer of 2014 was in tatters.[467]

In October 2019, President Trump authorized a US Special Operations Team raid on an ISIS compound in Syria and killed the ISIS leader Abu Bakr al-Baghdadi. *The Washington Post* referred to him as "an austere religious scholar." After critical public and political outrage, the *Post* revised its headline. *The New York Times* headline read, "ISIS Leader al-Baghdadi Is Dead, Trump Says."[468]

John Harwood, a journalist for CNBC, said, "It's great that Baghdadi is gone. credit to the skill and bravery of US special forces. It's very unlikely to influence public opinion much since a) most Americans don't know who he was and b) Trump has claimed over and over that he had already obliterated ISIS."[469]

Former vice president Joe Biden, Senator Chuck Schumer (D-NY), the Democratic leader, and other Democrats released statements praising the military and intelligence officials involved in the raid, without mentioning President Trump. Ms. Pelosi said, "The President was wrong to keep congressional leaders in the dark. The House must be briefed on this raid, which the Russians but not top

---

[467] *The Heritage Foundation: Did Trump Really Beat ISIS?*—January 2018
[468] *The New York Times: ISIS Leader al Baghdadi is Dead, Trump Says*—October 2019
[469] *Newsweek: Politicians and Pundits React* -October 2019

congressional leadership were notified of in advance, and on the administration's overall strategy in the region."[470], [471]

There can be only one explanation for the contrast in the reactions to the bin Laden and al-Baghdadi killings by the media and the Democrat politicians. Even upon the completion of a brilliant national military success, there is no pause in political party acrimony.

Presently, our military continues to be engaged in conflicts in Syria, Iraq, and Afghanistan.

>Only the dead have seen the end of war. (Plato)

As Scarlett O'Hara was heard to exclaim in the opening line of the classic film *Gone with the Wind*, "War, war, war…" I suspect that we have not seen the end of it.

Some wars are waged for principle, others without principle. Some wars are waged for a national security purpose, others without purpose other than nation building or regime change. Historically, wars have been waged for one of three reasons: territory, religion, or economy. There is no real *reason* for war, only the *why*.

Wars and conflicts drain America's blood and treasure. Their costs have been heartbreaking in terms of blood and massive in terms of increased national debt. Some wars were worth the price we paid, others not so much. Let's consider the outcome and perceived benefit of our major wars:

- The Revolution won our independence, a necessary result.
- The Civil War ended slavery, a positive result.
- World War I defeated the kaiser and restructured Europe. Some might argue that it created more strife than it resolved.
- World War II defeated Nazism and Japan's aggression, an essential result.

---

[470] *The New York Times: ISIS Leader al Baghdadi is Dead, Trump Says*—October 2019

[471] *The Washington Post: Trump Seizes on Baghdadi Raid to Paint Democrats as Dangerous Leakers*—October 2019

- The Korean Conflict, intended to bring democracy to all of Korea, failed. Korea remains divided.
- The Vietnam War, intended to defend democracy in Vietnam, failed. Vietnam is now totally communist.
- The Gulf Wars, intended to remove weapons of mass destruction, found that there were none. After fifteen years of battle, the region continues in chaos, and Iran is pursuing weapons of mass destruction.

Isn't it ironic that while most wars and conflicts were initiated by Democrat administrations for strategic benefit or moral imperative, the Republicans, in their insistence on a strong military, are viewed as "hawks"?

Our national adversaries are Russia, China, Iran, and North Korea.

- When China is permitted to build a military base on a man-made island in the South China Sea, peace is threatened.
- When Russia can occupy Georgia and annex Crimea with little, if any, resistance, peace is endangered.
- When North Korea and Iran can test ballistic missiles without opposition, peace is in jeopardy.
- When Russian planes and ships can interfere with US military operations with impunity, peace is imperiled.
- When aggression is met with timidity, peace is lost.

The Revolutionary War was inspired by common people who felt overtaxed, overregulated, and denied personal freedom. Could history repeat itself?

Today within the United States we seem to be engaged in an internal civil conflict inspired by philosophical differences in our political parties.

Sun Tzu wrote *The Art of War* around 500 BC. His belief was that "the supreme art of war is to subdue the enemy without fighting." I do not believe that there is an "art" of war, as his title suggested, only violence, death, destruction, and despair.

Recently, I was introduced to a poem written by English novelist and poet Thomas Hardy, who was commenting on the Boer War in 1902. He reminds us of both the absurdity and the irrationality of war and how, with a change in circumstance, today's foe might have been today's friend. I felt that Hardy's poem, along with the chilling prophesy of Albert Einstein, whose theories about nuclear energy helped lead to the invention of the atomic bomb, would be an appropriate way to finish this chapter.

# UNINTENDED CONSEQUENCE

## The Man He Killed
by Thomas Hardy

Had he and I but met
By some old ancient inn,
We should have sat us down to wet
Right many a nipperkin!

But ranged as infantry,
And staring face to face,
I shot him as he at me,
And killed him in his place.

I shot him dead because—
Because he was my foe,
Just so: my foe of course he was;
That's clear enough; although

He thought he'd 'list, perhaps,
Off-hand like—just as I—
Was out of work—had sold his traps—
No other reason why

Yes; quaint and curious war is!
You shoot a fellow down
You'd treat if we met where any bar is,
Or help to half-a-crown.

*I know not with what weapons World War III will be fought, but World War IV will be fought with sticks and stones.*
—Albert Einstein

# Epilogue

I found an opinion piece that serves as an excellent lead into this epilogue. It provides an insightful metaphor, written by Victor Davis Hanson, Stanford University professor and author:

> Sometime around A.D. 60, in the age of Emperor Nero, a Roman court insider named Gaius Petronius wrote a satirical Latin novel, "The Satyricon," about moral corruption in Imperial Rome. The novel's general landscape was Rome's transition from an agrarian republic to a globalized multicultural superpower.
>
> The novel survives only in a series of extended fragments. But there are enough chapters for critics to agree that the high-living Petronius, nicknamed the "Judge of Elegance," was a brilliant cynic. He often mocked the cultural consequences of the sudden and disruptive influx of money and strangers from elsewhere in the Mediterranean region into a once-traditional Roman society.
>
> The novel plots the wandering odyssey of three lazy, overeducated, and mostly underemployed single young Greeks: Encolpius, Ascyltos, and Giton. They aimlessly mosey around southern Italy. They panhandle and mooch off the nouveau riche. They mock traditional Roman customs. The three and their friends live it up

amid the culinary, cultural, and sexual excesses in the age of Nero.

Certain themes in "The Satyricon" are timeless and still resonate today.

The abrupt transition from a society of rural homesteaders into metropolitan coastal hubs had created two Romes. One world was a sophisticated and cosmopolitan network of traders, schemers, investors, academics, and deep-state imperial cronies. Their seaside corridors were not so much Roman as Mediterranean. And they saw themselves more as "citizens of the world" than as mere Roman citizens.

In the novel, vast, unprecedented wealth had produced license. On-the-make urbanites suck up and flatter the childless rich in hopes of being given estates rather than earning their own money.

The rich in turn exploit the young sexually and emotionally by offering them false hopes of landing an inheritance. Petronius seems to mock the very world in which he indulged.

His novel's accepted norms are pornography, gratuitous violence, sexual promiscuity, transgenderism, delayed marriage, childlessness, fear of aging, homelessness, social climbing, ostentatious materialism, prolonged adolescence, and scamming and conning in lieu of working.

The characters are fixated on expensive fashion, exotic foods, and pretentious name-dropping. They are the lucky inheritors of a dynamic Roman infrastructure that had globalized three continents. Rome had incorporated the shores of the Mediterranean under uniform law, science, institutions—all kept in check by Roman bureaucracy and the overwhelming power of the legions, many of them populated by non-Romans.

Never in the history of civilization had a generation become so wealthy and leisured, so eager to gratify every conceivable appetite—and yet so bored and unhappy.

But there was also a second Rome in the shadows. Occasionally the hipster antiheroes of the novel bump into old-fashioned rustics, shopkeepers, and legionaries. They are what we might now call the ridiculed "deplorables" and "clingers."

Even Petronius suggests that these rougher sorts built and maintained the vast Roman Empire. They are caricatured as bumpkins and yet admired as simple, sturdy folk without the pretensions and decadence of the novel's urban drones.

Petronius is too skilled a satirist to paint a black-and-white picture of good old traditional Romans versus their corrupt urban successors. His point is subtler.

Globalization had enriched and united non-Romans into a world culture. That was an admirable feat. But such homogenization also attenuated the very customs, traditions, and values that had led to such astounding Roman success in the first place.

The multiculturalism, urbanism, and cosmopolitanism of "The Satyricon" reflected an exciting Roman mishmash of diverse languages, habits, and lifestyles drawn from northern and Western Europe, Asia, and Africa.

But the new empire also diluted a noble and unique Roman agrarianism. It eroded nationalism and patriotism. The empire's wealth, size, and lack of cohesion ultimately diminished Roman unity, as well as traditional marriage, childbearing, and autonomy.

Education likewise was ambiguous. In the novel, wide reading ensures erudition and sophistication, and helps science supplant superstition. But sometimes education is also ambiguous. Students become idle, pretentious loafers. Professors are no different from loud pedants. Writers are trite and boring. Elite pundits sound like gasbags.

Petronius seems to imply that whatever the Rome of his time was, it was likely not sustainable—but would at least be quite exciting in its splendid decline.

Petronius also argues that with too much rapid material progress comes moral regress. His final warning might be especially troubling for the current generation of Western Europeans and Americans. Even as we brag of globalizing the world and enriching the West materially and culturally, we are losing our soul in the process.

Getting married, raising families, staying in one place, still working with our hands, and postponing gratification may be boring and out of date. But nearly 2000 years later, all of that is still what keeps civilization alive.[472]

A parable or a warning?

We have diminished as a nation by many measures: civility, sexuality, faith, economic independence, and national debt. Trust in our political leaders, our government agencies, the media, and commerce professionals has declined.

---

[472] *The Similarities Between Declining Rome and the Modern US*—Victor Davis Hanson—May 2019

## UNINTENDED CONSEQUENCE

While all noble causes, legislation has not always yielded its intended results:

- The Community Reinvestment Act led to the economic crash of 2007.
- The Social Security Act led to the expansion of benefits and the pooling of the Social Security Trust with the general fund, which led to the trust being underfunded.
- Medicare and Medicaid have been expanded to a point where the programs have become economically unsustainable.
- President Lyndon Johnson's War on Poverty cost over $50 trillion but did not measurably reduce the poverty level of the United States. As we address one aspect of poverty in our society, we seem abundantly eager to import more.
- The Food Stamp Program of 1964 was expanded to cover forty-eight million Americans by 2016, at a cost of $70 billion each year.
- We have instituted welfare programs at great cost with questionable results. We continue to deal with the unintended consequence of well-meaning programs and social engineering. Did Affirmative Action and welfare programs help or do harm?
- The Emergency Economic Stabilization Act of 2008, costing $700 billion, yielded little other than bailing out the United Auto Workers pension fund.
- The Economic Stimulus Program of 2009 cost $787 billion intended for "shovel-ready" infrastructure projects. It was redirected to "pork" and funded the hiring of additional government workers.
- The government takeover of student loans has led to over $1.6 trillion in debt, assuredly the next pending economic "crisis."
- The Affordable Care Act, intended to make health care more affordable and accessible, costing $100 million each year, has made health care America's number one concern

in the 2020 election. The act required billions of dollars in "bribes" to pass the legislation.
- The Department of Education federalized our public school systems, initiated Title I and Common Core, ultimately weakening public school curriculum.
- The Environmental Protection Agency, created in 1970, became an out-of-control regulation generating weapon by 2016.
- The Children's Health Insurance Program (CHIP) initiated in 1997 has grown beyond intent.
- The fecklessness of our immigration laws has resulted in an open southern border.
- *Engle v. Vitale* banned prayer in school and has led us to become a less faithful nation. We seem to accept a rising pitch of actions against Christianity and Semitism.
- The ACLU succeeded in allowing children to "opt out" of reciting the Pledge of Allegiance in school. Flag burning has become commonplace, and we have become a less patriotic nation.
- The sexual revolution lowered the bar of acceptable behavior and might have contributed to the need for a Me Too movement.
- *Roe v. Wade* gave women access to abortion, denying sixty million fetuses a chance at life.

Are you seeing the pattern here? The one consistent result in all these legislative initiatives, the one factor common to all, is that each has burdened our nation with unconscionable debt.

While there is no true evidence that Albert Einstein spoke these words, they are often attributed to him. In any event, while undoubtedly overused, I offer this thought: "The definition of insanity is doing the same thing over and over again and expecting a different result."

Noble ideas leading to legislation enacted with unintended consequence, resulting in unintended expense, followed by additional legislation required to address the unintended effect. All of which has led to unsustainable national debt and political tribalism.

President Trump did not make America immoral; he simply took advantage of the fact that it already was. We live in a time when we abuse our freedom, squander our affluence, and abandon our faith.

After eight years of liberal philosophical experimentation that cost the nation $9.5 trillion in debt, shall we countenance that again by choosing a far-left political strategy in 2020? There has been a decline in our mores, and we are now engaged in a cultural war.

President Trump's achievements are overshadowed by political philosophy. Ignore the noise and look to the policies that he had enacted. Look past his inelegant rhetoric and street-fighter counter-punching. Words or accomplishments—which is more important?

As a nation, we seem to have lost the wisdom and foresight that Jefferson, Madison, and Jay demonstrated in composing *The Federalist Papers* and the Constitution.

Vision is a rare commodity in today's Congress.

Our legislature dwells on what divides us rather than pursuing our issues of commonality. Congress ignored President John F. Kennedy's sage 1961 inaugural address counsel: "Let both sides explore what problems unite us instead of belaboring those problems which divide us."

Might we return to the era of "citizen-statesman" as opposed to "career politician"? Shouldn't the politicians crafting legislation be refocused upon, and subject to, the lawmaking before them, rather than their quest for reelection? Wouldn't legislation be more productive if it were driven by the needs of the people rather than by polls? Could it be time for stricter term limits?

As a nation, we appear to have a dearth of common sense. In my well-considered opinion, the future of our democracy and indeed our country is up to us; it is not preordained. It is within our national power and our national will to slow the progress of our trek into social and economic oblivion. I think so, I hope so, and I pray so.

The American people have become very mistrustful. The media and politicians rely on the apathy of the electorate. They encourage willful blindness. Many media outlets and politicians seem beyond irredeemable.

We must abandon our penchant to litigate rather than debate. Honest debate has become daunting and elusive. We must reset our "national rudder" deep enough in the water so that, while we might meander off course, we will not lose our direction. Political *opinion* should be rooted in *fact* rather than aspiration.

Our legislators need to recognize that our enemies are not one another; our true enemies are China, Russia, Iran, North Korea, and our spiraling national debt.

Liberal policies seem to be founded in rainbows and unicorns. Conservative policies appear more pragmatic and utilitarian.

In the 2020 presidential election primary, Democrat candidates are touting "Medicare for all" and "tuition-free college" as cures for ills created by other liberal programs, i.e., the Affordable Care Act and the government takeover of student tuition loans.

If we review our government's intervention in every major economic undertaking, we will see unintended consequences that have harmed the US economy and led to spiraling cost for the American consumer. In each instance, health care, education, and housing costs and values have been widely distorted by government intervention.

> One of the things the government can't do is run anything. The only things our government runs are the post office and the railroads, and both of them are bankrupt. (Lee Iacocca, business executive)

It cannot be disputed that proposed legislation, in any area of our government, must be accompanied by more realistic and effective cost projections. We must devise a method to avoid these repeated unintended consequences. The focus of our politicians has been on quick-fix legislation having a near-term "feel good" effect on smaller segments of our population with little consideration or regard for the longer-term consequence to the larger society.

Shouldn't we stop focusing on giving stuff away and concentrate on paying for the things that we have already given? Let's invest in prosperity and stop buying votes.

> God created every man to be free. The ability to choose whether to live free or enslaved, right or wrong, happy or in fear, it is something called freewill. Every man was born with freewill. Some people use it, and some people use any excuse not to. Nobody can turn you into a slave unless you allow them. Nobody can make you afraid of anything, unless you allow them. Nobody can tell you to do something wrong, unless you allow them. God never created you to be a slave, man did. God never created division or set up any borders between brothers, man did. God never told you hurt or kill another, man did. And in the end, when God asks you: "Who told you to kill one of my children?" And you tell him, "My leader."
>
> He will then ask you, "And are THEY your GOD?" (Suzy Kassem, *Rise Up and Salute the Sun: The Writings of Suzy Kassem*)

At some point, Americans will sensibly determine the future of our country. Hopefully, the moderate Democrats will decide the future of the Democrat Party.

Kimberly Strassel, author, columnist, and member of the *Wall Street Journal* editorial board, provided interesting insight within the introduction to her latest book, *Resistance (At All Costs)*:

> It is instead the reaction to Trump that is new and alarming, and that threatens to leave enduring marks. The term the haters have chosen for themselves—the Resistance—says it all. Throughout history, political resistance movements have existed to undermine occupying powers, as the French Resistance did in response to Nazi Germany. The very word suggests illegitimacy—a movement organized against an authority that has no right to rule. Yet whatever your

views of Donald Trump, he won his election fair and square, under an Electoral College that has governed our system from the start.

The mind-set nonetheless explains how the Resistance has gone so far off the rails. Those who view their targets or their actions as illegitimate view themselves as justified in taking any action necessary to get rid of the occupier. Whether that be turning the awesome powers of the Department of Justice and the FBI against an unconventional presidential campaign or ambushing a Supreme Court nominee with uncorroborated sexual-assault allegations, or using the impeachment process for political retribution, the Resistance views itself in the right. But these actions are not right.[473]

As we become an increasingly tribal America, there needs to be an end to this era of politics of personal destruction.

It appears that Americans have no limit to the level of hostile discourse that they will accept and participate in for the furtherance of personal political philosophy.

In a speech in Springfield, Illinois, Abraham Lincoln referred to the Bible passage Mark 3:25, "A house divided against itself, cannot stand."

We can be bigger and better; to do so, we must abandon toxicity and hatred and come together. The voters must decide our future. Do we want to continue political theater or pursue policy progress?

Parents must reassume their responsibility for molding their children into people of character, compassion, and empathy. All these attitudinal aspects in a young adult are developed by family and friends; it is a great obligation.

More broadly, *America* is an essence, a concept. We are an exceptional nation, and it is worth the struggle required to preserve it. We

---

[473] *RESISTANCE (AT ALL COSTS)*—Kimberly Strassel—2019

must create an inflection point and redirect the political course of our nation.

On September 12, 1962, President John F. Kennedy gave his famous "Moon Speech" at Rice University. His objective was to persuade the American people to support NASA's efforts to send a manned spaceflight to the moon. He said, "We choose to go to the moon in this decade and do the other things, not because they are easy, but because they are hard."

> The world isn't being destroyed by democrats or republicans, red or blue, liberal or conservative, religious or atheist—the world is being destroyed by one side believing the other side is destroying the world. The world is being hurt and damaged by one group of people believing they're truly better people that the others who think differently. (Andrew W. K.)[474]

Certainly, it will be hard. However, we need to pursue this goal of creating a "more perfect union" with imagination, fiscal responsibility, and vigor. Let us stop the pursuit of *political points* and attack our *national needs*. It is our shared values that make America great.

I am hoping to encourage people to think about events, circumstances, and the evolution of them. We are better than political party. We must think and reflect beyond that narrow delineation. Hope springs eternal. America has a decision in 2020. Do not let the opinions of others define who you are. We are each faced with a choice. Continue the way we have been going, allowing others to determine our path and suffer the unintended consequence. Or to understand the issues confronting us and choose the candidates that will have the greater longer-term vision, regardless of party. I am hopeful that fair-minded Americans will reflect and choose wisely.

---

[474] *Village Voice—Ask Andrew—My Dad Is a Right-Wing Asshole—August 2019*

We seem to take for granted what we have been given in the United States, and we are in peril of losing it. I do not believe that the electorate will vote against prosperity.

Americans were called to action in World War I, during the Great Depression, again in World War II and on 9/11. We responded as a nation then, and we are being called again to show our patriotism and save our nation now. I suspect that, with reasoned choice, we will have the temerity to respond again.

> Failure is simply an opportunity to begin again; this time more intelligently. (Henry Ford, inventor and founder of Ford Motor Company)

Government can be helpful, but too much government will be oppressive. Which is the greater good, dependency or self-reliance?

Diversity is an admirable thing, but in certain instances, uniformity is preferable. Charity is a blessed thing, but self-sufficiency is everlasting. Public assistance is a moral thing, but fiscal responsibility is an obligation.

> The great issues facing us today are not Republican issues or Democratic issues. The political parties can debate the means, but both parties must embrace the end objective, which is to make America great again. (Lee Iacocca, business executive)

The past need not be prologue. Our vote is our choice. Prepare, engage, and fulfill your responsibility.

> To solve big problems you have to be willing to do unpopular things. (Lee Iacocca, business executive)

> You can count the seeds in an apple, but you can't count the apples in a seed. When you teach, you never know how many lives you will influence… you are teaching for eternity. (Karen Jensen, author)

And so it is with this writing, as I had indicated in the prologue. This book is not intended to tell you *what to think*. Instead, it is meant to both *encourage* you to think and encourage you to question, challenge, validate, explore, and consider. I have attempted to recount the "how and why" we have come to this place.

Just as the rate of change in technology has been too rapid for us to absorb and employ, so, too, it is with the pace with which we are propelling our country toward socialism and incivility as a norm. I fear that these will be detrimental to our American way and lead to the bankruptcy of our nation.

In William F. Buckley's book *God and Man at Yale*, he noted, "Marx himself, in the course of his lifetime, envisaged two broad lines of action that could be adopted to destroy the bourgeoisie: one was a violent revolution; the other, a slow increase of state power, through extended social services, taxation, and regulation, to a point where smooth transition could be effected from an individualist to a collective society."[475]

I, for one, do not believe that this socialism blather will resonate with the people of America.

I am hopeful that I have informed you as to the perils of our current course. That course can be changed. Vote!

Being a citizen requires more than just being a resident.

> I did then what I knew how to do. Now that I know better, I do better. (Maya Angelou, poet)

> We must, indeed, all hang together or, most assuredly, we shall all hang separately. (Benjamin Franklin, patriot)

To paraphrase Ernest Hemingway in *For Whom the Bell Tolls*: "*The…(United States)…is a fine place and worth fighting for…*" The world is watching, and so are our grandchildren.

*Carpe diem.*

---

[475] *God & Man at Yale*—William F. Buckley, Jr.

# About the Author

William L. Kane Sr. was born in 1942, the youngest of eight children. He grew up in New Jersey and graduated from Tenafly High School. Bill, a veteran of the United States Navy, received his BS from St. Peter's College and an MBA from Fairleigh Dickinson University.

He has been married to Jo, his wife of fifty-four years, and they have two children, Bill Jr. and Sharon Ann, as well as two grandchildren, Ryan and Lilly Essmann.

Bill had been an adjunct professor at New York University School of Continuing Education and a lecturer at St. Peter's College. After a forty-year career as a business executive and management consultant, he is retired and resides in Port St. Lucie, Florida, and Harrington Park, New Jersey.